MAO TSE-TUNG AND I WERE BEGGARS

MAO TSE-TUNG AND I WERE BEGGARS

ILLUSTRATED BY THE AUTHOR

SIAO-YU

With a Foreword by *Lin Yutang,*
Preface by *Raymond F. Piper,* and
Historical Commentary and Notes by *Robert C. North*

SYU
SYRACUSE
UNIVERSITY
PRESS

This work has been published with the assistance of a Ford Foundation grant.

Copyright © 1959 by Syracuse University Press
Syracuse, New York 13244-5290

All Rights Reserved

First Edition 1959
17 18 19 20 21   6 5 4 3 2

∞ The paper used in this publication meets the minimum requirements of the American National Standard for Information Sciences—Permanence of Paper for Printed Library Materials, ANSI Z39.48-1992.

For a listing of books published and distributed by Syracuse University Press, visit www.SyracuseUniversityPress.syr.edu.

ISBN: 978-0-8156-0015-2 (hardcover)

Library of Congress Catalog Card 59-15411

In memory of my dear wife

Phyllis Ling-cho who courageously completed this
English translation before her serious operation

A hundred weeks have run like flowing water.
Everything thrown in the water is swept away,
But the current cannot move this sadness.
Her beautiful image floats in my memory.
My book will soon be published.
Her translation expresses her lovely spirit.
Her phrases serve as sad reminders.
I think of the chin* which remains.
I am touched by her complete understanding.

* A musical instrument.

Foreword

I take pleasure in saying a few words about the origin of this book. A few years ago the author and his wife were living in Cannes, and we had long and delightful conversations together. Both Mr. and Mrs. Siao are scholars and painters, and Mr. Siao in particular showed an extraordinary memory of men and events of the first years of the Chinese Republic. One of the most fascinating topics was his schooldays with Mao Tse-tung, now the dictator of Communist China.

The story of this book is thoroughly authentic, and is written by a person from the same province and the same region as Mao. Hunan is the province that has proverbially produced heroes and bandits. A Hunanese never says die. It takes a Hunanese to write about another Hunanese. I am glad to find that, though the author sharply differs from Mao in his political point of view, he has succeeded here in writing a true and unbiased biography of the formative years of Mao. The book, I believe, has a permanent, as well as current value. Mr. Siao is at present Director of the Bibliothèquè Sino-Internationale which was established in Geneva, but since the Swiss recognition of the Chinese Communist government, has been removed to Montevideo.

LIN YUTANG
Cannes, France
1956

Preface

Since I am the author's first American friend and since I knew his wife, Phyllis Ling-cho, for thirty-one years, I consider it a privilege to introduce Dr. Siao-yu to the English-speaking world and to relate the circumstances which have brought to public view this unusual book, a volume which will delight the reader at the same time that it will prove a significant historical revelation.

Miss Phyllis Ling-cho spent four years in the Teacher's College of Syracuse University from which she was graduated in 1930. Because her basic love was the art of painting, she also took instruction in the College of Fine Arts and studied my courses in aesthetics and philosophy. When she returned to China, she was appointed a Teacher of Pedagogy in the National Central University of Nanking.

In 1932, during a world tour to study living religions, I enjoyed the delightful experience of an unhurried sojourn in Peking. I was entertained in the spacious and peaceful home of my former student and friend, and became acquainted with her father, a great scholar, poet, economist and statesman. It was at this time also that I met her fiancé, Mr. Siao-yu, who with Phyllis became my almost daily guide and companion on excursions to view the wonders of this most beautiful of cities. On these happy, leisurely trips to visit palaces and temples our mutual fondness grew and our friendship was cemented, a friendship which has been continued through correspondence over the years.

When I first became acquainted with Mr. Siao, he had just completed three years of service as Vice Minister of Agriculture and Mines and was then filling three important positions: Dean of the National University in Peking, President of the University of Hwa Pei, and Director of the National Museum of Natural History. At this time also he was an active member of a commission devoted to preserving the art treasures and decaying structures of the newly opened palaces of the Forbidden City.

In June 1933 Phyllis Ling-cho and Siao-yu were married at Shanghai and in August they sailed for Europe. During the next twenty years, in Paris and elsewhere in France, Mrs. Siao devoted her life to painting, while she continued to share creative inspiration and counsel with her husband. She never returned to China. Three thousand paintings and drawings, as well as extensive poetry and prose, are left as a memorial of her artistic genius. But what is more, she was the rare and authentic aristocrat who both charms and blesses by her beauty, as well as by her wisdom, human sympathy, and geniality. Lin Yutang said of her: "She cultivated the poet's soul and the painter's eye for seeing the unseen."

During our happy association in Peking I came to realize that Mr. Siao's quiet reserve, unlimited kindliness, and goodwill concealed sound executive ability and immense knowledge, aided by a truly astounding power of memory. I have complete trust in his sincerity and in his devotion at all times to the welfare of his fellow countrymen.

Although I knew that Siao-yu had withdrawn from political life, I did not know of his early association with Mao Tse-tung. It was a great surprise to me therefore when I heard in a letter from Mrs. Siao in 1956 that she was busily engaged in translating from French and Chinese into English her husband's recollections of his student days with Mao, the Chinese Communist leader. These recollections had been set down as early as 1950 at the repeated urging of Siao-yu's friend, Lin Yutang. It was the hope of the author and his wife that such a book, published in this country, might provide the Western World with a better understanding of the problems of modern China. Although Phyllis Siao became ill during the work of translation, she succeeded by strength of will in completing it before she passed away in May 1957.

The reader will be startled as I was, when I first read the manuscript, by the fundamental opposition which exists between the minds of Mao Tse-tung and Siao-yu and which is vividly apparent in their conversations, especially during the period when they meandered as beggars among the farmers and villagers of Hunan Province.

The youthful personalities in *Mao Tse-tung and I Were Beggars* may at first seem strange to us in the West. We are amazed by the intensity and earnestness of their student arguments, by the nightlong, sometimes tearful, verbal contests between good friends, by a vacation spent in search of truth while begging their rice in the lush green valleys of inner China.

These young men are determined to win at any cost clear and workable ideas for improving the fortunes of their countrymen. Their objective is the total future welfare of China. There is no hint of academic play. They are not arguing for the sake of argument, although frequently they may be aware of the artistic qualities of their words and sometimes express an idea in poetry because for them a fine poem has superior expressive power. They are deadly serious about making right decisions concerning the philosophy by which they will live and by which their country may grow.

If such intensity seems strange to us, this strangeness gives way to a sense of familiarity when we recognize that these youths are struggling with problems which are basic to all of us. It is a positive and satisfying achievement for an Occidental to come to understand the sort of moralist and idealist which Siao-yu is. But Mao and Siao are not simple characters to grasp, because they epitomize the complications of our present-day life. Finally we ourselves also may come to the crucial forking of the ways when we must choose, whether on a small or on a larger scale, the Mao way or the Siao way. Either way is full of risk, struggle, and hard work. But the alternative is a drift toward nonentity or eventual slavery. In short, for every reader this book will be a serious but exceedingly stimulating experience.

It is stimulating also to discover that Siao possesses the fear-destroying faith and spiritual strength which spring from realizing the kind of moral harmony with the cosmos which Confucius taught. This prophetic insight made Siao the first Chinese to oppose Communism, even before the birth of the Chinese Communist Party. He has been true to his principles, his will is firm, and his courage admirable. Not only did he have to give up his intimate friend Mao, but he renounced his own brother who is a prominent Communist. If you ask Siao-yu about Emi Siao, he says simply, "He is my ex-brother. I have not known him for more than forty years."

In 1957, five months before her death, Mrs. Siao, in writing to me of the book, said: "Siao and Mao have two different ideas, two entirely different characters. We may say that if a person wants to be a Mao, the way is not easy. We ought to say that if one wants to be a Siao, that is more difficult. The things which Mao likes most: power, politics, quick success, they are what Siao dislikes most. Yet the same region produced these two entirely different persons."

How two good friends evolved into such antithetical people is the captivating story of this book. By recording their student years of mental growth and spiritual struggle Siao-yu has contributed greatly to the Western understanding of Chinese character and to the hard history of modern China. We are grateful to him for preserving these seemingly casual country-side conversations which underlie a movement that has shaken the world.

Robert C. North's illuminating Historical Commentary and Notes furnish fascinating corroboration of the importance of Siao-yu's story. Dr. North, Associate Professor of Political Science at Stanford University, is a known authority on the history of the Chinese Communist movement.

He has interviewed several leading Chinese ex-Communists, has made a study of the large collection of documents on Chinese Communism in the Hoover Library, and has written many books and articles on the subject, among which are *Kuomintang and Chinese Communist Elites, Moscow and Chinese Communists* (the first full-length story of the Communist conquest of China), the Introduction to *Red Dust* by Nym Wales, and *Soviet Russia and the East, 1920–1927,* of which he is a co-author.

As substitutes for precious early photographs which his enemies confiscated, Siao-yu, with exquisite artistry of brush and ink, has depicted many scenes of places and people in the story.

A limited Chronology at the back of the book is intended solely as a brief review of the major events in the narrative and in Mr. Siao's later life. It is regretted that a complete record could not be given here: an adequate account of Mr. Siao's accomplishments would require another volume.

In this book I discern two revelations of immense significance: first, the basic character and dangerous philosophy of Mao, the peasant-poet tyrant of Communist China; and, second, the story of the astounding power that students may come to exercise in shaping the destiny of a nation, indeed of the world.

RAYMOND F. PIPER
Professor of Philosophy, Emeritus
Syracuse University
August, 1959

Author's Introduction

This book was written neither in admiration of a hero nor in condemnation of a bandit. I had neither object in view. Moreover, to my mind, the line of demarcation between the bandit and the hero is at times faint.

No, in the following pages I have attempted merely to set down an accurate record of certain episodes in my life selected from the storehouse of memory as of certain interest to the public at large and in connection with current events in the Far East. More important than this, I feel it my duty, not only towards my own people but to humanity as a whole, to record a number of facts which may well be distorted to a greater or lesser extent in official histories—for I have already seen the germs of inaccuracy appearing in print.

My memory is one of my most precious gifts—I can still remember cradle days—and in writing these pages I have been able to relive the years Mao Tse-tung and I spent together with such clarity that no recourse to the diary I kept at that time has been necessary. This reliving of the past has afforded me many pleasant hours—although as those who know me well can vouch, I am far from being a day-dreamer.

I believe this is the first authentic account to be published to date of Mao Tse-tung's formative years and of the birth and organized development of the Communist movement in China. I sincerely believe I am the only person today who knows the details and secrets of these events and, since I am not in the political field, I can reveal them fairly and freely.

Since the Sino-Japanese war, in 1937 to be exact, when Mao Tse-tung appeared publicly on the scene, a number of friends—both Chinese and Occidental—begged me to write the memoirs of my life with Mao Tse-tung —known and unknown—and I commenced by writing the beggar episode directly in French. I had just completed this when my friend Mr. Lin Yutang asked me to write on the early life of Mao Tse-tung as the main article for a magazine he was editing. It was difficult to cut down the story and I set it all down in a further twenty-four chapters, but before I had finished the magazine ceased to be published.

I thus had two manuscript drafts, the first consisting of seventeen chapters in French and the second of twenty-five in Chinese, and I thought of completing both. My wife, meanwhile, had read the manuscripts enthusiastically and said she would like to translate the two into one English whole. That is how the present book came into being.

Up to Chapter 8 of this book, part of the story was told to me by Mao himself and part was related, sometimes as a joke, by friends and people in the country round our homes. I knew his younger brother Mao Tse-ta'n very well. I was told that while an officer in the army, he was killed by the Nanking Government forces well before Mao Tse-tung came to power.

From our meeting in the First Normal School—that is, from Chapter 8 —I wish to repeat clearly, I myself became an actor in the scene and can vouch for the truth of every word written. I have obviously recounted only selected episodes, since it would be impossible to set down all that happened in that fateful decade during which the two of us lived and worked together.

I have been most careful throughout this account to maintain the exact sense of all reported speech. The conversations recorded, it must be remembered, took place about forty years ago. If we were to discuss the same problems today, the views expressed would not be very different, but my point of view would be even more forcibly and maturely expressed.

For about twenty years, I have read articles and booklets in Chinese, Japanese and Occidental languages on the early years of Mao Tse-tung and the birth of the Chinese Communist Party. Often I could not control my laughter over the exaggerations and falsifications. The publications by the Chinese Communists are written under orders of the Party, which considers propaganda of more importance than truth. In all works published by the Communists they usually avoid using my name, though I worked and organized with their leader. If they do mention me, they place a word like "reactionary" before my name, because I was not a Communist and my name does not serve their cause. On the other hand, I do not hesitate to use Communist names in full in my book. I am writing true history and not propaganda for any cause.

This book is a sad souvenir for China as well as for me personally. My wife Phyllis Ling-cho had courageously completed the English translation on the eve of her serious operation. She had complete confidence that this book would be widely read because of its important message, but she did not live to see it in print. Besides her many poems and prose works in Chinese, this is her sole work written in English, though she had plans for many such projects which, alas, she was unable to realize.

It is appropriate that the book should be published by the Syracuse

University Press because my wife left her footprints at Syracuse University day and night for several years as a student. When she went to the United States for the second time, she exhibited her paintings and gave a lecture at the Museum of Art in the city she loved so much.

The appearance of this present account is in a great measure the result of Mr. Lin Yutang's insistence and I am deeply indebted to him for his kind Foreword.

I wish to record my most sincere thanks to Dr. Raymond F. Piper, Professor of Philosophy, Emeritus, for his very fine Preface and the brief Chronology and to Mrs. Lila K. Piper, for her gracious assistance in preparing the manuscript for publication. They are the first American friends to read this manuscript and have always shown their enthusiasm for the book.

I fully appreciate the wide experience and capabilities of Mr. Donald Bean, Director of the Syracuse University Press and Mrs. Arpena Mesrobian, Executive Editor. Their great faith in this book has been shown in the efforts they have expended in its publication. I also wish to express my sincere thanks to Dr. Robert C. North for his commentary appearing at the end of the narrative.

It is my hope that this account will be of interest to those seeking true information about the beginnings of the Communist Party in China. There is yet much to tell—perhaps in another book.

SIAO-YU
Montevideo
September, 1959

Contents

*A section of full-page illustrations by the author
follows the end of the narrative on page 206.*

MAO TSE-TUNG AND I WERE BEGGARS

1
Hunan, Land of Heroes and Brigands

Mao Tse-tung and I were both born in the province of Hunan, a land notorious for its heroes and brigands. There used to be a popular expression in China, and even the Chinese colonies in foreign lands, that "China can be conquered only when all the people of Hunan are dead."

More than two thousand years ago Hunan Province was a very strong country. At that time it was called Ch'u, and its traditional enemy was the neighboring country of Ch'in. A second popular expression, dating from that era, which has survived to the present day, is: "If only three Ch'u families are left alive, they will still be able to conquer Ch'in!" Siang is a third alternative name for Hunan, since the names of provinces varied with the dynasties, and in the year 1864, the Siang army destroyed the Taiping rebel forces which were threatening to overthrow the Ch'ing Dynasty, and thus gained great renown for this feat of arms.

Right on the northern boundary lies Lake Tungting, eight hundred *li* in circumference and connected with the nearby Yangtze Kiang (*kiang:* river) by numerous channels. The lake is fed by four big rivers named Siang, Li, Yüan and Tzu, which rise in the southern mountains and flow roughly parallel to each other from south to north, dividing the country into segments. The largest of these watercourses is the Siang Kiang, whence comes the old name of the province just mentioned.

The present name Hunan is a combination of the two words *hu*

3

(lake) and *nan* (south). Since the province lies south of Lake Tungting, the origin is quite clear. Hunan is located in Central China and, according to the official census of 1947, it has a population of 26,171,117. It consists of 77 districts, governed from the provincial capital, Changsha, and covers a total area of 204,771 square kilometers (79,062 square miles).

The mountainous character of this land, interlaced by its four mighty rivers, makes the Hunan landscape rugged, awe-inspiring, and extremely picturesque. The talented Chu Yüan (343–290 B.C.) was born here and his famous lyric poem, *Li Sao,* was a lament of the treatment he received at the court from jealous fellow officials and the easily influenced king. Finally realizing he would never be able to carry out his idealistic projects of reforming the country, he threw himself in the Mi-lo Kiang and the anniversary of his drowning is commemorated throughout China to this day, on the fifth day of the fifth moon, by what is now known in the West as the Dragon Boat Festival. The original ceremony of casting rice wrapped in bamboo leaves into the water has been transformed into the eating of sweetened rice from bamboo-leaf packets and water races in the dragon-decorated boats.

However, apart from providing inspiration for her poets and paint-ers, these rugged mountains from time immemorial supplied excellent cover for the numerous bandit gangs which thrive here. In fact, there have always been so many bandits that *Ch'un tao ju mao* is a common saying, which means, "The bandits are as thick as the hairs on your head." Indeed, Hunan came under the influence of culture and learn-ing very much later than other regions which were directly influenced by the doctrines of Confucius and Mencius, such as the Hwang Ho basin. It is interesting to remember that the Miao savages who domi-nated this area some three thousand years ago are the progenitors of the small groups of picturesque semilegendary tribes who today live in caves in the remote mountains, shunning all contact with the outside world.

The natives of Hunan, even the classically modest scholars, are still fond of boasting, *Iao tze pu pa hsieh!* which is, "Me? I'm not afraid of the Devil himself!" The Hunan people are distinguished throughout China for their inflexibility and their courage.

August 19, 1911, marks the first step in the fateful revolt against the Manchu rulers who had governed China since 1644. The outbreak, which occurred in Hupeh, was at first weak and isolated. But less than a fortnight later, on September 1, Hunan joined in after killing the General and a number of high Imperial officials and the revolution was firmly established.

Shanghai cargo boats of three to five thousand tons can navigate the Siang Kiang and there has always been a big export trade, chiefly in pork and bristle, with Europe. The Hunan pigs, fed on rice, are very famous for their delicious flavor.

In this strange land of Hunan, the locally grown peppercorns, which are pungent in the extreme, have become such a staple article of the people's diet that the little children begin eating them almost as soon as they learn to walk. Perhaps this pungent peppercorn may be regarded as symbolic of the vigorous, forceful character of its consumers. After becoming accustomed to this variety, there is no peppercorn in the whole world too strong for Mao Tse-tung and me, sons of the land of heroes and brigands.

In the heart of this land of hot peppercorns and savory pork, about two hours' steamboat journey from the capital, Changsha, there is a district named Siangtan. About forty or fifty kilometers beyond this, in the region called Yin Tien Shih, the traveler comes to a high mountain, with a lower one just beyond, and then another high mountain beyond that. There lies the valley of Shao Shan, not far from my old home. The mountains and hills in Yin Tien Shih have been compared with the exquisite petals of a lotus which combine to form the beautiful flower. On one of these petals a small human being was to be born on the nineteenth of November 1893 and here he was to pass his youth. The name by which this youth would be known to the world was Mao Tse-tung.(1)

2

The Farm Where Mao Tse-tung Passed His Early Years

Mao Tse-tung's father owned a small piece of land in Shao Shan, dedicated primarily to the growing of rice.(2) The family, who planted and cultivated the fields and then harvested the crop, lived very simply in their small house on the hillside. Both father and son were very stubborn, always quarreling, and never succeeding in coming to an agreement on any subject.(3)

Father Mao sent his eldest son to the small country school where the boy learned a few Chinese characters and was taught how to count. The father never intended his son to receive any more advanced education because he was needed to help on the farm, and they were much too poor at that time to hire a laborer. However, when the son had mastered characters sufficient to read simple stories, he came into possession of a novel which he was able to understand to some extent. Very few books were available in the small village where he lived and it happened that the most popularly read were two novels, the *Shui Hu*, and the *San Kuo Chih Yen I*. The first recounts the adventures of one hundred and eight brigands who had banded together; the second relates the tale of the wars between the Three Kingdoms. Mao Tse-tung became passionately fond of these two books and devoted every possible moment which he could spare from his work on the farm to reading them.

Meanwhile, Mao grew very tall and strong. When he reached the age of fourteen or fifteen, he was already as tall and as big as his father. He could carry on his broad shoulders two of the heavy manure baskets which had to be taken to the fields several times each day. His father was very happy to have such an efficient helper in his son, but Mao Tse-tung's thoughts were elsewhere. He would take his books with him to the fields every day, and whenever opportunity arose, he would steal away to his favorite hiding place under a tree behind an ancient tomb. Frequently he arrived at a state bordering on ecstasy as he followed, word by word, the lives and adventures of the great bandits, or read of the schemings and the stratagems in the wars of the Three Kingdoms.

His father, whose life was completely wrapped up in the daily routine of the work on the farm, began to notice his son's frequent absences and to worry about the farm work which remained undone.(4) Finally one fine day he caught Mao Tse-tung red-handed, sitting behind the tomb with a novel in his hand and the two empty manure baskets beside him. The father was furious.

"So you have decided to stop work, have you?" he asked.

"No, Father, I am only having a little rest," his son replied.

"But you have not carried any manure at all this whole morning!"

"Oh yes, I have. I have carried several baskets since dawn." Mao Tse-tung was referring to the big manure baskets, two of which are carried together, slung one at each end of a pole, and supported like a yoke on the shoulders.

"How many?"

"Five or six at least since dawn."

"Only five or six in half a day? And do you think that is enough to earn your living?"

"Well, and how many do you think you could carry in half a day?"

"Twenty! Or at least fifteen."

"But from the house to the field is a very long way."

"I suppose you think I should build the house right on the edge of the field to make your work lighter! Didn't I have to do just the same when I was a boy your age? It seems you no longer care what happens to your family. How do you think we're going to live? There you sit quite calmly as if you had not a care in the world! Have you no sense of gratitude? What good can it possibly do to waste your time reading those stupid books? You are not a child any more and if you want to eat, you must work!"

"Oh, hush. That's enough. You are always complaining," Mao Tse-tung replied.

After this scene, they went back to the house for lunch. About five o'clock, the son Mao disappeared again. This time his father found him easily. He went straight to the old tomb and the sight which had so aroused his wrath in the morning again met his gaze. There his son sat with his book in his hands and the empty baskets beside him.

The quarrel which had been interrupted in the morning began again:

"Has your mind been so completely turned by those bad books that you no longer pay any attention to what your father says to you?"

"No, Father. I do listen to you. I do everything you tell me to do."

"You know very well what I want. I want you to give your mind to the farm and to work regularly in the fields, and to read no more of these bad books."

"I will work regularly on the farm; but I want to read my books as well. I promise you I will work first in the fields and then I will read afterwards. When I have finished my work in the fields, I am free, am I not? Then you can't complain and scold. If I do my share of the work in the fields, you have no right to stop me from reading my books when my tasks are finished."

"But, my son, you carry just a few baskets and then you come and hide here to read."

"Before I came here to read, I did all that you asked," Mao Tse-tung replied quietly.

"And what was that?" the father demanded.

"After lunch, I have carried fifteen baskets of manure. If you doubt my word, you may go to the field and count them for yourself. Then you may come back here. But please leave me in peace now. I want to read."

His father gazed at Mao Tse-tung in open-mouthed amazement. Fifteen baskets represented really heavy work for half a day, and if his son spoke the truth, he certainly could find no cause for complaint. Baffled and sorrowful at this unusual son of his, he plodded his way to the field where the family was working and counted exactly fifteen baskets.

From that day, Mao Tse-tung read his beloved warrior and bandit novels in peace in his secret hiding place, after he had accomplished the work that his father had demanded.(5)

3
Mao Tse-tung's Struggle for Learning

Painfully pursuing the two old novels taught Mao Tse-tung many new word characters, and he discovered that he was experiencing much less difficulty with his reading. Thinking these things over while he did the daily tasks which he hated, he dreamed of himself studying in one of the lovely new modern schools where he could get more of this coveted book learning.(6) He nourished this fascinating picture quietly and secretly in his mind. Was it really as fantastic as it seemed? The more he dreamed and thought of it the less ridiculous and impossible it appeared. Gradually it became an obsession and he began planning and scheming.

The Ch'ing Dynasty was drawing to a close.(7) And the school system in China had gradually been reformed along more Western lines. The new "foreign schools," as they were called by the people, had sprung up everywhere, and it was to one of these that Mao Tse-tung dreamed of going. He had made up his mind to become a "foreign student." The very name appealed to his romantic imagination.

He did not dare to approach his father directly, but the idea preyed on his mind and obsessed his thoughts to such an extent that one day, without even realizing it, he let out his secret: He wanted to go to a big city and study in a "foreign school." His father regarded him in astonishment and dismay for a while, and then commented, "You want to go away to school? What imagination! What a ridiculous idea! Just use your common sense for a moment. What school could you attend? A primary school? How can a full grown man study with little children? A secondary school? But you cannot go to a secondary school without going first to a primary school. The whole idea is completely mad!"

"I want to go to a primary school," Mao answered. For reply, his father gave a loud and raucous laugh, as if to close the matter to any further consideration.

After this laugh, father and son did not speak to each other for a long time. But Mao Tse-tung spent more and more time in his private "reading room" behind the old tomb. His silence did not signify, as his father seemed to think, that he had resigned himself to spending the rest of his life in work on the family farm. On the contrary, the episode had served to crystallize his ideas and had enabled him to make a firm decision. The farm work which he had previously performed with a certain willingness now became abhorrent drudgery, and he thought of nothing but the day when he would leave it all behind him to go forth to the big city. He constantly turned the project over and over in his mind, wondering just how he would be able to make it a reality, but never for a moment doubting that it could be done. His father, meanwhile, was secretly congratulating himself on having so easily prevailed upon his son to listen to reason.(8)

Finally Mao Tse-tung completed his plan of action and decided to take the first practical step toward the freedom he was seeking. He went to visit several relatives and friends of the family and asked each one to lend him a bit of money without saying anything to his father. His scheme met with a certain amount of success.

With the money in his pocket, Mao gained greater strength and confidence, so that he felt certain that he could convince his father to agree to his plan to go and study in the city. One evening, while all the family was eating dinner, he suddenly, without preamble, declared, "I have decided to study in the Tungshan Primary School." His father, shocked and surprised, regarded him angrily but said not a word; so Mao continued, "In three days, I shall leave and go to the Primary School."

"Do you mean what you are saying?" asked the father incredulously.

"Certainly I mean it," replied Mao.

"Have you been granted a scholarship that you can go to school without paying? Or perhaps you have won a lottery ticket this morning and have suddenly become rich," scoffed his father.

"Don't you worry about the money. I shall not ask you to pay even a penny; and that is all I am going to say."

His father slowly got up and left the table to smoke his long Chinese pipe while he considered this new turn of events. Five minutes later, he returned and, while Mao and the rest of the family regarded him in silence, he asked, "Do you have a scholarship? How can you go to the Tungshan School without my having to pay? I know very well that when one goes to school, he has to pay for the lessons and also for his board and lodging. All this is very expensive. Little Wang has been wanting to go to school now for several years, but he has never been able to go. Unfortunately, primary schools are not free. They are only for the rich people, not for the poor such as you, I am sorry to say."

Mao smiled disdainfully as he replied, "Don't worry about all that, you will have to pay nothing. That is all."

"No," said his father with a sad voice, "that is not all. If you leave home, I shall be a laborer short. Who will help me work in the fields when you are gone? You tell me I will have nothing to pay, but you forget I shall have to pay another laborer to take your place. You know, my son, I cannot afford to do that."

Mao Tse-tung had not thought about that aspect of the problem, and he did not know how to reply. He realized that his father's contention was reasonable and true. What could he do now? It was always a question of money, and he felt very despondent. Also, he was angry and embarrassed because it seemed his father had outwitted him at the last moment. He needed time to think of a solution.

Finally he thought of Mr. Wang Chi-fan, a family relative, who, Mao had heard, liked to encourage and help ambitious youngsters to gain an education. Mao told Mr. Wang of his ambitions and his difficulties and asked him to lend him some money. Impressed by the youth's earnestness and determination, Mr. Wang agreed to comply with his request.*

When Mao returned home, he again started talking about the big city. His father sadly repeated that he could not let him go because he needed a laborer to help him on the farm. "How much would a laborer cost?" asked Mao.

"At least a dollar a month," replied his father. "That would be twelve dollars a year."

Mao Tse-tung quietly handed a package to his father and said, "Here are the twelve dollars. I shall leave for Tungshan tomorrow morning!"(9)

---

* Mr. Wang Chi-fan is one of the outstanding intellectuals of the present day and is a Director of Changsha College. The author retains very pleasant memories of his friendship.

4
On the Way to School

Next morning, Mao was up at dawn, full of his plans and his ambitions. While his father silently went off as usual to his field, Mao made packages of his few belongings. Within a few minutes, he had everything ready: a blue mosquito net, an essential article even for the poorest peasants during the Hunan summers; two white sheets, which had turned gray with the passage of time and many washings; and several old and faded tunics. All these were rolled up together into one bundle which he tied to one end of his carrying pole. To the other end, he tied a basket containing his two precious books, the *San Kuo Chih Yen I* and the *Shui Hu*.

His mother watched him anxiously and when he was all ready to go, she asked, "Are you going to say goodbye to your father?"

"No, I am not," answered Mao.

"Do you need anything more to take with you?"

"No, I have everything I need," answered her son.

Without another word or gesture of farewell, Mao left his old thatched home in Siangtan and strode off down the road, not even turning his head to look back at his old mother, standing in the door.

In the same way as he had previously been accustomed to carrying the double loads of manure, he now carried his luggage, suspended from a pole, his clothes on one end and his precious books on the other. But this load was very much lighter, with the two sides so well balanced that he hardly felt that he was carrying any weight at all.(10)

Only a few minutes' walk from his home, he met Old Wang, one of his father's neighbors, who stopped in astonishment to see Mao with his new shoes and socks on. In China, the poor farmer and his children wear socks only for very special occasions.

"Little Mao, how fine you look with your shoes on!" said Old Wang.

"I am going to school!" stated Mao proudly.

"Whatever are you going to school for?" asked Old Wang incredulously.

"To study, of course."

"You're going to study? You're going to become a scholar?" laughed Wang.

"Yes, and pray tell, why not?" asked Mao, his spirits somewhat dampened by this unexpected attack.

Old Wang laughed until the tears rolled unheeded down his brown cheeks, while Mao watched in embarrassment. When he finally regained his composure, he asked, "What school are you going to?"

"To the Tungshan Primary School in the big city."

"Oh, so you're going to a foreign school," he scoffed. "You want to become a foreign student who puts on a white uniform as one in mourning?" In China, white is mourning color, and in the modern schools, the pupils wear white uniforms in the summer. "Your father and mother are not dead," he continued. "Why do you want to go into mourning before they die? What madness is this? Does your father approve of your going to school? What good can come of these foreign customs? Has your father gone completely mad, too? I really don't know what our country is coming to . . . going to school!"

Mao was very angry now and he shouted, "You are just old-fashioned and out of date! You don't know anything!" and he strode off down the road, leaving old Wang staring after him in amazement.

Tramp, tramp, tramp, on and on he went. The road seemed endless. After crossing a wide stretch of monotonous fields, he climbed a mountain, only to see before him another apparently unending expanse of flat fields. He squared his shoulders, set his teeth and determinedly carried on, although he was already feeling very tired and footsore.

When Mao arrived at the foot of the mountain, he discovered a young boy who was quite smartly dressed seated on the ground with an old laborer, under a huge tree. Sitting down beside them, Mao addressed himself to the little boy, "I, too, am tired, and would like to rest a while with you. What's your name?"

The little boy looked uncertainly from Mao to the old laborer before he replied, "My name is Li Ta-fan. And what is yours?"

"I am called Mao Tse-tung. Where are you going? Are you a student? What school do you go to?" Mao hurled the questions at him for he was most anxious to cultivate his first contact with this new, strange world.

"I attend the Lienping Primary School. There are two primary schools in the big city. The one on the outskirts is called Tungshan."

Mao Tse-tung was delighted to have met a school boy who could tell him about Tungshan and about life in the foreign schools. He wanted to take full advantage of this opportunity to satisfy the curiosity which had consumed him for so long, and he set about plying little Li Ta-fan with questions. "How many students are there in your school?"

"About a hundred," answered Li Ta-fan.

"How big are they? Are any of them bigger than you are?"

"I am ten years old and am in the second-year class. In the third-year class, the boys are eleven or twelve years old, and they are a little bigger than I am. Lienping, you know, is a primary school for little boys."

"How many teachers are there in your school?"

"We have five teachers."

"Are they very strict?" Mao wanted to know.

"Yes, the teachers are quite strict."

"I have heard that caning the hands is the only method of punishment used in the modern schools. Is that true?"

"No, that is not so. We have one teacher, Pong, who often strikes us with his heavy stick. He is very strict and often hurts us."

"And do you put up with that without doing anything?" asked Mao in astonishment.

"Of course. What can we do?" asked Li Ta-fan.

"You shouldn't allow him to punish you like that."

"But we are just children, and he is a big man," answered Li Ta-fan in surprise at such an unheard-of suggestion.

"Yes, but there are many of you and he is only one. It would be easy to stop him."

"Yes, but he is a teacher, and we have to respect a teacher. You just don't understand."

"When he is cruel to you, do you still respect him?" asked Mao incredulously.

"All of us are afraid of him—all of my schoolmates. We dare not say a word against him. Oh no, there is nothing we could do."

"You boys are just fools," said Mao in great disgust at such a passive attitude.

"It's all very well for you to laugh at us. If you were in our place, you would do exactly the same."

"Oh, I would? If I were in your place, I'd kill him. It's really quite simple," declared Mao, maliciously.

"Oh, you are a very bad person," cried Li Ta-fan. "You frighten me! My mother warned me not to speak to anyone on the road. I don't want to talk with you any more. I'm going."

"Are you really afraid of me? You needn't be. You have the old man to protect you. Anyway, I was only joking when I said I'd kill the teacher. I want to ask you another question."

Li Ta-fan had stood up uncertainly, and now said it was time for him and the old laborer to continue their journey. It was still a long way to the big city. Mao Tse-tung said he would accompany them, since he was also going to the big city. And then they could continue their conversation. The boy did not reply and the three set off together toward the big city.

After walking in silence for a few minutes, Mao began to scold, "Why do you walk so slow? We'll never get to the city at this rate. You've got to walk faster! Now hurry."

"I can't walk any faster. I'm only a little boy, and I can't take such long steps."

"You said you were ten years old. You walk just like a baby," scoffed Mao.

"Don't bother about me. You just walk on ahead by yourself. I didn't ask you to walk with us."

"But I don't want to walk by myself. I want to walk with you. I want you to try to walk faster. Take longer steps. Go faster, faster, faster!"

The little boy began to sob as he walked. The old man, who had listened to the conversation, was very angry, but he dared not say a word. Mao was very big and strong, and the old man didn't fancy having an argument with one who boasted that he would kill a teacher!

Mao really was distressed, but he didn't know what to do. So he began to tease the child, "Crying because I tell you to walk faster! What a baby. Aren't you ashamed of yourself?" Then the three continued to walk in silence. After going about twenty minutes, they came to a little shelter by the roadside where several travelers were resting.

"Let's stop here for a few minutes," the child said to the old man, ignoring Mao.

Mao sat down beside them, and in his most pleasant manner asked, "Would you like something to eat? Perhaps you are hungry?"

Li Ta-fan refused but the old man suggested, "I think he is thirsty. I'm sure you must be thirsty too, after the long walk."

Mao understood what the old man meant, and he went off to buy three cups of tea in the kiosk, and as an afterthought, he got a small cake for the little boy. After eating and drinking together, the tension relaxed. Mao had achieved his object. He still had several questions to ask the boy and, as soon as they got back on the road, he started off again.

"Tell me, why do you go to the Lienping School instead of the Tungshan? Isn't the Tungshan a good school?"

"Yes, the Tungshan is just as good. I go to the Lienping because my uncle is a teacher there."

"Tell me, little boy, are there any big students of fourteen or fifteen at Tungshan?"

"Oh, I don't think so. It is a primary school for little boys."

"Do you have any friends at Tungshan School?" asked Mao.

"No, I haven't," answered Li.

By this time, they were getting quite near to the city gate. "I suppose you're going to the Lienping School now?" asked Mao.

"Yes, I am," replied Li. "Where are you going? Perhaps you have relatives in the big city and you are going to visit them?"

"No," answered Mao. "I don't have relatives in the big city. I'm going to the Tungshan School."

"You're going to visit someone there?"

"No, I'm going there as a student. I'm going to enter the school now."

"Oh, but that's impossible! You're too big. You must be joking."

"Oh no, I'm not joking. It's quite true. I'm going to enter as a student. Good-bye, Li."

"Good-bye, Mao."

5
Arrival at the Tungshan School

After saying goodbye to his new acquaintance, Mao crossed the river and followed a road which was paved with blue stones for two kilometers or more, when he stopped suddenly. Ahead of him, he saw an enormous building, standing alone in a big open space.(11) It reminded him, more than anything he had ever seen, of a Temple to the Ancestors. He had never seen such an enormous building before, and it was, above all else, the size which made him think of a temple, since a temple was the largest building he had ever seen in the country. Suddenly he began thinking of the old thatched house he had left only that morning. He stared a long time at this "temple," which was to be his school, comparing it in his mind with his home in the country.

The newly built Tungshan School was a renovation of the old Tungshan Academy. I had spent three years there shortly before Mao's unexpected arrival. Surrounding the building is an artificial river, in the form of a moat, about a hundred feet wide, crossed by a big, white stone bridge. I remember how I used to love to stand, all alone, on this bridge and watch the fishes dart to and fro in the water. They never seemed to be afraid of the shadows of my hand, even when I really tried to frighten them. Around the moat, there is a solidly built stone wall about fifteen feet high which entirely surrounds the school. We children used to call it the Great Wall of China.

Now that Mao saw the wall, the school looked to him like a fortified city. He squared his shoulders and walked bravely up to the first big gate in the wall, and slowly crossed the white stone bridge, paying scant attention to the beauty of the scene around him. Between the bridge and the main entrance to the school is a large open space, and when Mao arrived there with his luggage on his shoulders, several pupils were running and playing, since it was almost noontime. Mao stared at them curiously and they stopped their game to return his gaze, but having decided among themselves that he was a porter who had brought the luggage for one of their schoolmates, they

quickly returned to their play and Mao proceeded on his way.

However, in a few minutes a boy came running out of the big door, shouting loudly, "Come, all of you, quick! Come quick and see! A laborer wants to come to school, and he's quarreling with the janitor! Come quick and see!"

All the children made a mad rush toward the janitor's room, like a swarm of bees. They stopped and heard Mao say, "Why can't I go to school like other boys?"

They laughed loudly at that and one of them shouted, "You're big enough to go to the University!" Another said, "Why do you want to come to school here? We are not laborers." And the boys all laughed their approval.

While Mao argued with the janitor, a group of boys had been examining his luggage and had discovered the two old, well-thumbed novels in his basket.

"Are these all the books you've brought with you?" one of them scoffed.

"Do you expect to read these bad books in our school?" another wanted to know. "Don't you know that we're not allowed to read bad books like these?"

Laughing and talking, they crowded around Mao, who could not hear what the janitor was saying, till he suddenly called for silence.

"I beg you only to go and tell the Headmaster that I want to speak to him," pleaded Mao.

"I dare not go and disturb the Headmaster with such nonsense," replied the janitor. "You may be a fool, but I am not! What nonsense!"

"If you will not go and announce me, I'll go myself!" cried Mao.

"Just you dare try!" yelled the janitor.

"If you dare!" shouted one of the boys, and the others took up the chorus and shouted at the top of their voices, "If you dare! If you dare!"

Mao picked up his baskets and started toward the door, but the janitor barred the way, shouting, "Get away from this door! Tungshan is a school, not a lunatic asylum!"

The boys all laughed at this and yelled, "Tungshan is not a lunatic asylum! Go away. Go away!"

Mao hesitated and stopped. He did not know what to do next. He had not expected this sort of reception. In the meantime, one of the smaller boys had slipped away to find the Headmaster and had told him, "Oh, sir, a young bandit is trying to get into our school. Right now he is attacking the janitor. The janitor is trying to defend himself, and all the boys are trying to help him, but the bandit is big, and strong, and is quite savage. You should come and help us. Oh, please come quickly, sir!"

The Headmaster was naturally somewhat perturbed by this strange and naive announcement, and decided he had better go himself and see this "savage young bandit." He stopped to pick up his long pipe, which had a heavy brass bowl at the end of a meter-long bamboo stem. This pipe would come in handy if self-defense were called for.

Suddenly, a cry went up: "The Headmaster! The Headmaster is coming!"

As if by tacit agreement, the children formed a close group behind their Headmaster and maintained a most respectful silence. They all had great confidence in his strange long pipe, which it was known he had used successfully in the past to ward off attacks by animals!

"What is the matter? Why all the noise?" he asked, addressing himself to the janitor.

"Sir," he said, pointing toward Mao Tse-tung, scornfully, "this fool says he wants to enter this school, and he demands to see you. He is nothing but a rogue and a brute! Do you want to see him? Well, there he is!"

The Headmaster turned his gaze upon Mao, his moustache standing out stiff and straight from the sides of his mouth like the Chinese figure eight. Mao came straight toward him and speaking humbly, said, "Please, sir, allow me to study here in your school!"

The Headmaster gave no sign of having heard, but turning to the janitor, he said, "Bring him into my office."

Mao Tse-tung smiled to himself happily, hoisted his baskets up onto his shoulders and would have followed the Headmaster from the room, without waiting for the janitor. However, the janitor stopped him angrily, "Where do you think you're going with that luggage on your shoulders? Leave it here and come with me!"

Mao did not want to leave his precious possessions behind him. He was afraid that the boys, who had already been examining his things with great curiosity, might steal his two novels, and that he might never see them again. Hesitating uncertainly, he said, "I want to take my things with me."

The janitor was furious. "How can you take such things into the Headmaster's office?" he shouted. "Leave them here. Who do you think is interested in your precious possessions? This school isn't a madhouse. It's not a school for thieves either, leave your baskets here. I'm responsible for them. Yes, I'm responsible for them, I tell you!"

Mao hesitated just a moment longer, then carefully placed his things in a corner of the janitor's room and followed him to the Headmaster's office.

At this point, the school boys split into two groups. One followed Mao and the janitor down the hall toward the Headmaster's office, while the other went into the janitor's room where Mao had left his things. In a matter of seconds, the basket was emptied out upon the floor, and the precious books were hidden away in another part of the building. Mao and the janitor, proceeding on their way, were blissfully ignorant of what was happening.

When Mao entered the Headmaster's office, he repeated in the most respectful voice he could command, the request he had made a short time before, "Sir, please will you allow me to study in your school?"

The Headmaster stared at him unbelievingly and asked, "What is your name, boy?"

"My name, sir, is Mao Tse-tung."

"Where do you live, Mao Tse-tung?"

"I live in Shao Shan, about forty or fifty *li* from here."

"And how old are you?"

"I am just a little over fifteen years old, sir."

"You look big enough to be at least seventeen or eighteen years old."

"No, sir, I am just fifteen years and some months old."

"Have you attended your village school?"

"I studied for two years with Mr. Wang and I can read novels quite well."

"What kind of novels do you read, Mao Tse-tung?"

"I have read *San Kuo Chih Yen I* and *Shui Hu* quite a lot."

"Have you read the primary-school books?"

"No, sir, I haven't read them."

"Are you able to read the second-year school books?"

"Most of them. There are some words that I don't know yet."

"Have you learned any mathematics?"

"No, sir, I haven't."

"How much history and geography do you know?"

"I haven't learned any history or geography yet."

"I want you to write two lines of classic characters."

Mao took the pen and wrote some words in a very clumsy fashion. His hands were large and tough, much more accustomed to hard work than to holding a pen.

"No, it's no good. You cannot come to this school. We have no primary classes for beginners. Besides, you are too big to go to a primary school."

"Oh, please, let me enter your school. I want to study," pleaded Mao.

"You could not follow the classes. It's quite hopeless."

"But I will try. Please let me stay."

"No, that's impossible. You could never follow the classes. It would be a waste of your time."

"But I will try very hard. . . ."

At this point, Hu, one of the masters, who had overheard part of the interview, came into the room. He was quite impressed by Mao's obvious keenness, and he proposed that they grant his request. He suggested that Mao be allowed to attend classes for a five months' trial period. If by that time he had not shown progress so that he could make the grade, he should go.

The Headmaster consented to the experiment on that basis, and further suggested that Hu give Mao some private lessons.

And so Mao Tse-tung entered Tungshan School, but only on a temporary basis, for a half year.(12)

6
Departure for Changsha

Mao worked desperately hard at his lessons, and by the end of the five months, he had made such progress that it was decided he should be allowed to stay.(13) His classmates, who had been quite afraid of him in the beginning, adopted a more friendly attitude toward him and before long, they returned his two novels which they had hidden. Mao was surprised to discover that now he could read them much more easily than he had before.

Soon he was regarded by his companions as an authority on the history of the Three Kingdoms and the story of the Hundred Bandits. He often recounted episodes to them from his books, and they would listen to him with rapt attention.

It happens, however, that *San Kuo Chih Yen I* is not the true story of the Three Kingdoms. It is merely a highly romanticized version of the historical facts. This was something that Mao could not admit. The tale had assumed such importance in his life that any doubts cast on its veracity assumed the proportions of accusations against his own personal truthfulness. He often held heated discussions with his history teacher on this subject and with each argument he became more stubborn in the maintenance of his own personal views. He even went so far as to suggest to his schoolmates that they start a movement to get rid of the teacher. One day he went to see the Headmaster about their difference, but the more the Headmaster tried to explain the misunderstanding the more stubborn and determined Mao became. He informed his schoolmates that the Headmaster, who was deliberately protecting the teacher because they were cousins, was really not very well informed in the true history of those times. He urged them to band together to get rid of this headmaster. He even produced a petition addressed to the mayor of the city asking that the Headmaster be replaced and he urged all the students to sign it. When no one wanted to sign, Mao was furious. "You're nothing but a bunch of cowards," he yelled at them. "A lot of useless cowards!"

The little boys stood staring at him like a flock of sheep because they were afraid of his brute strength. Only little Wang, who had become one of Mao's closest friends, plucked up courage to open his mouth. "I don't see how you can possibly know more about history than the Headmaster does," he said. "He has a degree and he's written a lot of books on history. My father is always telling me how much he knows. I don't think you know more than the Headmaster does!"

"Wang!" shouted Mao. "You don't believe me? But surely you can read my books."

"Tell me, Mao, what books?" asked little Wang.

"The *San Kuo Chih Yen I!*"

"But, Mao, hasn't the Headmaster told you that the *San Kuo Chih Yen I* is only a romantic novel? It is based on history but it is not a true account."

"But it is history, I tell you. History! It's just nonsense for you to say it's not true. Of course it's true!" he shouted. Then suddenly changing to a sneering tone of voice, "Little Wang, how clever you are! You know so many things! You must be a very great scholar like the Headmaster! Are you his nephew?"

Little Wang knew Mao was being sarcastic and he replied, "No, you know I am not his nephew!"

"Oh, then you are undoubtedly his stepson."

"Mao, why do you say such things? You know I am not his stepson."

"Why not? I say that little Wang is the stepson of Kung Chi-an, the Headmaster!"

"And I say that Mao Tse-tung is the Headmaster's grandson!"

Mao, who couldn't stand to have anyone cross him, was furious. He flew into a rage, shouting, "Traitor! Traitor!" and threw a chair at Wang, who quickly moved to one side and escaped harm.

"I'm going to report you to the Headmaster," cried little Wang.

"I'm not afraid of him," boasted Mao, "but if you do go, I warn you, I shall kill you!"

Little Wang was really frightened by this threat and now he began to cry quietly. The other boys, meanwhile, looked on without saying a word, like spectators in a theater.

Suddenly, Mao turned his attention away from Wang and toward Chang. "Little Chang, what a coward you are," he said.

"Why?" asked Chang.

"Why? You have often boasted that you were a good friend of mine, but it seems you forgot that you were my friend when Wang was arguing with me just now. Why didn't you back me up? When I threw the chair at him, if you were my friend, you would have thrown another. You are not a true and loyal friend."

"No, no, no, Mao," protested Chang. "I've always been faithful and true to you. I thought what little Wang said was right just now. That's why I didn't say anything against him. But neither did I say anything against you, who are my friend."

"Oh, so you think Wang is right, do you? Good! Now I know whose side you are on. You're a traitor, Chang, and I shall kill you. Just you watch out!"

"No, no, please, Mao! I do want to be on your side. Really I do. I shall fight little Wang any time you ask me to. I really am your true and faithful friend."

From that time Mao lost the sympathy of his teachers and his schoolmates. Even the protestations of little Chang to the effect that he was Mao's friend were no longer sincere, since they sprang from fear rather than from true feelings or sentiment.(14)

The feelings of fear and animosity which he had stirred up in the Tungshan School were so strong that Mao finally decided to leave for good. One fine day, he packed up his simple belongings and set off on foot for Changsha, the capital city.(15)

7
Revolution

After the summer vacation in 1911, Mao Tse-tung arrived in Changsha, and shortly afterward, on the nineteenth day of the eighth month of the old Chinese lunar calendar, the big revolution broke out in Wuchang, the capital of Hupeh Province, and in the neighboring province of Hunan. The rebel leaders very quickly began recruiting students to form a fighting force, and, as soon as news of this appeared in the newspapers, many students from Hunan set out for Wuchang to join the army. Mao, who had already run into financial difficulties in the city, was one of these. However, soon after they arrived in Wuchang, fighting broke out in Hunan. Here the provincial government was quickly overthrown and the commander-in-chief of the army and the high officials sent by the Emperor were killed. A students' army was quickly recruited and I was selected as one of the commanding officers.(16) We were assigned to and placed under the order of a general, a well-known teacher of gymnastics who had taken an active part in the planning of the revolution. Mao Tse-tung and his comrades, who had been unsuccessful in their attempts to enlist in the Wuchang army, heard of the fighting in their own native province and quickly returned to Changsha.(17)

The revolution spread rapidly throughout the whole of China and very soon the Central Government was established in Nanking. Life in the colleges quickly returned to normal, and the student armies were dissolved. Mao Tse-tung had been unsuccessful in his attempts to enlist in either the Hupeh or the Hunan army, and now with the return to normal conditions, he was faced with acute financial difficulties. He lacked sufficient money to remain in the provincial capital where living was expensive, and he could not decide what to do.

One day as he was wandering aimlessly through the streets, lost in his thoughts, he came to the Tien Hsin Ko, the "building which reaches the heart of the sky." The Tien Hsin Ko, which is Changsha's skyscraper, stands on the great wall near the south gate of the city and is a seven-floor tower constructed in the form of a pagoda.

Because he had nothing better to do, Mao Tse-tung climbed up to the top floor in order to admire the splendid view below. He looked out toward the west and his attention was drawn to the Siang Kiang, the most important river of the province, which flows quite close to the city. A few miles beyond was Yao-lu, the "foot of the sacred mountains," which is itself a really high mountain. From this height, Mao was able to follow with his eye the mountain chain for several hundred miles, even as far as Nan-yao, "the holy mountain of the south," which is one of the five great sacred mountains of China. This chain is famous for its awe-inspiring, wonderful landscapes. At the foot of Yao-lu, Mao saw a large white house, the provincial college, previously a famous academy for advanced studies, and which, during the Sung Dynasty (A.D. 960–1276), had had the great philosopher Chu Hsi (A.D. 1130–1200) as principal. Mao gazed at the building for a long time, then turned his eyes to the city itself, which had the appearance of a huge bowl. The numerous roofs of houses below made him think of the scales of a fish and suddenly he realized how high he must be above them; how high he was above all the rest of humanity.

From this reverie and from his fantasies engendered by the view from the west window, he was awakened by the sound of steps behind him. Turning his head, he was happily surprised to see his three comrades, Tan Wu-pien, Liu Hong, and Pung Shih-liang, students whom he had met on his way back from Wuchang to Changsha. Liu Hong, who was quite rich, had promised to lend Mao some money. Mao greeted them enthusiastically, and Liu invited all of them to the tea-room on the floor below. They sat together around the little table while a waiter brought them four cups of the best tea and two large plates of peanuts and watermelon seeds. The four friends chatted happily as they ate.

Tan Wu-pien was a great talker who would carry on all day and all night almost without interruption. Sometimes he became so excited that the saliva ran down from the corners of his mouth without his even realizing it. His surname Tan means Talker and Wu-pien means "he who understands the changes and vicissitudes"; but his friends like to mispronounce this name just a bit so as to make it mean "limitless." Thus he became the limitless talker. Tan was almost as large as Mao, with a big head, broad shoulders, and the beginnings of a hunchback. His very flat nose almost disappeared between big eyes and mouth when he was talking. Because of this peculiarity his schoolmates called him Wu-pi, which means "no nose" and phonetically sounds very similar to his real name.

Liu Hong, who was very tall and slenderly built, was nicknamed "the bamboo." He had a very amiable disposition and took great pleasure in inviting friends to have meals with him. His friends called these invitations "eating in the bamboo."

Pung Shih-liang, who was undersized, only about half as tall as Mao, was very lively and spirited, and his nickname was "Monkey Pung."

On this particular day they drank "in the bamboos" and almost as soon as they were seated, Tan Wu-pien began to talk. "Now," he said, "our country has become a republic. We no longer have an emperor. We are all equal. The land is ours. We are the masters, and the officials are servants of the state. Even the President of the Republic is just a servant! We could all be President. You and I, we could become President. Let me repeat that, we could be. . . ."

"I would like to be President first!" interrupted Monkey Pung.

"Monkey Pung," reprimanded Tan Wu-pien, "you think I'm just joking; but I assure you, I'm speaking quite seriously."

"No," answered Monkey Pung, "I didn't think you were joking. I know you are speaking seriously. So am I. I seriously want to be President of the Republic first. Can't I be President before you? I promise you solemnly, here in the Tien Hsin Ko, with Liu Hong and Mao Tse-tung as my witnesses, that you will be my Prime Minister when I am President of the Republic!"

Mao Tse-tung, who had been listening to Tan Wu-pien with great interest told Pung, "Let him talk. What he says is all quite true and I am very interested. Let him talk."

Tan was the son of a mandarin and he knew much more about politics, government, and history than his friends did. Mao was completely fascinated. He loved to watch the movements of the wide mouth as Tan talked, and he was absorbed in the subject. Now he asked, "Tell me, exactly what would one have to do to get elected President of the Republic? Would he have to study a lot? Should he learn all about foreign countries after he finishes his studies at the

University? Just what should one do?"

"No," replied Tan, "it is not necessary to study to get into power. Did the rulers of the Ch'in dynasty study, for instance Emperor Shih Huang (246–210 B.C.) or the Empress Han Wu (140–88 B.C.)? Wasn't Genghis Khan (1277–1294) a common soldier? All of us really know a lot more right now than any of them did. To become President you don't have to be a scholar. Politics is a different matter altogether!"

"Well, what does one do then to get political power?" asked Mao.

"Politicians must fight," replied Tan. "A politician must attack fearlessly anyone who attacks or opposes him. Other men also want to become President and he must overcome them. He must fight all who stand in his way and he must win at whatever cost. Sometimes it may be necessary to kill and to become a merciless assassin!"

"But in politics, how does one attack one's adversaries?" asked Mao.

"That is a very important question, Mao," answered Tan. "You can't attack them with your two bare hands. It is necessary for you to have many loyal partisans who march to victory with you and who are willing to work for you. You have to gather these partisans together. In a word, you have to organize a political party!"

Mao Tse-tung took in all this information greedily and very frankly expressed his admiration for Tan's great wisdom.

8
Back to School

During the first year of the Republic, 1912, the city of Changsha founded a Fourth Normal School, with Mr. Chen Jun-lin as Director. Mr. Chen was a well-known educator, who also operated a private school, the Ch'u Yi. We became fast friends and about three years later he invited me to accept a position as senior master in the Ch'u Yi private school.

When Mao Tse-tung entered the Fourth Normal, his first teacher was Chen Jun-lin. Among the many deans in this college was one named Wang Chi-fan, a friend of mine who used to loan money to Mao.

The Fourth Normal had been in existence for only a few months when the Hunan government decided to amalgamate it with the First Normal, where I was a student. One morning I saw all the furniture and movable equipment arrive for installation in our school, and the combined schools became the First Normal. Mr. Wang Chi-fan, the dean, was also transferred together with the students, who numbered about two hundred. First Normal had previously had about a thousand students, but now the combined registration made it the largest school in Changsha.

The students from Fourth Normal were not as well dressed as First Normal, since we all wore uniforms. Their clothes differed in both type and color, and they looked like raw army recruits. One of these "recruits" was a tall, clumsy, dirtily dressed young man whose shoes badly needed repairing. This young man was Mao Tse-tung.(18)

Mao was not unusual in appearance, as some people have maintained, with his hair growing low on his forehead, like the devils pictured by old-time artists, nor did he have any especially striking features. In fact I have never observed anything unusual in his physical appearance. To me he always seemed quite an ordinary, normal-looking person. His face was rather large, but his eyes were neither large nor penetrating, nor had they the sly, cunning look sometimes attributed to them. His nose was flattish and of a typical Chinese shape. His ears were well proportioned; his mouth, quite small; his teeth very white and even. These good white teeth helped to make his smile quite charming, so that no one would imagine that he was not genuinely sincere. He walked rather slowly, with his legs somewhat separated, in a way that reminded one of a duck waddling. His movements in sitting or standing were very slow. Also, he spoke slowly and he was by no means a gifted speaker.

From the first day, I knew that he was Mao Tse-tung and he knew that I was Siao Shu-tung, which was my school name, since we were distant neighbors in the country region from which we both came. Our homes were approximately thirty kilometers apart, and we lived in neighboring districts. I came from Siangsiang, and he lived across the border in Siangtan.

Though we knew each other by sight, we had never spoken except for an occasional smile or a short greeting when we met in the school corridors or on the school grounds. At that time, since I was a senior student, he did not dare to speak first to me; and I knew nothing of his personality nor his ideas. As my studies kept me very busy, I had neither time nor desire to form trivial friendships with those in lower classes.

Later, however, an incident occurred which increased our acquaintance considerably. It took place in the schoolroom where the best essays were exhibited. Each student in the fifteen or twenty classes in the school was required to write an essay once a week. The best from each class was handed to a teachers' committee which chose three, four, or five to be hung in the glass-covered exhibition cases in the large display room, for all the students to read as models. Often my essays were thus honored, and Mao became my most enthusiastic reader. His essays were also selected on several occasions and I read them with interest. Thus I became acquainted with his ideas, but what impressed me most at that time was his awkward style of handwriting. With his clumsy brush strokes, he never managed to keep quite within the lines of the squared paper, and from a distance his characters often looked like haphazard arrangements of straws. Finally he spoke to me, with a smile of apology, "You can write two words in one small square while I need three small squares for two words." What he said was quite true.

From reading the essays, we learned of each other's ideas and opinions, and thus a bond of sympathy formed between us.

Of course Mao knew all that time that I was the top student in the school and I knew that, according to prevalent criteria, he was not too bad himself. Every morning I used to hear him reading aloud from the old classics and I know he studied hard. But of all the subjects in the curriculum, only his essay-writing was good. He received no marks at all for English, only five out of a hundred for arithmetic, and in drawing the only thing he managed was a circle. In these subjects he was always among the bottom few in the class. But at that time, essay-writing was considered all-important. If the essay was good, then the student was good. So Mao was a good student!(19)

Several months after our brief exchange in the display room, we met one morning in one of the corridors. We were both walking slowly, since we were not going to class, and Mao stopped in front of me with a smile, "Mr. Siao." At that time everyone in the school addressed his fellow students in English.

"Mr. Mao," I replied, returning the greeting and wondering vaguely what he was about to say, since this was practically the first time we had really spoken to each other.

"What is the number of your study?"

"I am in study number one," I replied. Naturally he knew this quite well and the question was merely an excuse to start conversation.

"This afternoon, after class, I'd like to come to your study to look at your essays, if you don't mind," he asked.

"Of course I shall be pleased to see you," I replied, because it was customary for good friends to ask to read each other's essays, and his gesture implied both admiration and respect for the writer. Mao Tse-tung's request was at the same time a manner of offering me his friendship, which I accepted. I did not, however, ask to see his work, for that would have been considered most unusual on the part of a senior student.

Classes finished for the day at four o'clock and Mao arrived at my study within the hour. My friends had all gone out for a walk; so I was left alone waiting for his visit. During our first talk, no mention was made of our home country, and we confined our conversation to a discussion of the organization, curriculum, and teachers of the school, stating frankly our opinions of the merits of each. We agreed on gymnastics in which subject we had four teachers, one of whom specialized in military drill, another in dancing. But we did not like them and we found it difficult to show any respect. They were too smartly dressed for teachers, and we suspected their moral standards were not what they should have been. In the mornings they often missed classes because they had stayed up too late at night playing cards; so they could not waken.

Mao and I enjoyed our first talk. Finally he said, "Tomorrow I would like to come and ask your guidance." He took two of my essays, made a formal bow, and departed. He was very polite. Each time he came to see me he made a bow.

9
Our First Discussion

Next day, after classes, Mao Tse-tung again came to see me and said, "I like your essays very much and I'd like to keep them a few days longer. Would you like to go for a walk with me after dinner?" I agreed, and suggested that I wait for him in the common room. It was a very popular custom for students to take a walk after dinner.

First Normal was the only really modern construction in Changsha and people used to call it the "occidental building." It was surrounded by a wall, and outside the main gate was a road from which branched a number of lesser streets. There were several low hills behind the school which were known as the Miao Kao Feng. The city itself lay to the right, while to the left was a flight of some five hundred stone steps leading to the railway, and a little further on one came to the banks of the river Siang Kiang. The Siang Kiang is the longest river in Hunan Province and is navigated by a constant stream of boats of varying sizes. In the middle of the river is a long island on which thousands of orange trees have been planted, giving rise to the popular name Chu Chou, Orange Island. When the oranges were ripe, from a distance the isle looked like a golden-red cloud floating on the water. In the poems which Mao and I composed at this time, we often made reference to the "orange clouds" and the "orange-cloud isle." Three miles further on was Yao-lu Shan, quite a high mountain.

While some students preferred the excitement of the city, others chose to walk in the opposite direction in order to admire the beauty of nature: the river, the mountains, and the little clouds which seemed to float out from amongst the peaks. Often on Sundays some of us walked ten miles along the river banks to a place which was called the Hou Tze Shih, Monkey Rock, from the striking resemblance of an enormous gray rock to the figure of a monkey. We learned to judge distances quite accurately from the size of the monkey.

The scenery along the river banks was exquisitely beautiful and we were full of poetic ideas. I jotted down many verses in my diary and it is sad to think that all those old notes were, I understand, destroyed by the Communists when they occupied my home. Little did they realize that a great many of these poems were written jointly with Mao Tse-tung and that there was also a collection of several hundred letters which he had written to me. I remember especially one large notebook on which he had inscribed a phrase which he was fond of using, *i chieh jui i,* "all in one." The Communists are said to have no time for old writings, which have always been regarded as treasures, and they have burned great quantities as waste paper. Even though they did not realize the value of the documents, there seems little excuse for this sheer vandalism.

I still remember the beginning of one of the poems Mao and I composed one day as we were strolling along the river bank. It was quite a common practice for two people to collaborate in the composition of poems in China, and, translated literally, it ran something like this:

Siao: *Clouds come out from between the mountain peaks,*
Man returns from the river bank,
The clouds float along a thousand miles away.
Mao: *Man observes the distant sails*
While the evening sun casts its glow over the lonely village.
Siao: *A bell tolls in the old temple*
And the weary birds are returning to the deep forest.
Mao: *A woman can be seen in the tall building. . . .*

I do not remember seeing the woman Mao mentioned and I do not recall what follows.

Mao Tse-tung and I were together at this school three and a half years, and our evening walks became a regular habit. However, it was not often that we wrote poems, since our greatest pleasure was in discussions, in hearing each other's opinions of things in general.(20)

Our first after-dinner discussion along the river bank lasted two hours. Mao started by saying he liked my essays. My Chinese-composition teacher, Wang Chin-an, a famous literary man, who came from the city of Ningsiang, had often remarked that my work reminded him of the writings of Ou-yang Hsui, one of the greatest literary figures of the Sung Dynasty. Mao, sincerely or as an intentional compliment, said he agreed with Wang's opinion; that Mr. Wang understood me very well indeed. Even now, after forty years, I still remember both Wang's and Mao's words as if they had been spoken only yesterday.

I had loaned Mao two exercise books which contained more than twenty essays. The title of the first was, "Comments on Fan Chung-yen's inscription on Yen Kuang's tomb." Mao's ideas of this particular inscription, which is recorded as a piece of classic literature, differed from those I had expressed in my essay and we spent the whole evening discussing our divergent points of view. The story of Yen Kuang is as follows:

Kuang Wu Huang Ti, one of the greatest emperors of the Han Dynasty, ruled for thirty-three years (A.D. 25–57). He had, before assuming his high office, been known as Liu Shiu and had maintained a very intimate friendship with the scholar, Yen Kuang, who was also a high official. When Liu Shiu became Emperor he invited Yen Kuang to help him govern the country. Yen Kuang arrived in the capital and slept in the same bed with his imperial friend. As proof of their extreme intimacy, it is told that during the night, he unconsciously placed his feet on the sacred body of the Emperor. Kuang Wu Huang Ti asked Yen Kuang to be his Prime Minister. When he saw that his friend hesitated, he even offered him power and authority equal to his own. But Yen Kuang did not want to lead a political life. He considered it a base profession and was quite sure that if he accepted his friend's proposal, no one would believe that his purpose was entirely honest and altruistic. Therefore; he refused.

Kuang Wu Huang Ti begged him again and again, but he could not alter Yen Kuang's decision. He left the capital, located at Lo Yang at that time, now in the province of Honan, and returned to Fu Ch'un in the mountains of Chekiang Province. There he lived a quiet and retired life, spending much of his time fishing in the river. To this day, there is a part of the Fu Ch'un River known as Yen Ling Nai, in commemoration of the fact that it was one of his favorite spots. He died when he was forty years old, but his action became legendary. During the Sung Dynasty, a temple was built in his honor and the Prime Minister, Fan Chung-yen, an important literary figure of the day, was invited to write the dedication. This latter became very famous and was in time included in all literature classes as a "selected passage." It was common practice for Chinese composition teachers to require their students to write an essay on their impressions after reading the story of the two famous friends of the Han Dynasty, and it was such an essay that appeared on the first page of one of the exercise books which I had loaned to Mao Tse-tung.

Fan Chung-yen's dedication contained only two hundred nineteen words, and the theme was his admiration for both the Emperor Kuang Wu and for his friend Yen Kuang. Both demonstrated unusually high qualities, the Emperor in respecting the wisdom of the sage, and Yen Kuang in refusing to be tempted by the offer of power and worldly vanity.

When I read this dedication, I did not agree with Fan Chung-yen. I explained in my essay that I believed the Emperor had merely asked his friend to help him in his difficult task and that the request should not necessarily be interpreted as homage to superior wisdom. Nor did I think Yen Kuang's purity was so great as we had been given to understand. If he knew he was not accepting the invitation to become Prime Minister, why did he visit the Emperor and sleep with him? Was not that action an expression of his vanity?

Mao Tse-tung held a different opinion. He thought when Liu Shiu was made Emperor, that Yan Kuang should have become Prime Minister as Chang Liang, a friend of Emperor Kao Tzu, who had lived two hundred years earlier in the same dynasty (206–195 B.C.). I contended, "It is clear that you fail to grasp Yen Kuang's point of view."

We had a long discussion and finally I said, "If Yen Kuang could hear your ideas, he would say you were despicable." I spoke the words so sharply that Mao was embarrassed and blushed; so I tried to joke to put an end to the discussion, "All right," I said, "if you become Emperor one day, you will see that you will not invite me to go and sleep with you in the same bed, and put my feet on your body!"

10
The "Confucius" of the First Normal School

"Confucius" was the nickname given to one of the teachers in First Normal School by the students because of his impeccable conduct. He did not know that I was married and he tried to interest me in his daughter, Yang K'ai-hui. However, after his death, he became father-in-law to Mao Tse-tung. The real name of "Confucius" was Yang Huai-chung.

Mao Tse-tung often remarked that Yang Huai-chung had been a great influence in his life. He was also known as Ch'en-chi, and he came from the Pan Tsang village of the district of Changsha. He called his study the *Ta Hua Chai* and he wrote this name on all his notebooks.

Mr. Yang was a very learned person and he was endowed with a strong personality with which he enforced upon himself a very strict moral code. His conduct was at all times beyond reproach. He was so familiar with the doctrine of Confucius that his friends and his students regarded him as if he were a reincarnation of the great sage.(21)

He had spent his youth studying philosophy and when he was thirty years old, he began to study English. Later he traveled abroad, first to Japan, then in Great Britain, where he obtained a degree in philosophy at Edinburgh University. Subsequently he undertook further studies in philosophy in a German university. Thus he had acquired quite an appreciable knowledge of both oriental and occidental standards. During the first year of the Republic, he returned to Changsha from Germany and was immediately invited by First Normal to accept a teaching position.

First Normal was the richest school in Changsha. Not only did students receive free board and lodging, but also their books and clothing. Under the Emperor, they had also received pocket money. For this reason, as may be imagined, it was not easy to pass the entrance examination. Each of the sixty-three districts of Hunan Province submitted the names of their twenty best students, but not more than five of these passed the preliminary examination. When I took this examination in Siangsiang, eighty of the hundred aspirants were eliminated. In the second examination, only a fifth of the five hundred passed. Students were thus carefully selected, and the same may be said of the faculty, who were well-trained and some of whom were famous personalities. They received good salaries and when vacancies occurred, teachers were often drawn from a distance, such as Shanghai, or Anhwei, and other provinces. This explains why Mr. Yang remained in Changsha where he taught logic, philosophy, and education.

After the summer vacation when I returned to school, I found the students discussing the fact that we were to have a new teacher who was said to be especially good. Naturally everyone was curious to see what he was like. When classes began, we saw him coming toward us in the distance. He walked very slowly and, when he entered the classroom, we saw that he was about fifty years old, clean shaven, with a swarthy complexion. His eyes were deep set and rather small. He spoke awkwardly and read the whole of his lecture, without repetition and with no opportunity for explanation or discussion. The hour passed and everyone was deeply disappointed. Within the week other classes also commented on the poor impression made by Mr. Yang in his classes. Heads of the classes held a meeting and as a result urged the Director to ask Mr. Yang to change his method of teaching and to explain his text. A fortnight later at another meeting, it was proposed that the Director be asked to dismiss Mr. Yang, and if he refused, all the classes threatened to strike. At the time I was president of these delegations and I opposed the suggestion. I contended that although Mr. Yang did not speak fluently, if one read his printed text, he would find it most valuable. These texts were the result of his own study and experience and were very different from those which were merely composites of others' books. I felt that we should wait till the end of the semester to see what practical results we had accomplished before making a drastic decision. Ch'en Chang, the head of the second class, agreed with me and eventually they accepted my suggestion and settled down to work.

After this meeting I talked with several of my best friends, Hsiung Kuang-ch'u, Ch'en Chang, and others, to discuss how we could get our schoolmates to understand Mr. Yang's teaching and to appreciate it. The only way seemed to be to persuade them to read his written texts carefully. Also, it was important for us to explain and interpret Mr. Yang's "Confucian" personality to them.

Mao Tse-tung had not yet had an opportunity to attend Mr. Yang's lectures since he taught only the upper classes and when he first came to school Mao was three years below me.

Within two months, everyone who attended Mr. Yang's lectures admired and respected him. Although he did not talk much in class, each short statement meant a great deal. His really was the Confucian style of speaking. Within a year, the entire school accepted him and he became the "Confucius of First Normal School." Other schools in Changsha invited him and he conducted classes as far away as the high school at the foot of Yao-lu Mountain. Soon he was known to students throughout the city as "Confucius."

Every Sunday morning my friends, Hsiung Kuang-ch'u, Ch'en Chang and I visited Mr. Yang's home to discuss our studies together. We read each other's notebooks, talked over our problems, and returned to school after lunch. Many of the phrases in my notebook pleased Mr. Yang so much that he copied them for himself. He was pleased with my work, and on my examination papers, he often gave me the maximum mark of 100 and added "plus 5." Once Mao Tse-tung wrote an essay which he called "A Discourse on the Force of the Mind" (hsin li lun) and Mr. Yang gave him the famous 100 plus 5 mark. Mao was very proud since it was the only time he received such a high grade, and he never tired of telling people about it.

Mr. Yang wrote several works which were never published but which remained in manuscript form. After his death, his son Yang K'ai-chih sold them to Mr. Yi P'ei-chi, an ex-Minister of Education, without realizing that, since his ideas were very different from Mr. Yang's, this gentleman would not appreciate the true value of the writings. Apparently the works were lost after Mr. Yi P'ei-chi's death.

After six years of teaching in Changsha, Mr. Yang received a telegram from Chang Shih-chao, former Minister of Education in Peking, advising him that he was invited by the President of Peking University to go there to teach. He left Changsha for Peking in the summer of 1918 and took a house in the Tou Fu Ch'ih Hutung where he remained several months. Soon I went to Peking and lived in Mr. Yang's house and later we were joined by Mao Tse-tung. So we all three lived together for a time.

In January 1919, I left for Paris and several months later, I received a letter telling me that Mr. Yang was dead. While he was in Changsha, he had had an especially large tub made for him. He filled it with cold water and each morning took a bath, immersing himself completely. He continued this practice of a cold bath in Peking, saying, "Every day one must do something difficult to strengthen one's will. Cold water not only strengths the will; it is good for the health!" I think the cold bath in the icy Peking winter may have been one cause of his death.

In his diary, Mr. Yang paid me a compliment which he repeated on several occasions in public: "My three most notable students, of the several thousands I taught during my six years in Changsha, were first, Siao Shu-tung; second, Ts'ai Ho-shen; and third, Mao Tse-tung. The three best women students were Tao Szu-yung, Hsiang Ching-yu, and Jen Pei-tao."

11
Miss Yang K'ai-hui, Who Married Mao Tse-tung

Mr. Yang had two children—a son, K'ai-chih, and a daughter, K'ai-hui. K'ai-hui was the younger. She was rather small in stature and round-faced. She looked somewhat like her father, with the same deep-set, smallish eyes, but her skin was quite white, since she had inherited none of his swarthiness. In 1912 when I first saw her, she was seventeen years of age and studying in the Changsha Middle School.

From that year, when my two classmates, Hsiung Kuang-ch'u, Ch'en Chang and I visited Mr. Yang's home every Sunday morning to discuss our studies, we had lunch with them and then returned to the school. At the table we were always joined by K'ai-hui and her mother. When they entered we merely bowed our heads politely in greeting but none of us ever spoke. Every week for two whole years we ate our meal rapidly and in silence, not one of us ever uttering a single word. Naturally we did not ignore each other. We could hardly act as if no one else were at the table, and sometimes our lines of vision crossed, especially if two of us started to help himself from the same dish at the same time. We communicated only by means of our eyes and eyebrows, but we never smiled at each other. Again in 1918, when I stayed in Mr. Yang's home in Peking, we observed exactly the same table manners.

Mr. Yang himself never spoke a word and we all respected his silence and ate as rapidly as was possible. The atmosphere reminded one of people praying in a church. Mr. Yang paid a great deal of attention to matters of hygiene but apparently he did not realize that it is better for one's health to talk and laugh normally during meals, that a happy atmosphere aids digestion.

His wife, who was always very kind, was an excellent cook and gave us plenty to eat. We were especially appreciative, since the school food was far from good or satisfying. My two friends and I ate much more than usual every Sunday when we visited Mr. Yang and sometimes we had to restrain ourselves in order not to appear too greedy by eating up everything on the table. We suggested that we should pay for the meals each time we went and Mr. Yang said we could if we liked, since that was the custom in some foreign universities, but it must be very little—a token payment and nothing more.

The three of us always went and left together. Only once, in 1912, after lunch, when Mr. Yang had accompanied us to the door, suddenly he asked Hsiung to stay behind for a moment. Hsiung sat down and we left alone. I supposed that Mr. Yang had something to say which he did not wish us to hear; so we said nothing about the matter.

When I was in Paris in 1919, I was surprised to receive a long letter from K'ai-hui telling the details of her father's death. She knew how much I admired and respected Mr. Yang and she realized that the news of his death would affect me almost as if he were my own father. Her letter was very sad. We had never spoken to each other before and this was the only letter I ever received from her. At the end she wrote that she was returning to Changsha, but she gave me no address; so I was unable to reply.

After Mao Tse-tung returned to Changsha in 1920, he married K'ai-hui.(22) They had two children and one, after a visit he made to Moscow, is today called "Prince Mao" by non-Communist Chinese. However, K'ai-hui was not Mao's first love. In our group of school friends was Miss Tao Szu-yung, the girl named by Mr. Yang as one of his best students. Miss Tao was a very superior person. In 1920 she and Mao organized a cultural bookstore in Changsha but they had very different ideas and later they separated on friendly terms. Miss

Tao founded a school, the Li Ta Hsüen Yüan, in Shanghai, where she lived until her death. She was much older than K'ai-hui, his second love.

In 1920, when I returned to Changsha from Paris and Peking, I asked for news of Mrs. Yang and K'ai-hui because I wanted to visit them. He told me that they lived a long way off in the country and said nothing about his love affair. Later, he did confide in me. At this time, I asked Mrs. Huan, a friend of Mrs. Yang's, to deliver a little gift to her in my behalf. I was sorry I had not replied to K'ai-hui's letter and I felt guilty because I had not offered to take care of her father's manuscripts.

In 1927, in Nanking I learned that the Hunan Provincial Government was about to arrest K'ai-hui, since she was the wife of Mao Tse-tung, a Communist. I did everything I could, including writing many letters and telegrams to influential people, in an effort to save her life, but to no avail.

In 1936, when I was in Paris for the third time, my old friend Hsiung Kuang-ch'u came to see me. Naturally, we spoke nostalgically of our old school and we shared our feelings of sorrow for Mr. Yang's family, agreeing that it was terrible that K'ai-hui should have been shot. Hsiung Kuang-ch'u heaved a great sigh and said, "The one who killed K'ai-hui was Jun-chih." (Jun-chih was Mao's second name.)

Finally I asked him a question I had thought about for a long time. I said, "About twenty years ago, I wanted to ask you something, but I didn't. Now I wish you'd tell me something. Do you remember one day when we three were leaving Mr. Yang's house together and he called you back? What did Mr. Yang tell you? What was the secret?"

He answered without hesitation, "Mr. and Mrs. Yang wanted you to marry their daughter K'ai-hui," and he added that K'ai-hui herself had this wish. "I had to tell Mr. Yang that you were already married. That was why I said nothing to you at the time."

So that was it. Now I was silent, thinking. I was sorry I had not known this thirty-three years earlier. Mr. Yang had now been dead twenty-six years and his daughter, eighteen. K'ai-hui had written me a long letter which I had not answered. When I returned to Changsha, I had not even visited her and sent only a small gift to her mother. She must have thought that I had no feelings, that I completely lacked sympathy. In my guilt, I mused, "If I had not been married, if I had accepted her love, she would not have been arrested as Mao Tse-tung's wife and been shot. It might have been."

One day in Geneva, my wife, Siao-ying (the courtesy name of Mme. Siao-yu), and I were talking about Mr. Yang's family. She was deeply touched and said "Was it not a predestined tragedy? It is really very poetic."

Immediately I took out my pen and composed some lines which, translated literally, read as follows:

Beautiful dreams are very difficult to realize in this life.
I think sadly of something which happened forty years ago.
I gave no indication that I liked her, but she did.
It was impossible for us to fly side by side like a pair of birds as she
    wished, because I was married.
Our hearts were never in contact.
How can I make her happy?
Another had no heart; he abandoned his wife for the sake of am-
    bition (Mao).
His wife still hates him in the other world.

12
Our Mutual Friend, Ts'ai Ho-shen

In relating the beginnings of the Chinese Communist Party, mention must be made of our friend Ts'ai Ho-shen, who was the first Chinese to accept, unreservedly, the principles of the Communist doctrine. He played a very important part in the conversion of Mao to Communism.

Ts'ai Ho-shen, whom we called Ho-shen, was born in my home district. He was tall and slender, and his two front teeth protruded noticeably. He was strong-willed and, though one rarely saw him smile, he was very kind to his friends.

Ho-shen and I were schoolmates in First Normal, but he was two classes lower and later he transferred to the Yao-lu Shan Higher Normal School. His mother conducted the school in our town, and we called her "Aunty." She also had a daughter, Ts'ai Ch'ang, who is now President of the Communist Women's Association. When Ts'ai Ch'ang was a girl in her teens, we used to call her "Little Sister." She was very strong-willed like her brother, though she was quite small and did not resemble him physically at all. I was very fond of Ho-shen and respected his family.

Ho-shen was handicapped by a lack of initiative and drive, and he was averse to asking any help or favors of others. As a result, he remained without a job after graduating from Higher Normal, and he lived with his mother and sister who had rented a house at the foot of Mount Yao-lu. They were desperately poor and often had no rice to cook on the fire.

I had a regular income, since I was teaching in both the Hsiu Yeh and Ch'u Yi schools, and I had my living quarters in the latter. Mao Tse-tung knew of my friendship with Ho-shen and one day he came very hurriedly to see me in the school, and said, "Have you had any news from Ho-shen?"

Surprised, I replied that I had not seen him for quite some time, and waited for his news.

"Well," Mao Tse-tung continued, "someone told me that the family has no rice and that Ho-shen is so worried at home thinking that he is a burden to his mother that he has taken a basket full of books and left for the Ai Wan T'ing under Mount Yao-lu." Ai Wan T'ing is the Pavilion of the Evening Breeze, a small pointed-roofed shelter supported by four columns and open to the air. "He has nothing but the winds for his meals and he sleeps in the open air."

"Have you seen him?" I asked.

"No, I haven't seen him. Ch'en told me about it."

"Why don't you go and see him?" I asked.

"It's quite useless for me to go. There's nothing I can do to help him," shrugged Mao, leaving the responsibility with me.

After Mao had gone, I asked for a short leave from duty and immediately set out across the river toward the Yao-lu. As I approached the pavilion, I saw Ho-shen seated on the stones, with his back against one of the columns. He held his book in one hand and was reading so earnestly that he did not hear me come up. He appeared for all the world like a statue. When I spoke his name, he looked up, startled, and said, "How do you find time to come all this way across the river to see me?"

"I asked for the day off," I answered.

"No doubt you are going to the Yao-lu Academy?" he asked.

"No, my friend, I was not going to the Academy. I came especially to see you. And I also want to visit Aunty Ts'ai," I replied.

"What is the news? It's such a long time since I've been to town, and we have no newspapers here."

"There's no special news," I said. "Do you live in this pavilion? No doubt it is very nice and cool, but it will not be quite so pleasant if it rains."

"But it's not the rainy season now."

"I came here to invite you to come and live at our school, the Ch'u Yi. I feel very lonely there. Just outside my bedroom is a little cubicle with a bed in it. You could do your reading there, and after classes we could chat together."

"But it's not your home," he protested. "You're living in a school and I don't want to make trouble for you."

"But it would be no trouble at all. The building where we have our dormitory is just as if it were my own home. It will be no trouble at all. You'll feel right at home immediately. Come. You must come with me now. Today."

"I must go back to arrange my things first. I shall go with you tomorrow," he replied.

It was agreed and we set off together to see Aunty Ts'ai. Ho-shen held his broken basket of books together very carefully. When we arrived at his home, Aunty Ts'ai called her daughter to gather some twigs from the mountain trees, and very shortly, with a happy smile "Little Sister" brought me a cup of boiling water. They could not afford to buy tea. Aunty apologized for not "having time to go to town to buy tea" and asked me to accept the hot water. I gave her an envelope with four dollar notes in it, explaining, "A little gift for Aunty."

"Oh, thank you," she said. "But you shouldn't do that!" Carefully, she put it in her pocket.

She guessed, no doubt, that it was money, but she did not know how much. At that time four dollars was quite a generous sum with which mother and daughter could buy food for at least two months. Soon she went into the house and returned a moment later with a cheerful smile on her otherwise inscrutable face. She made no comment, but I knew that she had opened the envelope.

"Aunty Ts'ai," I said, "I have come to take Ho-shen back to school with me. He is lonely here, and I am lonely in the school after classes; so I have come to fetch him to live with me."

"Oh, that will be fine," Aunty Ts'ai exclaimed. "He has been very lonely and worried here. That's why he went to live in Ai Wan T'ing!"

Next day Ho-shen brought his small bundle of belongings to the school and settled himself in the little room outside my dormitory. There he had a table and a bookshelf, and there was good light for reading from the window. Outside the window was a beautiful flowering tree.

Mao came again to see me in the afternoon while I was still on duty; so we had opportunity for only a few words, but when my class finished and the students left, we had a long talk. Mao proposed that Ho-shen prolong his stay and the latter was delighted to hear this.

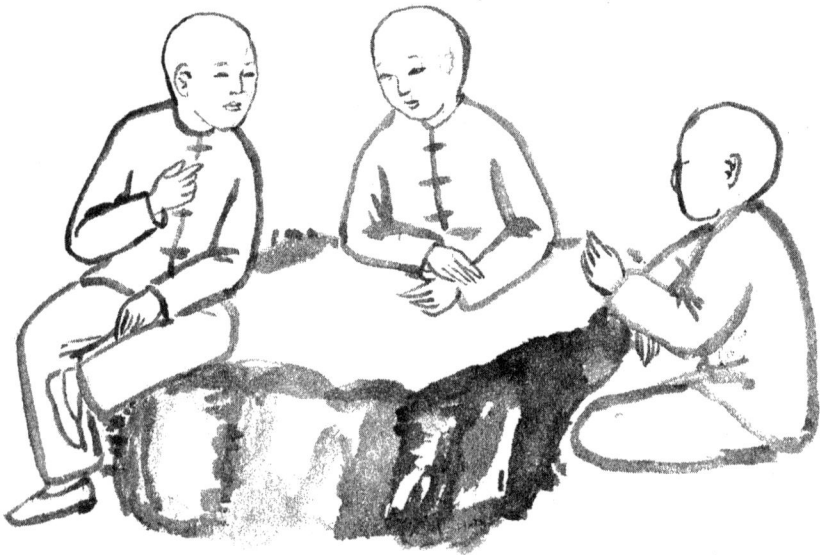

Later we all dined together before Mao returned to First Normal where he was still a student.

Since I had to have my meals with the students, Ho-shen was obliged to eat alone in my room. I had asked the cook to prepare his food, but I learned that he was eating only one meal a day, at noon. Afternoons, he went out and did not return till after dinner. When I asked why he did not have dinner with me, he replied, "In the afternoon I like to go to the library to read. Sometimes I go home. Of course I eat dinner at home and then I come back here to school."

This seemed very strange, since his home was very far away and he had to cross the river. How could he return home for supper every day? I could not imagine where he could get a meal in town. No, he must be eating only one meal a day.

Shortly afterward the cook jokingly commented on my friend's appetite. "What a big eater your guest is!" he exclaimed. "I used to give him half a little *t'ung* (small pail of food), but now he eats three or four people's portions."

On hearing this, I had little doubt that Ho-shen was eating only one meal a day and I asked him again where he ate at night; but I saw that he did not care to answer; so I said no more. He probably hated to have me pay for his meals and he wanted to save me additional expense. Yet he did not want to explain his motive. Needless to say, I was touched by this episode and I asked the cook to give him an extra meat dish so as to provide a satisfactory daily diet. This gave some idea of Ho-shen's stoicism and integrity in friendship.

Later he and I created a "half-day work" movement for students and in 1919, he, his mother, and sister went to France, where he lived in the Montargis Middle School, studying French. There he fell in love with our best woman colleague, Miss Hsiang Ching-yu. Since I was in France at the time, Ho-shen told me all about his love affair. The two of them wrote a booklet about it, entitled "Alliance toward High Things." When they asked my opinion, knowing that they were living together as man and wife, even though they were opposed to the principles of marriage, I replied, "You two are my best friends. I wish to congratulate you both and dedicate a short phrase to you—'alliance toward low things'—the name of your booklet with just one word changed."

Previously Ho-shen had frankly expressed his distaste for the so-called capitalist system. This had been his own frank opinion long before the Russian Revolution, but he had not discovered how he could do anything about it. With the establishment of the Russian Communist Government it was, therefore, logical that he accept their doctrine wholeheartedly and unconditionally. I tried to tell him to study and analyze the Communist principles before accepting them, but he insisted there was no need since the truth of them was quite obvious. The French newspaper, *Humanité*, was full of Communist propaganda and although Ho-shen had by no means mastered the French language, he pored over this paper every day with a dictionary in his hand. Since he did not understand too well, he made many mistakes in translation, but he would not admit his errors, even to himself. He had preconceived ideas and nothing could shake his conviction. But when we had discussions, they were always pleasant and amiable. Although our opinions differed very considerably, we respected each other's ideas and until Ho-shen's death, our friendship remained firm and intimate.

While he was living among the Chinese students in France, he organized the propagation of the doctrine through selected Communist comrades. Among those most strongly influenced by him were Hsiang Ching-yu, Li Wei-han, Ts'ai Ch'ang, and Li Fu-chun. Mao Tse-tung was strongly influenced through letters from Ho-shen.

In 1921, Ho-shen and his family returned to Shanghai, where he became editor of the Communist Party's newspaper *Hsiang Tao* (*The Guide*).

While I was teaching at the French-Chinese University in Peking in the year 1925, I received two long letters from him. His sweetheart, Hsiang Ching-yu, had been arrested in the French Concession in Hankow and he asked me to help her. Though I did all I could, she was finally shot. I was very sorry, for, even though we held different political views and philosophies, she was a good friend.

Ts'ai Ho-shen died a few years later. Though he was one of the founders of the Chinese Communist Party, Ho-shen remained a dear and highly respected friend to the last.

13
Yang Tu

In less than half a century after the birth of the Republic of China, two men had conceived plans to overthrow it, and both were successful in carrying out their individual schemes. Strangely enough, both men came from the same district of Hunan Province, Siangtan. One of these was Yang Tu, the other Mao Tse-tung.

Though these men did not know each other, I knew both of them. Fundamentally they were very different in their manner of thinking, though there were certain points of resemblance, and in relating the story of Mao Tse-tung's youth, mention should be made of Yang Tu.

Yang was almost twenty years older than Mao. He belonged to the previous generation, and in later years, it was his political ambition to be able to influence to some extent his fellow Siangtanite, Mao Tse-tung. No doubt neither sympathized with the other's ideas, but that is not a part of this story.

I remember when I was a very young lad, hearing people in the Tutor School say, "This Yang Tu is a man of exceptional talent." But at that time I did not know what they meant. That was when he achieved second place in the notoriously difficult Imperial Examinations, attaining thereby the highest educational honor possible under the old system. His reputation was well known and much talked about throughout the country.

Though the Chinese Republic was established in 1912, internally the country was very unstable, and Yang Tu maintained that until education became more general, it was impossible to practice successfully a democratic republican form of government. He believed that the masses had to be educated in order to be able to govern themselves, and in the meantime, that the republic should be changed to a limited monarchy system like those in England and Germany at that time.

In 1913, he started to put his ideas into action. First, he brought together five well-known public figures in Peking to form an association which they gave the name *Ch'ou An Hui*, "Stabilization of the Country." This group proclaimed the President, Yüan Shih-k'ai, to be

Emperor. Yüan Shih-k'ai himself was, of course, quite agreeable to the change and the plan found quite wide acceptance. The establishment of the republic was thus followed within four years by a return to the monarchy, the name given to the new system being translated as "the first year of the New Era." Yang Tu became the Emperor's Prime Minister.

Many high ranking army officials, however, did not approve of the change in government, and just eighty-three days after he was put on the throne as Emperor, Yüan Shih-k'ai was overthrown by a popular revolt, organized by this army nucleus. A republic was once more proclaimed and Yüan Shih-k'ai, it is said, died of a broken heart.

Though Yang Tu's political activities had seemingly ended in failure, he lost none of his political ambition. At that time Mao Tse-tung and I were still students in First Normal and we followed these events in the newspapers day by day with keen interest, discussing what was taking place and endeavoring to forecast what the future might hold in store. Our attitudes were, however, fundamentally quite different: Mao was very excited and enthusiasic about Yang Tu and his political action, while I was inclined to be rather cynical and impatient with his political scheming. I really considered Yang Tu a rather despicable person, completely lacking in personal pride, integrity, and dignity, and as for Yüan Shih-k'ai, I felt that he had shown clearly in a number of ways that he was not worthy of the name of Emperor.

After Yüan Shih-k'ai's untimely death, many people, following the Chinese custom, composed memorial couplets for him. For Yang Tu, even with his high educational honors, the task was not easy; but everyone looked to him for the official memorial couplets, since he had been Prime Minister and people felt that he was most capable of composing a fitting memorial. The first part of his couplet (*tui tzu*) said: "The republican government was bad for China, but China has been unjust to the republican form of government; this will be seen clearly a hundred years from now." The second half ran: "Your Majesty owed a debt to monarchy, but monarchy owes nothing to you; from your place in the other world, you must agree with this." Later he wrote two short poems on his fan which, translated literally, reads as follows:

With success you become an emperor or king,
With failure you remain a common man.
But in the end, the grave claims all alike.
I exchange my post of counselor to the Emperor
For retirement to fish peacefully on the Five Lakes,
As did Fang Li.

To serve a master with whom one has an intimate acquaintance
Is a difficult task.
Wang Man and Chang Liang died unhappy
After dedicating their lives to their Emperor Masters.
The will of Heaven will decree further troubles for the country.
*But I am no longer to be a Kung Ming.**

In 1926, the army chief, Chang Tso-lin, formed a government in Peking and proclaimed himself Marshal. It was proposed that Yang Tu should be Minister of Education and he asked me to help him. At that time, I was a revolutionary who lived in constant fear of arrest by Chang Tso-lin's secret police; so I acceded to his request with pleasure, since I was thus assured of protection in case of need. Yang Tu and I had many long talks on the subject of Communism, which Chang Tso-lin was attempting to stamp out unmercifully. In fact, anyone even suspected of being an active member of the movement, who fell into his hands, was summarily shot. At that time, the Communist leader was the director of the Peking University Library and a good friend of mine. Later, he was strangled on orders from Chang. Many quite innocent people were killed during this period because they were suspected of being in sympathy with the radicals and Communists. Mao himself was in hiding and I was without news of him.

One day when Yang Tu and I were talking, he warned me of possible danger, and the following conversation took place: "Tzu-cheng," he said, "you had better be careful. People are saying that you have Communist tendencies and in some quarters it is being suggested that you are a Communist spy."

"How strange," I answered, "why should they suspect me?"

"Because your talk is inclined to be radical and in the university, it

* Kung Ming was the famous Prime Minister under Liu Pei.

is said, you often favored the Communist students. However, the most important reason is that you are Mao Tse-tung's best friend and you have often been heard to say that he has his good points. It would almost seem at times that you are campaigning for him," warned Yang Tu.

"It is true that I was Mao Tse-tung's best friend, but I never became a Communist."

"But, my friend, how can you be such a good friend of his? I have heard that he has no sentiments whatever!"

"We were schoolmates," I explained, "and he seemed to have been attracted to me. We got to enjoy the discussions we used to have and naturally, in time, we became very close friends. I admit that Mao's conduct has sometimes indicated that he can be quite hard-hearted, but they can't say that he has no feelings or sentiments at all."

"Well," continued Yang, "I read in the paper that his hair grows very low down on his forehead, and that he has a very ugly face."

"That's perfectly ridiculous! He's really not at all bad looking. In fact, he's quite a normal person."

"They say he wants to kill his own father," reported Yang.

"It's a fact that Mao doesn't get on too well with his father," I agreed, "but that's no reason why he should want to kill him."

"I've also heard that he did very poorly in school; is that so?"

"In general he did not do too well, but his language and literature were good and he wasn't bad in history."

"Can he write essays, and does he do well in calligraphy?"

"Essay writing was always his best subject in school, but his hand writing was always very poor. He couldn't seem to master the art of penmanship. The characters were too large and messy."

"Does he have a good foundation in the classics and philosophy?" Yang inquired further.

"I should say not! He never did read much from the classics and he never cared for studying from books. However, he does very well in discussion and can write a long essay without saying anything worthwhile, in the fashion of many Chinese scholars."

"This is the first time I've heard anyone say anything good about Mao Tse-tung," explained Yang. "But you must not talk about this anywhere else. It would be very dangerous and it would increase the suspicion that you are a Communist."

"Thank you for the warning," I said warmly, "I know I cannot speak freely to everyone, but if I can't talk, I can't tell lies either!"

"The ancients said, 'Evil comes out of the mouth.' In these times, it's probably better not to talk very much. Between ourselves, of course, we can say anything." Then he asked, "Tell me, what do you really think of this fellow, Mao Tse-tung? Has he any real ability, knowledge, natural endowment, or talent? What I mean is, does he have any real talent?"

"What is talent?" I asked. "Who is a genius? That's a very difficult question to answer. I do know, first, that Mao is a person who takes great pains to plan very carefully whatever he undertakes and that he's a great schemer and organizer. Second, he can estimate quite accurately the power of his enemies. Third, he can hypnotize his audience. He's really got a terrific power of persuasion and there are very few people who are not carried away by his words. If you agree with what he says, you are his friend; if not, you are his enemy. It's as simple as that. I came to realize what sort of person he was a very long time ago. If you say he has talent, that he's a genius, then Chang Hsien-chung and Li Ch'uang, the two famous bandit chiefs, were also geniuses. Their talents are similar. Likewise you can say that Liu Pang and Liu Shiu, the two emperors in the Han Dynasty, were successful men; but had they been less lucky, they would have been bandits. Then no one would have said they were geniuses. You wrote a poem that expresses the idea quite accurately, 'To become a nobleman or a king is success; to remain a common man is failure.' From ancient times it has been said that heroes all like to interfere with other people's business. The hero is one of the world's madmen. He is always a source of trouble. If there were no brilliant individuals nor madmen, the world would remain at peace."

"Let's not discuss the philosophical aspect for the moment," interrupted Yang. "Do you think that Communism can be put into practice?"

"That depends upon the method of government in operation, and upon the political stability of the country," I conceded. "If the people are restless and dissatisfied with their form of government, then Communism may spread very rapidly. Remember how the Six Countries were conquered by the Ch'in Dynasty? That event should more correctly be designated as a failure on the part of the Six Countries than a victory for the Ch'in. The same thing may happen again. If the Communists are successful in China, it will be because their opponents make the same mistakes as did the Six Countries."

Later events proved this to be the case. At the time of this conversation, the Communists did not anticipate that they could ever dominate the whole of China.

14
Our All-night Talk on the Miao Kao Feng

The daily routine for students of the First Normal was very rigid and their activities were strictly scheduled to the last minute: the times for entering classrooms, the reading rooms, dining room, and the dormitory were all fixed and were indicated by sharp blasts on a trumpet, in imitation of the army bugle. When the trumpet sounded, the thousand or more students all gathered together like so many ducks and they were directed by ten disciplinary officers. Mao and I strongly objected to what we considered unnecessary insistence upon discipline, and we often failed to obey the trumpet blasts. For a time the disciplinary officers reprimanded us, but finally the Principal conceded that since we were good students, and since our conduct records were good, our failure should be ignored.

Our main reason for completely ignoring the trumpet blasts was our desire to carry on uninterruptedly with our conversations. We felt that these talks were very important and of great significance and that there should be no break in their continuity.

As stated above, we always got together after supper and had long discussions while we walked along the river bank. In the summer time, after the rest of the students went to the big study or to the reading room, we often went out and sat on the grass up on the Miao Kao Feng. The Miao Kao Feng was a small hill about two or three hundred meters in height situated just behind the school, and only a few minutes' walk from the gymnasium. From this hill we looked down on the tall school building below us and on across to the peak of Mount Yao-lu. Often we went to the top of this hill at night and watched the little lights of the ten thousand homes of Changsha shining below us away beyond the school, as we sat and talked under the moon and stars.

I remember very well one particular occasion which was quite memorable. We had walked as usual up to the top of Miao Kao after supper and had found a comfortable seat on the grass. We were deep in conversation an hour or so later when we heard the trumpet. "They must be going into the Common Room now," we said. Later, the trumpet sounded again. "Now they will be going to the dormitory."

Half an hour later, a final blast of the trumpet: "They'll be putting out the lights now!" And still we sat there talking. Soon the whole school was enveloped in darkness and we knew that we were the only two students not in bed. Later we learned that our absence was noted, but at that time, we were too deeply engrossed in our talk even to think of any consequences of our being out after lights.

This was the period when Yüan Shih-k'ai was President of the Republic and as usual we were discussing the events that were reported each day in the newspapers and trying to forecast China's future. I remember our discussion this night quite clearly. "Just think how Yüan Shih-k'ai could influence the future of China!" I exclaimed. "But he's nothing short of a criminal. And those army chiefs are simply his puppets!"

"Apart from Yüan Shih-k'ai there seems to be no one capable of carrying out the reforms that China needs," Mao pointed out. "K'ang Yu-wei has some good ideas but he's out of date; and as for Sun Yat-sen, he's the real leader of the revolution, but he doesn't have any military power."

"Some brand new influence is needed to reform China!" I said.

"Of course, a new force is required," agreed Mao.

"To reform the country, each individual citizen must be reformed and each one must cultivate his own character," I pointed out.

"It's a matter of many people getting together to work out one predetermined fixed idea," Mao stated. "We two could do almost anything!"

"No, we two are not enough," I replied. "There must be many people, all of whom have the same ideas that we have. We two must organize them. They will be our comrades."

"Let's study our schoolmates first. There are more or less a thousand of them here. We'll see how many we can find to join us."

"We must choose only the best and most intelligent," I pointed out, "only those who have very high ideals."

"We know those who are most intelligent, that's easy," Mao said, "and we are acquainted with their conduct. But it's not so easy to know their ideals."

"You and I will have to talk with them and discuss the problem in a general sort of way and then we must select those whom we consider to be the very best. After that, we can talk with each one individually," I suggested. "For instance, there's Ts'ai Ho-shen in the Higher Normal School. We both know quite well that he shares our ideas. Then again, there's Hsiung Kuang-ch'u and Ch'en Chang and Ch'en Shao-hsiu I'm sure we could count on all of them as our first comrades. In the lower classes, you know the students better than I do and you can select them."

Mao agreed, saying, "Yes, I have one or two fellows in mind now that I can try to talk to."

We were being carried along by our plans, and I continued, "From the thousand students in the school, we should select only ten to start with. We have plenty of choice and the selection must be made very carefully. It will be too bad if we can't find ten among the thousand. We can form an association with this nucleus of ten and when they are well organized, we can start recruiting more members."

Mao suggested, "The association must have a good name. And rules! Why don't you start writing down some rules?"

"Since it is to be an association for the purpose of study, we might call it the *Hsin Min Hsüeh Hui,* The New People's Study Association."

As the night wore on, we continued. "I think the Association should have three aims," I remarked. "First, to encourage good moral conduct among its members; second, to interchange knowledge and third, to form strong bonds of friendship."

"I think you should write the details out in the form of a draft and then we can study them again more carefully," Mao suggested.

We discussed in detail how we should go about increasing our membership in the Association and finally, we decided that there were no more suitable candidates within the school and that we should have to look outside. This would not be easy and we discussed the various possibilities for a long time.

In the end, we decided to write down a summary of our aims, including that of saving our country, and our reasons for forming the Association. We decided that this should be written in very clear and concise form and then sent to the students' associations in other schools for their consideration. Those who agreed with the principles and aims were to write to us and we would go to see them and talk the matter over with them before they were taken into membership.

Mao was to write a letter which we would have printed and sent to all the schools in Changsha. The letter was short and very simple, the general idea being, "Today our country is in a very critical condition. None of the members of the central government can be depended upon. We want to form an association of all those with views similar to our own. The principal aims of the association will be self-improvement and reform of the country. All those who are interested in this idea are requested to write to us and we shall discuss it personally and make further plans." This was rather an audacious open letter and we were afraid people would just laugh at us. Because we did not think it advisable to sign our own names, we chose a pseudonym, *erh shih pa pi*, the "twenty-eight strokes," in honor of Mao, whose full name is written with twenty-eight strokes. Perhaps this was an omen, since this term *erh shih pa pi* later came to be widely used as a synonym for Chinese Communism, the first ideogram of which is composed by coincidence of the form signifying twenty-eight.

While Mao wrote the first draft of the letter, I jotted down a set of rules for our *Hsin Min Hsüeh Hui*. When we had finished, we exchanged our work, read over what the other had written, and made a few corrections and suggestions. By this time it was dawn and suddenly we heard below us the loud trumpet blast. It was morning. That was the signal to get up; so we set off down the hill toward the school. We had spent the whole night working on the first steps of our project to reform China.

15

The Hsin Min Study Association, Embryo of Chinese Communism

The Hsin Min Study Association was organized by Mao Tse-tung and me in 1914. In the beginning, it was merely a society of carefully selected students of good moral character who had ideas and ideals similar to ours. The aims would be stated simply as the betterment or improvement of each individual, strengthening his moral and spiritual fiber and improving his education, as well as bringing about needed reforms in the country, but without expressing any political opinions nor affiliating with any party. Later, however, Mao Tse-tung and other members of the Association developed political ambitions and they accepted the Communist doctrine. At the present time, a great many of the top rulers in Peking are former members of the old Hsin Min Study Association; while the others, the more scholarly, idealistic element, have remained loyal to the Liberals. Our Study Association must be regarded, therefore, as the embryo of Chinese Communism since, when the Communist doctrine began to awaken active interest, the nucleus of the movement was already in existence in our group. I have called it the embryo of Chinese Communism since I think this is the most appropriate term; although some years later other separate terms appeared, the Hsin Min remained the principal nucleus.(23)

I well remember the spring day when I finished composing the Association's rules. They were only seven clauses and all were very simple. Mao read them over without making any comment and then we rechecked the individual merits of the colleagues we had nominated to be charter members. We agreed that they were all satisfactory. There were nine of them; so all told, our Association consisted of just eleven charter members; but in the ardor of our youth, we considered ourselves eleven "sages," guardians of the wisdom of the ages! We also considered ourselves brothers, who had the same ambitions and ideals, and who felt great respect for one another.

One Sunday morning, in one of the classrooms of the First Normal School, the eleven of us met together very solemnly for the first official meeting. I distributed the printed copies of the rules of the Hsin Min Study Association and asked for suggestions, questions, or comments. There were none. Each one paid the small membership fee and I was elected as their first secretary. We decided not to have a president; so the meeting was closed. Such was the genesis of our New People's Study Association. Although no speeches were made, a closer bond had sprung up among us, and our ambitious ideas and enthusiasm for the movement took on new impetus. All of us felt that from now on, we were carrying the weight of an additional responsibility on our shoulders.

Mao Tse-tung had said nothing at the meeting. We all knew the purposes and what the members were expected to do and we believed that each one should act in a practical manner without any show of empty talk. The Association had only one member who liked to talk just for the sake of talking and this was Ch'en Chang, who was famous for making long speeches. Our schoolmate, Ch'en, who came from the Liuyang District, had struck up an acquaintance with me and we had become close friends. Even he, however, made no speech on Organization Day. He later became one of the early Communist organizers and was shot in 1928 by the Nationalist Government.

After the formation of the Association, meetings were held about once a month. They were not secret gatherings but we tried to make as little show as possible, since, as the membership was strictly limited, it was difficult to avoid having some students feel jealous or slighted because they had not been invited to join. The biggest problem we had to tackle at this time was how to recruit new members of the type we desired. When a potential name was submitted, it was put to a vote and if anyone raised an objection, the proposed member was rejected. To obtain admission to the Association, the membership had to be one hundred per cent in his favor.

Professor Yang Huai-chung, who knew of the Association and of our strict method of selecting members, told me Hsiung Kuang-ch'u and Ch'en Chang had reported that, in the city of Changsha, there were three girl students, Tao Szu-yung, Hsiang Ching-yu, and Jen Pei-tao, who seemed to possess all the attributes required by us, as well as being first-class students. Later I proposed their names at a meeting and they were unanimously voted into membership.

Tao Szu-yung came from the Siangtan District and was one of the kindest, gentlest persons I have ever known. She joined the Hsin Min Study Association in 1914, and about six years later, she and Mao Tse-tung opened a bookstore in Changsha to which they gave the name *Wen Hua Shu Chu* (Library of Culture). They were deeply in love, but because they held different political ideas, she finally left him and founded a school, the Li Ta Hsüeh Yüan, in Shanghai. She died in that city in about 1930. She was one of the first women members of our Association, also one of the first members to reject Communism.

Hsiang Ching-yu was another attractive, intelligent girl. Her literary work and calligraphy were excellent and she possessed a natural gift for speaking. Her fair complexion needed no cosmetics to enhance its natural charm, and she treated her friends with warm affection as brothers and sisters. In 1919, she went to France under the "student-worker" plan and there she fell in love with Ts'ai Ho-shen. She was one of the first women members to accept Communism. As mentioned earlier, she was shot by the Nationalist Army in Hankow, despite my efforts to save her life through an appeal to the French Legation. Her being a Communist did not lessen my esteem for her, and I was deeply moved by her tragic end.

Jen Pei-tao, the third girl, was an unusually fine person, who came from Siangying District. These three girls were just like sisters. Miss Jen, like Miss Tao, rejected Communism in due course. After graduating from the Higher Normal School, Miss Jen went to the United States for further study in an American university. When she returned to China, she worked in many schools both as teacher and director, and today she is not only a member of the legislative body in the government in Formosa, but she holds a professorship there also.

After these three girls had become members of the Hsin Min Study Association, I suggested that Miss Ts'ai Ch'ang, sister of Ts'ai Ho-shen, should also be invited to join us. The others, including her brother, thought she was too young, since she was just fifteen or sixteen, and since she was only in the first year of the Middle School. A few years later, she went to France as a student-worker and then she did become a member. At the present time, she is a leader of one of the Communist women's organizations. We all greatly admired Ts'ai Ch'ang's firm character and her honesty and, as we had great respect and affection for her mother and brother, we called her our "little sister." We treated her, in fact, as if she were our own little sister.

Though I have lost more than a thousand photographs of my original collection, I do still have one group picture which included Hsiang Ching-yu and Ts'ai Ch'ang snapped together at this time.

At the time of the formal organization of the Chinese Communist Party in 1920, the membership of the Hsin Min Study Association numbered more than a hundred. In 1919 and 1920, Ts'ai Ho-shen and I enlisted some thirty new members in France and Mao Tse-tung returned to Changsha where he recruited nearly a hundred new members. His main interest was in creating a strong organization, and as a result, he paid little attention to the qualifications of moral conduct and high ideals on which I had insisted when the movement was in its infancy. He campaigned quite openly and actively and accepted anyone who had ideas similar to his own. He was impatient to put theories into action and started to publish correspondence of the Association in the form of a newspaper. Many of my letters were chosen for this purpose, including one in which I stated that I did not believe that Russian Communism was an adequate means of re-forming China. Up to that time, the Hsin Min Study Association had been one united body with all the members completely free to express their own political ideas.(24)

In 1920, the split began to appear. Those favoring Communism, led by Mao Tse-tung, formed a separate secret organization. I was prob-ably the only non-Communist who was aware of what was happening, since Mao told me all about his new organization, hoping that I would join them. At the same time, he was confident that I would do nothing to betray them, even though I was not in sympathy with them.

The new group regarded me very much as a big brother and since they listened very seriously to everything I said, Mao was afraid that I might dissuade some of his new converts to Communism from their convictions. He did not, however, dare to remonstrate with me openly for fear of losing the confidence of the members. He did tell them, when I was absent, that although I was a person greatly to be respected and a good friend of his, that I had bourgeois ideas, that I was not one of the proletariat, and for this reason, that I was unwilling to accept Communism.

A rather amusing but significant incident occurred one day which will illustrate our difference. Ho Shu-heng, whom we called Hu-tzu (The Moustache) because of his thick dark moustache, was about ten years older than Mao and I. Though he was a friend to both of us, he was somewhat more intimate with me because he had been a fellow teacher of mine in the Ch'u Yi School for a couple of years. On this particular day, he told me, "Jun-chih (Mao's other name) is secretly criticizing you among the members, saying that you are bourgeois and that you don't agree with Communism. What he really means is that he doesn't want them to have any confidence in you, but to follow him alone."

I told Mao what Ho Hu-tzu had said and he confirmed it without hesitation. I asked, "Why do you say I am bourgeois? If I have ever said I did not agree with Communism, you know that it is the Russian Communism that I am opposed to. I am, as you know, very much in favor of the principles of Communism and I believe that Socialism should gradually be converted into Communism."

Mao Tse-tung said nothing for the moment and Ho Hu-tzu laughed loudly, "Siao Hu-tzu" (here the term "moustache" was respectful and intimate), he cried, "When you are not here, Jun-chih (Mao) wants me to go one way, and when Jun-chih is not here, you try to persuade me to go another way; when neither of you is here, I don't know which way to go; and now that you are both here with me, I still don't know which way to go!" This caused a great laugh but it was quite true.

Ho Hu-tzu, although he spoke in jest and only for himself, had, nevertheless, been acting unconsciously as spokesman for practically all the members of the Hsin Min Study Association, since there was a noticeable element of indecision at that time. However, Ho had been the only one who spoke out frankly and sincerely to call attention openly to the division of opinion between the two leaders and the consequent split in the group.

16
A Summer Vacation in School

Summer vacation was about to begin. A notice appeared on the bulletin board to the effect that all classes had completed their examinations; that we were to have two and a half months' holiday; and that all the students were expected to leave the school within three days.

Everyone commenced to pack, smiling happily in anticipation of soon being at home for vacation. Books were taken from study halls and packed away in suitcases, of which there were more than a thousand in the big baggage room. For two days, crowds of excited students walked in and out of this room continuously and it was almost like a big Customs Office. Everyone talked and laughed noisily. Classes were over and everyone was in a holiday mood. "Have you written to your wife? Does she know you're coming home?" "Is your fiancée coming to meet you?" and other similar comments could be heard all day long.

Finally, all the studies were emptied. That is, all except mine. All my books, brushes, and ink were still on my table and my book case was still full. Mao Tse-tung came in to talk with me. When he saw that I had not started to pack my things, he sat down and said, "Mr. Siao, when are you going home?"

"I have decided not to go home," I replied.

"Are you really going to stay at the school? When you spoke about it last month, I thought you were just joking."

"No," I continued, "I have decided to stay here for a couple of months and then to go home for about twenty days. It will be quiet here at the school for these two months and I shall be able to do a lot of studying."

"What is your plan for these two months? What do you plan to study?" Mao inquired.

"I mean to study algebra, geometry, English, and geography by myself for the next semester, and then I shall probably read some philosophy also."

"I see. And will the Principal allow you to stay in the school?"

"Yes, last night I went to see him and told him what I wanted to do. He said it was against the school rules, but since he believed I really wanted to study seriously, he would give his consent. He told me the porter would be here as well as the four domestics; so I shall not be here alone. He said he would tell the servants to sleep near my dormitory to look after me. Some of the cooks will remain, too; so they will be able to cook for me. But, of course, I have to pay my board. The school cannot be responsible for any extra expense."

"That sounds good. I should like to stay with you, too. What do you think?"

Mao Tse-tung was my best friend; so I was delighted, and said as much, "Come, hurry and see the Principal at once. I'll go with you if you like. I might be able to help. It will be good to have a friend and companion here with me. I do hope you can stay."

"But tell me," Mao Tse-tung hesitated, "how much will you have to pay the cook for your board?"

"I have to pay two dollars and fifty cents a month. Each meal will consist of soup and one other dish."

"Two dollars and fifty cents a month! That means five dollars for the two months!" exclaimed Mao. "That's too much!"

"No, it's not. I think it's quite cheap! But don't worry about the cost. If you don't have enough money, I shall lend it to you. Come now, let's go at once and see the Principal."

We went off to see the Principal, who granted Mao's request without question. When the other students heard that we were staying, two more wanted to stay with us, and they asked me to go with them to see the Principal. Again he agreed and so it was that we four remained behind during the summer vacation. Although I knew the other two fellows quite well, they were only slightly acquainted with Mao. We considered them rather ordinary and not of high enough caliber to be elected to membership in the Association.

In the summer, the weather was so very hot that it was impossible to work in the afternoons. We studied during the morning and after lunch we would chat, but sometimes it was too hot even to talk. The temperature rose so high that we would perspire freely even when we sat quite still and did nothing.

Our work during the morning was not the same for all of us. I wanted to study English and algebra to start with, but Mao was not at all interested in them, and he did not wish to look for a method to study mathematics and English by himself. He spent most of his time reading old classical essays and history. During our rest periods, I passed the time practicing calligraphy, but Mao was very awkward at this and he never did manage to improve his ugly characters.

Mao Tse-tung's reason for wanting to stay at the school during the summer vacation was quite different from mine. He had no warm sentimental feeling for his home and at the end of the summer, if he had gone home, he would have had to help his father in the fields, cutting and harvesting the wheat. Working on the farm now held even less appeal for him than it had when he first decided to leave home and go to school. However, his only pair of shoes was very badly worn and cut. Both shoes had holes in the soles; so later he would have to go home at least once to get a new pair made.

At that time, practically all the students wore homemade shoes and it was quite unusual to see shop-made shoes in the school. Wearing store shoes indicated unnecessary expense and a desire to show off, and consequently the wearer was usually looked down upon. One of the two fellows who had elected to stay in the school with Mao and me appeared with a beautiful pair of shop-made shoes. For us, these fine shoes had less value than the old worn-out pair which Mao had on. When our companion realized how we felt about his shoes, he did not put them on again, while Mao's torn ones took on a veritable halo of glory!

In such reduced company, differences of character were much more apparent than during school time. I felt almost a moral obligation, or at any rate, it was an ingrained habit, to keep my desk, my books, and my room as tidy as possible, even though there was no one to inspect it each day. Mao's desk, on the other hand, was always in complete disorder. The same was true with our studies; mine was always orderly and neat, but Mao's was invariably untidy and he never once thought of sweeping it. Once I said jokingly, "If a great hero does not clean and sweep out his own room, how can he possibly think he is capable of cleaning up the universe?" To which Mao replied, "A great hero who thinks about cleaning up the universe has no time to think about sweeping rooms!"

The hot water system did not function during the holidays; so we had to heat what water we wanted on the kitchen stove—each man for himself. I had a bath every day, but Mao used to let several days pass without a bath despite the terrific heat. He complained that I took too many baths—"So much unnecessary trouble!" he said. I used to retaliate by telling him, "Jun-chih, you smell awfully sweaty!" which was only too true, but he was not at all sensitive about it, nor about being told that he smelled. Nor did my telling him change his slovenly habits. At first, all four of us sat at the same table for our meals, but after a time, the other two decided they preferred to sit by themselves at a table some distance away. Mao could not understand what had prompted this sudden decision!

Not only was he content with being dirty himself, but he objected to my cleanliness. For instance, I always brush my teeth after meals and he would mock me, saying, "After eating, you have to brush your teeth! That's typical of the son of a rich father! You're quite the gentleman, aren't you!" He started to nickname me "son of a rich father"; later he was to call me "bourgeois" (*shen shih*), but at this time he had not yet learned that word. There was no doubt that for him, cleanliness implied a bourgeois type of mentality; but I could not see why belonging to the proletariat and being a Communist prevented one from having a free will in such matters, or compelled one to be dirty.

In school, we had to wash our own clothes and I quite enjoyed this task because it was a change from studying, but Mao hated it. Although we had such different personalities, backgrounds, and personal habits, and did not hesitate to criticize each other, we never really quarreled. We were, in fact, quite fond of each other and felt mutual respect. After an exchange of personal criticism, we ended up laughing, and we always liked to joke, because it provided some relaxation and a change.

Our serious discussions were not in the least influenced by these small differences of opinion and habit. We had a long talk every afternoon, usually not about any specific subject, but just whatever occurred to us at the time. More often than not we discussed the latest news which we had read in the papers.

We talked a lot about Germany, since at that time, the Chinese felt a special respect for Germany and Japan, though we realized that Japan imitated Germany. Mao Tse-tung, of course, adored Bismarck and Wilhelm II, but I did not care for the type of character displayed by these two gentlemen. We had several hot arguments about them and these finally got us back to the subject of the educational system in China.

In the Normal School, the aims of education were considered of the greatest importance, and on a large scroll over the entrance to the Ceremonial Hall was written in large characters: "The first aim of our educational system is moral training; second, industrial; third, military; and finally, aesthetic training to perfect the virtues." This was Ts'ai Yüan-p'ei's declaration when he was the first Minister of

Education for the Republic of China in 1912. The reference to military training was, of course, in emulation of Germany and Japan, but Mao thought it most admirable. I did not agree. I remember, during one discussion, I said, "Ts'ai Yüan-p'ei's declaration is sensible enough, but I think it is very commonplace. Only one point, the idea of aesthetic training, raises it somewhat out of the purely commonplace and conventional. Some time ago, he wrote a good essay on this subject, 'Aesthetics in Place of Religion.' "

"But," Mao insisted, "military education is much more important. If the country is weak, what's the good of talking about aesthetics? The first and most important thing to do is to conquer one's enemies! What does it matter if you have an aesthetic education or not?"

"The perfection of the virtues is emphasized in the ancient poems, in the classics, and in music. It's all the same idea."

"If the people are weak, what is the use of perfecting the virtues?" asked Mao. "The most important thing is to be strong. With strength, one can conquer others and to conquer others gives one virtue." Thus our basic philosophies differed, but in the delights and enthusiasms of our youth, we were probably unaware of the depth of our differences.

17
The Hsiu Yeh and Ch'u Yi Schools

The two middle schools of greatest repute in Changsha City were the Hsiu Yeh and the Ch'u Yi, though there was one other called the Ming Te.

Two months before my graduation from First Normal in 1915, I was invited to teach in the Hsiu Yeh, and I spent just one semester there. In January, 1916, I went to teach in Ch'u Yi and I continued in the Ch'u Yi for more than two years.

I was the only graduate from First Normal that year who was invited to teach in these schools and my fellow students considered this to be a very great honor. Mao Tse-tung was very impressed. Remarks he made to me on several occasions left no doubt that he had great admiration and respect for learning and intellect, in spite of his alleged feeling for military education. The talks we had during this period of my teaching could usually be divided into three distinct categories: ways of self-cultivation; the reform of China; and a discussion of study and the latest news.

Mao was very curious to know just how teachers lived. One day, shortly after I had taken my position in the Hsiu Yeh, he began questioning me, "How many pupils do you teach?"

I explained that there were fifty-eight students in the class of which I was head teacher.

"How do you manage to look after fifty-eight students and still have time to teach?" he wanted to know.

"All head teachers have to take classes as well," I explained. "Just now I'm teaching several important courses: Chinese language, moral training, and history."

"How many hours do you teach each week?" he wanted to know, showing signs that he was visibly impressed.

"I teach twenty hours a week. Apart from that, of course, I have to correct essays. My students write two each week. And then there is the preparation."

"That means, besides your teaching, you have to correct a hundred and sixteen essays every week?" he asked.

"Yes, and after correcting the essays, I have to explain points to each pupil individually."

"Why should the pupils have to do two essays a week?" he wanted to know.

"Because it is very good practice for them."

"You work too hard!" Mao concluded.

"Although I have a great deal to do as teacher, I do find pleasure in it. It is stimulating and challenging. And then, too, the students like me and I like them. That's important. In this school we're just like a big family. It's really most interesting to observe the progress one's pupils are making," I explained.

"I think the educational system should be reformed. The teacher has to work too hard!" insisted Mao.

"The teachers are really treated very well," I continued, patiently. "The funds available are limited and they really can't pay for more teachers. That's why each one of us has to teach several subjects. I enjoy my work."

About midnight on this same day, some time after Mao left me, a fire which broke out in the students' dormitory spread rapidly to the teachers' residence and caused considerable damage. I lost my suitcase and my bed clothes, but I did manage to save my books.

Mao read about the fire next day in the local newspaper; so in the afternoon, he came around to see me again. "Did you lose much in the fire?" he asked, quite concerned. "But I suppose the school will pay for all the damage and loss of the teachers' belongings?"

"No, the school isn't going to pay for any of the damage suffered by the teachers," I said, telling about my personal losses. "Not only that," I continued, "but this morning, the Principal called all of us together and asked us to contribute from our salaries to help cover the losses of the students. Some of them are very poor, you know."

"But you can't do that! That's too much to ask! Surely you are going to protest!" shouted Mao, greatly disturbed.

"It's really nothing of great importance. It's not worth making trouble over," I explained. "This is just the beginning of the term. I shall carry on teaching for another five months, and then I can decide at the end of the term whether I shall continue or not."

Shortly after this incident Mao came to see me again and asked, "Do you find it interesting to be a teacher?"

"Yes, indeed," I said, "I find it very interesting. You soon get used to it, and one is never bored. Shall I tell you of a rather amusing incident which occurred just the other day?"

"Yes, do, what was it?"

"I think I told you that in my class there are several students who are older than I am. It's often quite obvious that they resent me and that they don't like the idea of having a teacher who is younger than they are. Quite often before class begins, they write something on the blackboard to irritate me, but I pretend not to see it."

"Yes," Mao agreed, "it's best to pretend not to see it; to ignore these things."

"I never punish them."

"But do they write insulting things?" Mao wanted to know.

"No, sometimes they just try to pick extremely difficult passages of literature for me to explain. When I first took the class, I could see that they were very surprised at my youth. When the Director introduced me to them, he said, 'Do not be misled by Mr. Siao's youthful appearance. I am fifty years old, and I still consider him my Chinese language teacher.' These words of praise completely reassured most of the pupils as to my capabilities, and the atmosphere of the class eased noticeably. But these few older students constantly tried to make things as difficult as possible for me. A few days ago, they had a good chance."

"That was good of the Director to give you such a fine introduction," conceded Mao. "But go on, tell me what happened."

"One of the pupils died and the boys wanted to hold a memorial service. Of course, they knew I could write essays, but the writing of couplets (tui tzu) for the dead is a task usually confined to older and very experienced scholars who can compose in classical language. They presumed that I would not know how and they would be able to humiliate me before the whole school."

"Since you are the Chinese language teacher, you could not refuse their request, if they asked you. But, you are really gifted for that," Mao replied.

"But you don't know how they went about it! Just the day before yesterday, I was sitting in the teachers' rest room after class at eleven o'clock in the morning. Four of these older students came there to see me. They bowed, and one of them said, 'Sir, our classmate Jen has died and we are going to hold a memorial service for him. We wish to write a couplet for the occasion but we don't know how to compose one. Please, sir, will you write it for us?'

"Of course, I was surprised and pleased to have them ask me, and I had not heard of the memorial service. 'Very well,' I said. 'When do you require it?'

"They all answered together as if they had rehearsed, 'The Memorial Service is to be held at four o'clock this afternoon.'

"Of course, I realized immediately, but too late, that this was a trap. That they had deliberately planned to try to make a fool of me. They could have asked me a week ago to compose the couplet for them, but they had deliberately left it till the last moment, hoping that even if I were able to produce anything at all, I would make a very poor showing. However, nothing was to be gained by remonstrating with them; so I must make the best use of the short time at my disposal to compose something really good, if I did not want to be made a laughing stock. I asked them, 'What relation was Jen to you?'

"They answered that he was their schoolmate, nothing more, and that he came from the same district. I told them that I'd write the couplet in a little while and waited for them to go. But they had not finished. 'Please sir,' they asked, 'will you write it for us in your calligraphy, also. Not later than two o'clock this afternoon, please, because we want everything in the Ceremonial Hall by three.' I tried hard not to show my uneasiness and displeasure with the request, and said I would do it.

"I lay down on the sofa there in the teachers' rest room after they left. My mind was a blank. Through the window I watched the fluffy snowflakes floating idly past. The heavy leaden sky seemed to press down as if it would crush the school, and an air of melancholy pervaded everything. Immediately, I had an idea for the first line: *We weep for our schoolmate, and for our country; the winter day gives birth to tears of sadness, which fall on the plum blossoms of the snow.*"

"That's very good for the first line," Mao said, "but the second part is always much more difficult."

"Yes, and after that first line, my mind again went completely blank. I just couldn't think how to start the second line. Half an hour passed and still I hadn't written a single word. I began to get worried and annoyed. The time was too short. After lunch, at one o'clock I had a class; so I had only an hour and a half in which to think of something really good. Then I had to go to the lavatory. I often get an inspiration there, and this time the god of the lavatory smiled on me. I had an inspiration and wrote out the last line!"

"Tell me, what did you write?" asked Mao.

"I wrote: *The gods gave this man life, but they also decreed his sojourn here be short; awe-inspiring are the decisions of heaven. Who can jump free from the circle of life and death?* I felt quite pleased with this last line." I concluded.

"You should. It really is excellent!" exclaimed Mao. "What did your pupils say?"

"At exactly two o'clock, the four students came again, followed by a group of lookers-on. They tried not to show their surprise that the couplet was completed. One of them said, 'Please, sir, write quickly!' I asked if the ink was ready and if they had prepared the squared cloth for me to write upon. 'The ink is all ready,' they said, 'but we haven't finished the cloth because we didn't know how many words there were to be on each side.'

" 'There are just twenty words in each line,' I told them. 'Please hurry and draw the lines. Quick! Quick!' They prepared the cloth very quickly and I wrote out the couplet. They thanked me and went off to the Ceremonial Hall to hang it up."

Mao asked if there were any other really good couplets in the Hall; so I told him the rest of the story.

"At two o'clock, all the classes were dismissed; so that preparations for the memorial service at four o'clock could be made. About three, I went to the Ceremonial Hall. It's a very large room and there were more than two hundred couplets for the dead boy, hanging on the four walls. Everyone was looking at them and commenting. Big Beard Wang was there, too. We gave him this nickname because he had a long, thick black beard. He had obtained the highest degree in the Imperial Examinations and he is the head Chinese language professor. Naturally, he's considered the supreme authority on matters of literature in the school. When I entered the room, I saw him in the distance, reading my couplet with a crowd of students around him. He was explaining it to them. Then he read it aloud, giving it the full rhythm as if he were singing it. When he finished, he turned to the students, 'Good! Very good, indeed! Who wrote it?' One of the students said, 'It's Mr. Siao's.' Then someone saw me and, with Mr. Wang leading, they all came toward me. Mr. Wang said, enthusiastically, 'Excellent! Excellent! There's no doubt at all that your couplet is the best in the room! It's admirable!'

"The looks of astonishment on the faces of the students were most amusing. Then the Principal came up and congratulated me very warmly. At four o'clock the service started, with the Principal presiding. Then, after the ceremony, he made a speech in which he again praised my couplet. All the people in the hall kept looking at me while he talked and it almost seemed that the meeting was being held in my honor instead of as a memorial service for the dead. After the service was over, Mr. Wang took my hand and we went out together first, followed by the Principal. I felt as if I had just received a greatly coveted diploma in literature.

"As you can imagine, I have had no further trouble with those older students," I concluded. "They all treat me with great respect, bowing to me whenever we happen to meet, either in the school or out on the street. They are so quiet in the classroom, it's just like being in the church!"

Mao thought quietly for a moment and then he spoke, "I can understand how difficult it must be for the student to believe everything the teacher says. But it is vitally important for the teacher to create confidence in his students."

Time passed rapidly and soon my first semester of teaching came to a close. One day I met Mr. Wang, Mao Tse-tung's uncle, who asked me if I was happy in the Hsiu Yeh School. I told him that though I was quite happy in my work, I was also very tired, and that I had not yet decided if I wanted to continue teaching the next year. He told me the Ch'u Yi School needed a good teacher, and he invited me to accept the post there. I thought it over for a time and, since the Ch'u Yi was a school of excellent standing, I decided to accept the position.

18

The Beggar Life

In January of 1916 I started teaching at the Ch'u Yi School. The next year when the time came for the summer vacation of almost three months, I felt that I needed a change. So I decided to spend the summer as a beggar.

The attraction of the beggar's life for me was the ability to overcome physical and psychological difficulties inherent in living outside the accepted pale of society. In China and in the East generally from time immemorial, begging has been considered a profession, rather than, as in the West, a mark of poverty or improvidence. It is fascinating to try travel about the country without a cent in one's pocket.

At this particular time Mao was still a student in the First Normal, but he came often to see me and to chat.

One day he said, "Summer vacation is drawing near. When do you finish your classes?"

"We're having examinations now and vacation will start in a week," I replied.

"Ours will start in a fortnight," Mao added.

"Will you spend your summer at the school again as you did last year?" I asked.

"I haven't decided what I'll do this summer," Mao answered. "What are you going to do?"

"I have a new plan for this summer," I told him. "I have decided that I'm going to try being a beggar."

"A beggar? What do you mean by that? I don't understand. Why do you want to be a beggar?" He shot the questions at me incredulously.

"Yes, I shall be a beggar. I shall go a long way away without taking a cent with me and I shall beg for my food and lodging. All the same I expect to have a most interesting holiday and visit many interesting places!" I explained.

"I still don't understand," Mao continued. "If you don't find anyone to ask, or if people don't want to give you anything, how are you going to get along? You won't like going hungry."

"Ah, that's the most interesting part," I explained. "I want to find how people react toward me. Do you really think beggars starve to death?"

"No, that's true. You don't hear of them starving."

"Not only that, but they are the freest and the happiest men alive! Remember the saying, 'After three years of life as a beggar, one would not accept even a post as mandarin'? Now tell me why do you think they say that?"

"Why, that's because an officer has responsibility while a beggar has none," Mao replied.

"No, not only that," I explained. "An officer is tied down by restrictions and a beggar is completely free. I have experienced the happiness and complete freedom of the beggar's life. Do you know what it feels like?"

"No, but I can imagine it just as you do."

"But, I am not imagining. I have really lived the life of a beggar," I said.

"You mean you have actually been a beggar?"

"Yes, of course. You didn't know about that, did you? I have never told you about that episode in my life."

"Please," said Mao, "tell me that story. It must be very interesting."

"It was four or five years ago and I was a beggar on two different occasions. I had been meditating on the freedom and happiness of beggars and I decided I'd like to give their way of life a practical trial. The first time I was a beggar for only one day, but the second time it was three days.

"The first time I set off early in the morning and walked out into the country till I felt hungry, when I began to beg for food. At the first house they didn't give me enough; so I went to a second. There the food was dirty; so I went to a third place where I was allowed to eat as much as I wanted. After that I walked back home. In the evening I was hungry again and I begged for some rice. Finally I arrived home by the light of the moon."

"But when people saw you, did they really take you for a beggar?" asked Mao.

"It was interesting to observe their reactions. Some people were cold and would have nothing to do with me. Others asked if I could read. Apparently they suspected that I was a *sung tzu hsien sheng* (an intellectual beggar who gave symbolical gifts of a verse on a cheap scroll, composed and written by himself, in exchange for food, lodging or money). However, I simply said I had no money, that I was hungry and had nothing to eat. Some were quite sympathetic, chatting with me as I ate. In one house I was given a whole bowl of rice, vegetables and a fried egg. The head of that household was an old lady who had two sons studying in the city. She asked me several times how it was that I was so poor that I had to beg. I had a very interesting talk with her and gained further insight into the psychology of society."

"That is really very interesting. What a pity you had only one day," Mao said.

"Yes, that's why I did go out again for three days. This time it was more difficult because I had to find a place to sleep."

"But how could you beg for a place to stay overnight?" asked Mao.

"Why not? Let me tell you. It was summertime, not too cold at night, and there was a moon. It was a wonderful experience. Walking slowly alone across the deserted countryside I seemed to be the only person in the world—walking in a void, no obstacles, no worries, completely free. Far behind and forgotten were the noise and bustle of everyday life, with only the stars and the moon in their blue velvet setting for companions. I had never before experienced such a sensation of peace and separation and I decided to walk all night. When dawn came, I lay down on a grassy bank and slept soundly till noon. Then I got up to beg for food. The second night was dark and somber without a moon. Before long I came to a high mountain and as I walked along beneath it, I saw a huge rock, blacker even than the sky, jutting out above me. Deep shadows and strange shapes were beginning to frighten me and I wasn't happy as I had been the previous night."

"But weren't you afraid of the tigers and other wild animals that live in the mountains?" asked Mao.

"To tell the truth, I began to recall all the stories I'd ever heard of mountain tigers and I imagined that there were tigers really prowling around in search of prey. As I stood there hesitating about whether to go on or turn back, I saw a point of light in the distance and I set out toward it. The light from a lamp was shining from the window of a small farmhouse. This indication of the presence of other human beings was most reassuring and I hastened forward. A few moments after I knocked on the door, I saw through a wide crack a young girl of seventeen approaching, carrying a small lamp in her hand. She peered out at me without opening the door and asked what I wanted. I told her I was a beggar who had lost the road and was looking for a place to pass the night. She stared at me a moment, then turned and went back into the house. I realized that she was afraid to open the door to a stranger and had gone to call her father. Soon an old man appeared, carrying the lamp, and asked who I was, where I came from, and was I alone or did I have a companion? My reply seemed satisfactory and he let me in. We entered a large room and he held the lamp high while he studied me carefully from head to foot. I looked at him in the same manner. He was obviously a farmer, about fifty years old and had almost no hair save for a straggly little moustache. He smiled gently and I knew then that he had decided that I was not dangerous. I turned to look at the girl who stood by the table. Her hair was tied at the back into a long pigtail and she wore a blue cotton dress with trousers of the same material. From her sunburned, almost swarthy complexion it was easy to see that she worked on the farm, but her eyes were large and bright and her teeth were white and even. She was watching me and our eyes met for a moment.

"Turning to her father, she asked, 'Papa, have you asked if he wants something to eat?' I said I had not eaten but that I was not hungry. The girl, without comment, quickly left the room while her father and I continued our talk. Soon she returned and smiling, handed me a cup of tea. 'The rice will soon be ready,' she said. The farmer asked about my family and why I was a beggar; so I told him I was studying in a school. He told me his wife had died the previous year and he had only the one daughter. They worked the land together for a living. When the daughter brought me a bowl of rice and vegetable, her father said, 'Daughter, this young man is no beggar; he's a student.' She smiled and said 'Master Siao, please eat your supper.' We all talked as I ate, after which we all went to bed. I was extremely tired and they were in the habit of going to bed early.

"Next morning everyone was up at daybreak and I wanted to say 'goodbye' and be on my way, but they begged me to stay. Finally, after I had eaten lunch with them, I thanked them for their kindness and set off toward home. We still keep up our friendship."

"Ah," exclaimed Mao, "now I know why you're so interested in living a beggar's life! You still want to see the farmer and his daughter!"

"Last winter I did go to see them on my way home," I explained. "I took them a few gifts. The daughter was married and had a baby two years old and the father was living with them. This time I want to take a new road. I want to see new things and have all new experiences. The most interesting aspect is the overcoming of difficulties and there is nothing more difficult than trying to live in the society of others without money. I want to see how I can overcome that difficulty."

Mao was enthusiastic. "It sounds very interesting. May I go with you?" he asked.

"Of course, if you like. The beggar life is really for only one person and for never more than two. But the two of us should get along very well."

"Good! I do want to go with you. When do we start?"(25)

"My summer vacation begins next week but I shall wait a week till you are free and then we can decide definitely on the date and complete the details."

19
Two Beggars Set Off

The date was finally fixed and since the idea was mine, it was decided that we would start out from Ch'u Yi School where I lived. Mao arrived early in the morning on a beautiful summer day. He wore his old school clothes which consisted of white shorts and tunic, both very old and worn. Being a teacher, I wore the traditional long robe in the school; but for this occasion I had changed into a coarse old jacket, shorts and cloth shoes. Mao always shaved his head, soldier fashion; so the day before I had done likewise. My disguise was thus complete.

Mao had brought an old umbrella and a cloth bundle containing a change of clothes, a towel, notebook, writing brush and the ink box. The less we carried the lighter we could walk; so we had agreed to take nothing more with us. I had bought an umbrella and my bundle was the same as Mao's with the addition of some stationery and a rhyme book, just in case I was inspired to write a poem.

I had left my money with the school manager and now I put the loose coins from my pocket into my desk. Neither of us was to take a cent on the journey, nothing but the umbrella and a bundle of clothes.

When we were all ready, I said, "Please wait for just a moment. I want to go and see the Director and tell him good-bye."

When the Director's servant saw me, he opened his eyes wide, staring at the old, worn out garments which I wore. He hesitated, apparently wondering what to say. Finally he asked, "Mr. Siao, what is the matter? What has happened? Have you had—have you had a fight with someone?"

The only explanation he could think of was that I had put on these clothes to fight a duel and that I now had come to tell the Director. "Who would I want to fight with?" I asked. "I just want a few words with the Director."

The Director was as surprised as his servant with my appearance. "Mr. Siao!" he ejaculated. "How are you? What has happened? Why are you dressed like that?"

"Nothing has happened," I answered calmly. "I'm just going on a journey."

"Where in the world would you go in such clothes?" he asked.

"I want to get acquainted with our province; so I have decided to travel on foot. This dress is most comfortable for walking," I explained.

"You must be very careful on the road," he continued, quite concerned for my safety.

"Thank you," I replied. "I have a companion, Mao Tse-tung, who is going with me."

"Oh! The young man who comes here to visit you so often? He was a student of mine when I was Director of Fourth Normal. A strange fellow! A very strange fellow. You're going with him? Two strange fellows! Very good. But do be careful all the same."

· Returning to my room from the Director's office, I came face to face with one of my best students in the large hall. He stared at me in open-mouthed astonishment, and then at a distance of some ten steps, he bowed to me. As we came abreast, I asked him why he was in school, since all the students had gone on vacation the week before. But suddenly he became mute and he said not a word. His face turned a deep red, he dropped his head, and he dared not look at me. I understood without his speaking that he was thinking how ugly and undignified I looked, dressed as a laborer, but he dared not ask any questions. When I spoke again, he lowered his head still further, made a deep bow, and walked rapidly away.

When I returned to my room, Mao and I discussed which way we would go when we started out, to the right or left? It mattered little since begging would be the same in either case, but there was one difference. If we turned right, we should be outside the city and out in open country after a ten minutes' walk. To the left, we would have to cross a wide river, the Siang Kiang, within ten minutes.

Mao said, "You go first and I'll follow."

"I want to go left and cross the river," I said.

"Very well," he replied, "we'll go left. But why do you want to cross the river?"

"If we turn right, it's all flat open country with no obstacles, and it would be uninteresting. If we go left, we have to find a way to get across the river and that will be our first obstacle."

Mao laughed loudly and said, "That's true! We're going to avoid the easy path and look for difficulties. Good. Let's go! To the left."

When we had picked up our bundles, I locked the study door and we were on our way. We put our umbrella over the right shoulder and

slung our bundles over the end, close to our backs; so the weight was better distributed and it seemed lighter. I had learned this trick in my former experiences as a beggar. I suggested that Mao should lead the way, but after a bit of argument, he insisted that I lead and he would follow; so we set off, I walking in front and Mao behind me. For the whole month that we were beggars, we walked in that order with but very few exceptions.

As we were going out to the street, the gatekeeper came and stared at us in astonishment. His mouth slowly opened but no words came.

I spoke to him, "Old Lu, I'm going on a journey and if letters come for me, do not forward them. I'll be back at school in a month."

He still stared at me with open mouth as if he had not heard me; so I asked, "Old Lu, do you understand what I am telling you?"

He answered as if in a daze, "Yes, Mr. Siao. Yes, yes. . . ." Several laborers in the gatekeeper's room followed us with their amazed glances and we continued on our way. They were wondering, I'm sure, what could have happened to the usually dignified teacher for him to have dressed up and gone away in such a strange manner?

But from then on, we were no longer the focus of persons' stares, because there were many, many people on the highway wearing old worn out tunics and shorts. We were right in style.

20
We Overcome Our First Obstacle

Only a few minutes' walk from the Small West Gate of Changsha City took us to the banks of the broad Siang Kiang. At this point the river is five or six hundred meters wide and we knew it was very deep because we had often seen large steamships go past. Since we could walk no further, we sat down on the grass and watched the flow of the river waters.

"How can we get across?" we asked simultaneously. There were three possibilities. First, swimming, but neither of us knew how to swim and besides, we would get our things wet if we attempted to swim and carry our bundles—so swimming was out. Second, if we walked about half a mile up the river we could take the free ferry; but neither of us wanted to take that way out. It seemed too easy and we seemed to be evading the obstacle that way, instead of overcoming it. Third, there was a small rowboat service, but the fare was two coppers. That was very cheap and many people crossed that way, but we had not a cent. We were indeed penniless beggars.

We sat watching these small boats fill up with passengers and set off for the other side. One left about every ten minutes. We watched one particular boat cross three times and we knew that looking would not get us across. We had to act. Mao suggested that we go down and talk to the ferryman, that we tell him we had no money and ask him to take us across.

To his suggestion I replied, "I doubt that he will accept. And if he refuses, what shall we do then?"

"Well," said Mao, "I'm not afraid. I'm going to ask him." He walked resolutely down to one of the small boats tied up near us and very politely asked the boatman to take us across without paying because we had no money.

The young boatman replied very firmly and emphatically, "If you have no money, you will have to take the public ferry. It is only a few minutes' walk from here."

When Mao returned and asked what we should do next, I said, "I knew he would not take us. My idea is for us to walk down and get into the boat as if we were ordinary passengers. When he collects the fares, we'll be half way across and we can tell him then that we have no money. It's very unlikely that he will turn back and he wouldn't push us out of the boat; so we'll get across. He won't bring us back again because he'll want our space for other paying passengers. Come on, let's try it out."

We jumped up and quickly boarded one of the small boats that had just arrived from the other side. We elbowed our way ahead of the other passengers and went right up to the bow. Since there were no seats, we all stood packed together till about fourteen had boarded and the boat was full. "We're off!" shouted the boatman as he pushed against the bank with all his force with a long pole. Quickly the boat glided forward and soon we were in mid-stream.

A little girl of five or six reached out a plate to us for our fares. Each passenger tossed in his two *t'ung yuan* and there was a continuous tang, tang, tang, as the coins fell in. When she reached us, the tang stopped. The boatman, watching, said, "Will the two distinguished looking gentlemen please pay the little girl? Two *t'ung yuan* each, please."

"I'm afraid we have no money," answered Mao. "Please will you not take us across?"

"What? No money?" asked the boatman, incredulously. "Then why did you get on this boat? I can't carry passengers without paying. Please give her the money quickly."

"Really it's quite true," I broke in, "we don't have a cent between us. Please take us across now and in a month when we return we shall pay you back double."

"How do you think I can remember you in a month's time?" he asked. "If you have no money, you could leave me one of your umbrellas."

"Oh, no," answered Mao. "We need the umbrellas on our journey. Besides, an umbrella costs fourteen *t'ung yuan* and the trip on the boat for two of us is only four!"

"But if you don't pay, you can't cross the river!" shouted the ferryman.

"Do you say we cannot cross the river?" I asked. "We are in the middle of the river now. What will you do?"

"You are robbers!" said the ferryman. "I've a good mind to turn and take you back."

At this, all the others loudly protested. They had listened with amusement to our conversation, but now they shouted, "No, no. We're in a hurry. We have paid our fare! Be quick and get us across."

Among the passengers was a kind old man who now stepped forward. "I'll contribute two *t'ung yuan* toward their fare," he said, "and the other passengers can pay the other two. We don't want to go back."

Several other passengers agreed to that, but Mao and I cried, "No, no! We do not agree. You must not pay for us!" Then I had an idea, "The boat is in the middle of the stream. The boatman can rest while we row across. That way we'll be working our way across."

But the ferryman did not agree. "I'll still be four *t'ung yuan* short, and I don't need a rest," he said. "If my best customer wants to pay for you, why don't you let him? You're just trying to make things difficult for me! You're just plain robbers!"

By now the passengers were shouting impatiently, "Let's get moving!" and the old man assured the ferryman that when we reached the other shore, he would see that the trouble was all cleared up before he left the boat.

As soon as the other passengers were off, the ferryman pushed the boat about twenty feet from the shore lest we try to escape. Meanwhile the old man quietly offered again to pay the money for us but Mao insisted that we would return in a month and would pay the boatman at that time.

I broke in with, "Sir, if you pay the four *t'ung yuan*, it will be like giving us a slap in the face. We shall be offended."

The ferryman heard the last of our conversation and he shouted, "What's that about a slap on the face? If you don't pay up, I'll give you more than a slap!"

"If you want to fight to settle it, we're not afraid," said Mao.

By this time a number of people were waiting on the bank to take the ferry across and another little boat was already in mid-stream on its way over. The boatman realized that if the other boat got to shore first, he would lose those customers; so finally he gave us up as a bad job and he pushed to shore again, telling us in no uncertain terms exactly what he thought of us!

As soon as the boat touched shore, the old man, Mao and I jumped

ashore and, as we gave the ferryman a sweet smile, we said, "Thank you, and goodbye."

The old man went quickly on his way and we set off along the road which stretched in front of us. We didn't know where it would take us. We just knew it was a road from Changsha to the District of Ningsiang.

"It was very kind of that old man to offer to pay our fares," I said as we walked along. "And since we are beggars, we could have accepted; but that would have been too easy. We must try to do things the hard way."

"It's too bad all those people were waiting for the ferry," mused Mao. "If no one had been there, we might have had a good fight with the boatman!"

We strolled on toward Ningsiang District.

21
The Second Obstacle: Hunger

Modern motor highways were undreamed of at that time and this main road was only a meter wide, paved with slate slabs down the middle to form an uneven but relatively clean path during the wet season. On both sides of the road were fields of young rice plants. At the crossroads were stone signposts with chiseled characters, but often we didn't look at these; rather, we looked at the roads and took the one that was widest.

Though the sun was very hot and we had no hats, still we did not need to use our umbrellas to protect our shaven heads. It was our feet that felt the heat most! The slate seemed to be red hot, and though it was quite smooth, we preferred to walk on the grass at the side of the road. When we left the school, we wore heavy-soled cloth shoes; but after we crossed the river, we changed to straw sandals.

As we walked along, the long straight road ahead seemed to pull us like a magnet. The flatness became monotonous, but soon we saw a mountain ahead which we would have to climb! When the scenery changed, we were quite happy again.

But the road through the mountains grew wearisome, too, and we longed for the flatness of the plains. When we walked through the flat plains, we remembered the beauty of the mountains. Nature seemed to be familiar with this peculiarity of man and had kindly alternated the long stretches of flat plains with the beautiful mountains. Soon we lost count of the number of fields and mountains we passed on our journey.

We talked of all sorts of interesting things as we walked. Time had ceased to exist. Neither of us wore a watch and we judged the hour by the length of the sun's shadow. When the shadows began to point eastward, we judged that it must be two o'clock, and suddenly we realized that we had not eaten and that we were hungry! When we were engrossed in our talk, we had not noticed the time but now we felt real hunger pangs in our empty stomachs and the more we thought of it, the hungrier we became. Our feet, too, became hotter and more tired with every step.

Soon we came to a little eating place alongside the road where it was customary for travelers to stop and rest even though they did not expect to eat. We dropped thankfully into two seats out of the sun and it was so pleasantly cool that we were sound asleep with a breeze fanning us gently and quietly. I have no idea how long I slept, but when I awakened, Mao Tse-tung was still sound asleep. Soon, however, a big, heavy cart passed close beside us and the vibration and the noise wakened him with a start.

The woman who ran the eating place studied us curiously, no doubt thinking it strange that we should arrive so obviously tired and hot, yet buy no refreshment. She now inquired if we had had tea, but we thanked her and said we were not thirsty. It was quite true that we did not want tea; what we did want was some good solid food for we were ravenously hungry! Should we beg her for some food? She looked kind and probably would have given us a bowl of rice, but to ask her directly was too easy; so we said nothing. She must have guessed our situation for soon she brought us two cups of tea explaining that there was no charge. We gratefully gulped down the hot tea, but shortly regretted it because it just served to increase our hunger.

"Come on," said Mao. "Let's start begging. I can't wait a second longer. I'm starved. Let's start with those farmhouses."

"The trouble is," I explained, "each family will give us only a small quantity of food and we shall have to go to four or five houses before we can satisfy our hunger. Again, some people will probably give us uncooked rice as a symbolical gift and that will be of little help to us. No, I think the best plan would be for us to find if any family of intellectuals live near here. If so, we shall pay them a visit. No doubt we will have better luck there."

Mao turned to the woman and asked, "Do you know of any family of intellectuals living near here?"

"Oh yes," she said, "about half a kilometer from here is a family called Wang. They have two sons studying in Changsha. Their neighbors are called Tsao. The head of that family is a doctor and his son, who is fifteen, is also studying medicine at home. In the hills at the back of my restaurant lives an old gentleman called Liu. He is an Imperial Doctor of Arts and a retired Prefect. He has no son, but several daughters, all married."

"Jun-chih," I cried, "Dr. Liu will be our host today! We shall direct our first attack upon him. I think the best approach would be for us to write a poem to present to him in which we tell him the purpose of our visit in symbolical language."

"Good idea!" agreed Mao. "Let's see, the first line could go: *Toiling over the mountains, following the rushing streams, we finally reach a famous district.*"

"That's good," I approved, "The second line, *With sticks of bamboo and straw sandals we come from afar to pay homage to the great scholar.* Then we could continue with, *The road we have traveled was deep in white clouds like a celestial sea.*"

"We could finish it with, *And the dew from our wet clothes soaked into our hungry bodies,*" finished Mao.

The reference to the clouds was an allusion to the fact that Liu was a scholarly hermit, living in his distant mountain retreat far from the petty struggles of humanity, while the mention of our "hungry bodies" and "long journey" seemed obvious enough.

When the poem was finished, we read it through several times, quite pleased with ourselves. "Imperial Doctor Liu ought to admire our prowess!" said Mao. "We'll soon see what sort of literary critic he is." We read the lines again, which in Chinese really sounded very good, and both of us laughed heartily, forgetting our hunger for the moment.

Opening my bundle I took out my brush, ink, paper and envelopes, and in my very best calligraphy, I carefully wrote the poem which we both signed with our real names. On the envelope, I wrote, "To Imperial Doctor of Arts Liu." The woman, seeing us address an envelope, came to the table to ask if we were writing letters home. "There's no post office here," she explained. "You'll have to take it to Ningsiang Town to post it."

Thanking her kindly, we went out to the road, turned left and climbed the slope behind the restaurant. Soon we reached the top, and from there we saw a big white brick house at the foot of the hill. Knowing that it must be Dr. Liu's residence, we set off toward it.

The low hill back of the house was covered with trees forming a uniform green background against which the white brick house stood out clearly even from a great distance. The windows and columns at the front were red and the long white surrounding wall with its even black tiles, made one think of a walled city. To the right was the entrance gate with big trees with red blossoms on each side. Before the wall was a large pond almost covered with large green lotus leaves and exquisitely beautiful red blooms. From the distance the scene looked like a richly colored painting; but it would have required an expert artist to do it justice.

When we reached the stately residence, we saw that a red band had been painted on the polished wood of the gate, and this band bore characters printed in black. Those on the right were: *"Chao jen ch'iu yüeh,"* which means "May the autumn moon shine on us," on the left: *"Hui wo ch'un feng"* or "Give me the spring breeze." We admired the beautiful calligraphy which we presumed must be Liu's, since under the old system of Imperial Examinations, calligraphy together with literature and poetry was one of the main subjects. For this reason, the *Han Ning*, the Imperial Doctors of Arts, were all master calligraphers. We hoped that Liu, as a connoisseur of calligraphy and poems, would be pleased with our efforts which we were about to present to him.

The outer gate was closed and locked. Looking through the crack, we could see a second gate about ten meters further on which was also closed. We could see through into a large courtyard in which stood the house with its doors and windows all wide open. We banged on the outer gate three or four times with our hands and immediately some big dogs in the second court began to bark furiously. We were astonished to hear so many dogs, just a bit scared because they sounded so savage, and we wondered if they could get out. When we stopped knocking, the barking ceased. We had had no previous experience with dogs, so we stopped to talk the matter over. Our umbrellas were useless as weapons because an attacking dog would break them immediately; so Mao got two strong, hard sticks from the dry branches of the trees nearby. Each was about two yards long and as hard as steel.

These clubs gave us assurance and we banged on the gate with them. The more we banged, the louder the dogs barked. But we were not afraid now and we continued our knocking in spite of the horrible howls. After five minutes of this pounding the only result was that the dogs seemed to be getting tired and made less noise. A few minutes later, looking through the crack, we saw an old man dressed in a short tunic coming from the house. He must be Liu's servant. He came slowly across the court toward the gate, followed by half a dozen huge hounds in a variety of colors, all barking furiously. Opening the second gate, he came to the main gate before which we were standing. There he stopped and asked with a rough voice what we wanted. Speaking through the crack in the gate, Mao answered, "We have come from the capital and we have a letter for Dr. Liu."

I slipped the letter through to him, and in a kinder voice he said, "Please wait a moment," and he turned back to the house. No doubt he thought we had brought the letter all the way from Changsha, and we smiled at the thought. The dogs seemed to have realized from their master's voice that we were friends and now they stood wagging their tails in quiet welcome.

As we sat down on the stone steps to wait, all was quiet except for the singing of the birds in the trees back of the house. After waiting patiently for more than ten minutes, Mao wanted to start banging the gate again, but I told him to wait awhile, that Dr. Liu was undoubtedly admiring our poem and our calligraphy. After a further long wait with nothing but silence, we lost our patience and we started banging on the gate once more, and the dogs started their barking. Almost at once the old man came out and opened the gate. "Please come in, masters," he said, and we followed him through the two gates into the inner court. "I was a bit late returning because my master just wakened from his afternoon sleep. He washed his face before reading the letter, but when he read it, he told me to ask you to come in immediately."

He ushered us through the middle door in the front of the house and on into a large room on the walls of which were hung many scrolls of calligraphy and paintings. We could not examine these in detail, however, because the old man hurried us on through this room and into another smaller one. There he left us. We supposed this was Dr. Liu's private room; so we remained standing.

When Liu finally came out, we saw that he was an old man of about seventy, short and thin and slightly hunch-backed. The white hairs on his head and chin were so sparse they could almost be counted. On the top of his head, he was quite bald. He wore a long, white robe and carried a white silk fan in his hand. We bowed low before him, but he stood staring at us in obvious surprise: "Why are you dressed like that? Have you had an accident? What very strange clothes! But please sit down! Sit down!"

After we were seated, Liu continued, "Did you meet robbers on the way?"

"No, we had no trouble," answered Mao.

"Where have you come from? Where are you going?" asked Liu.

"We have come from Changsha and we are going to Ningsiang Town," I replied.

"What do you do in Changsha?"

"We're students in the capital," said Mao.

"Do you perhaps study in one of the foreign schools? You can write poems, too, I see. You write very good poems, and your calligraphy is very good, also," Liu continued, studying us as before.

"Not only do we learn to write poems in college, we study classics also," I explained.

"Ah, so you study classics? What kind?"

When Mao told him that we studied the Thirteen Classics and

Lao Tzu and Chuang Tzu, he was very pleased. "If you study Lao
Tzu and Chuang Tzu whose do you consider to be the best of the
commentaries?" he asked.

"The best commentary of Lao Tzu is Wang P'i's and that of Chuang
Tzu is Kuo Hsiang's," I answered.

He seemed pleased with my answer, "Quite right! I agree! Where
do you come from?"

"My friend Mao Tse-tung comes from Siangtan District and I come
from Siangsiang, but right on the border. We really live quite near
to each other."

"Siangsiang is where the famous Tseng Kuo-fan was born," Liu
commented.

"Yes, my great grandfather was tutor in Tseng Kuo-fan's family," I
said.

"He must have been an excellent scholar to teach in the Tseng
family. Please wait a moment," he replied, rising and leaving the
room.

We waited as patiently as possible under the circumstances. It was
difficult to concentrate on the beautiful paintings and scrolls of exquisite calligraphy when our stomachs were rumbling with their
emptiness. However, we comforted each other with the thought that
he had probably gone to tell his cook to prepare a rich meal for us,
and that would take some time. Surely he could not have misunder-
stood the meaning of our verse! That must be the explanation. That
was why he was gone so long. But the more we thought of food, the
hungrier we felt!

Finally Liu returned, walking toward us with a smile. He did not
mention food. He simply withdrew his hands from the wide sleeves
and held out a packet wrapped in red paper. He offered it smilingly,
without a word. From its size I realized immediately that it was
money and when I took it in my hand, by its weight I realized that
it was a generous sum. We both thanked him for his kindness and said
goodbye. He accompanied us to the door and handed us over to the
old man who took us through the courtyard and the two gates. As
soon as we got outside, we hid behind a tree and opened the packet.
We had suddenly become rich! The packet contained forty copper
mei!

No need to discuss what we should do: we hurried as fast as we could go, back to the wayside restaurant where we asked the woman to prepare us a meal as quickly as possible! Soon our rice arrived with bowls of peppered vegetables and soya beans. After we had devoured three bowls apiece, we felt satisfied. The meal had cost us four *mei* each; so we still had thirty-two *mei* left!

After a short rest we started off on our way, always taking the widest road when there was a choice. We had no idea where we were going nor what adventures might lie ahead. When the sky darkened, we decided to spend the night in a little inn by the side of the road.

After we had eaten supper, we talked of our plans for next day. Suddenly we remembered that our friend Ho Shu-heng whom we called Hu-tzu (The Moustache) lived in this district and we should visit him. I had his address in my diary and the innkeeper thought it was about seventy kilometers away. That would be just a good day's walk from the inn. Tomorrow night we should be with our Ho Hu-tzu.

22
Ho Hu-tzu's Home

Early next morning, we had a quick wash and set off for Ho Hu-tzu's home. It was to be our habit to walk ten kilometers each morning before breakfast. It was the habit in Hunan to eat a heavy meal in the morning the same as for lunch and dinner. This custom was very different from the usual breakfast of watery rice or congee, which was customary in Peking, Shanghai, Soochow, and other cities. To eat this congee in Hunan implies that one is very poor since Hunan is one of the big rice producing areas and one must be in the last stages of final misery not to be able to afford a good bowl of rice each meal.

We walked along lightheartedly because we were rich: we did not need to beg today. Also, we knew that when we arrived at our friend's home about nightfall, we would receive a generous and happy welcome! We felt almost as if we were going home.

As we walked, we talked together about the life of Fang Pi-tsung, a strange man who not only was my cousin, but had married my older sister. Mao had heard of him and was very interested in all the details I could tell him of his life. He was the fourth grandson of my maternal grandfather and when I was a child I called him Chen Chiu-ko, Big Brother Chen Chiu. My father was famous for his literary works when he married, but he was not very rich. Therefore, Grandfather Fang gave my mother some land as a dowry, so she would have something in case of need. Thirty years later she needed money to enable my brother to have an education, and the land was sold. By this time, the Fangs also had become poor; much of their land had been sold; and Fang Pi-tsung was unable to complete his studies.

He started a grocery store, later began weaving, then turned to sewing, building houses, and finally making furniture. The strange thing about this was that he attained proficiency bordering on perfection in all these crafts despite the fact that he had never studied them. In China it was the custom for sewing and weaving apprentices to study under a master for at least three years but Fang Pi-tsung had become an expert after only a few days' study. He could imitate any sort of handcraft with incredible perfection.

Mao Tse-tung wondered how this gift could be explained and considered it a pity that he should have been born in China where this sort of genius was not appreciated and cultivated. "Why if he'd have been born in Italy, he might have become another Michelangelo!" he suggested.

I pointed out that when Fang was a small boy he had been very fond of making toys of wood and bamboo; so he was given a collection of small tools: hammers, knives, saws, a plane, and so on, to work with. He had a miniature factory. But although he was a genius in handcraft, he was no good at all in calligraphy or painting. Mao contended that this was due to faulty education along certain lines.

Five or six years after this conversation Fang Pi-tsung arrived in France at the same time as Chou En-lai, Li Li-san, Li Wei-han and Ts'ai Ho-shen under the student-worker scheme. After four years spent in France, he returned to China where he died at the age of forty. His son, named Lian, had exactly this same manual ability. During the Sino-Japanese war he was attacked by bandits in north Szechwan and was killed, before he was thirty years old. I promised

Mao Tse-tung that I would introduce Fang Pi-tsung to him later but the opportunity never came and they never met.

That day we talked about Fang Pi-tsung off and on till midafternoon. The sun was very hot; so we sat to rest in one of the roadside teahouses; but the shade was so pleasant that we fell asleep. When we wakened, it was late and the innkeeper told us we still had to go forty kilometers to Ho Hu-tzu's place.

Now we walked in silence, concentrating on keeping up a good pace and getting to Ho Shu-heng's by night. In the evening, we reached a restaurant where we ordered a supper of rice, vegetables and fried eggs, and the owner told us he thought we still had to go about twenty kilometers further on. Eating supper quickly, we set off at a steady pace. When we came to a crossroad with a number of narrow tracks leading off in every direction and with no signposts, we had no alternative but to wait till someone came along and told us to take the track that led up over the hills. Ho Hu-tzu lived in an out of the way part and when we got into the hills, we came to another crossroad. We had seen no people, so we debated which to take. Both tracks looked alike. Finally we turned right, out of the hills, hoping to meet someone who would tell us where to go.

The moon was shining now but in the mountain forest it was dark and many animal noises could be heard. We were not afraid, however, because this was a small forest and there would be no tigers. Also there were two of us. When we had walked an hour, the hills ended and the track petered out. Before us was a broad plain across which led a wide road and in the distance we saw two houses without lights. The people had retired. Since we had no idea where we were, we went to the nearest house and knocked. We were told we had taken the wrong fork in the hills—we should have turned left—but we could cut across to Ho Hu-tzu's home which was about fifteen kilometers away. The Chinese saying, "In a hundred-mile walk, the first ninety is half way" was appropriate on this occasion.

Since we met no one on the road, we had to ask our way several times at houses where the road branched. Finally, when we were sure we must be at our destination, we asked, "Is this Ho Shu-heng's house?" After many negative replies, they said, "No, it's the house just up the road there!"

At last we had arrived! We rushed to the door and knocked excitedly. "Ho Hu-tzu! Ho Hu-tzu!" we called loudly. "Get up and let us in!"

A light went on in one of the rooms and Ho Hu-tzu appeared at the door and embraced us with a happy laugh. "Siao Hu-tzu! Whatever are you doing out this way? And Jun-chih has come too? I never dreamed of seeing you two out here! Come in. Come in!"

As we entered the big room, his father entered from another door. He was a typical farmer of about fifty years. Our friend's brother came in; we had met him when Ho Hu-tzu taught at Ch'u Yi School. His twelve-year-old nephew appeared next; I had known him as a student in the Ch'u Yi School. Then Ho Hu-tzu asked his wife and sister-in-law to come and be introduced. It was like a family meeting to welcome long absent members. We felt as if we had really come home.

When introductions and greetings were over, Ho Hu-tzu asked, "Where have you come from, Siao Hu-tzu?"

I told him we had come from Changsha and Mao added, "We walked all the way from Changsha especially to visit you!"

"I am not worthy of that honor," said Ho Hu-tzu. "You are very welcome and we are delighted to see you, but why did you walk? You must be exhausted!"

"Oh," I answered, "the walking was not bad at all. In fact, we are thinking seriously of making a walking tour of the province."

"You see," added Mao, "we are making an experiment. We are trying to travel as far as we can without money. We are living like beggars."

Ho Hu-tzu was visibly shocked. "Living like beggars?" he asked.

"Yes," I continued, "we left Changsha without a cent in our pockets; so we should have to beg our way."

"But I still don't see why you want to do that!" said Ho Hu-tzu.

"The idea is to see if we are equal to solving difficult situations; to see if we can live and travel as we want, even if we have no money. In a word, we are trying to learn to overcome difficulties," I explained.

Ho Hu-tzu sighed, "What strange fellows you are. What strange things you do!"

When the younger brother brought a bottle of wine, we protested that we had eaten supper, but we all drank a little wine and ate some fruit before we went to bed at about two o'clock. We were dead tired after our day's walk of about eighty kilometers and we knew that we had already disturbed them too much for one night.

23

From Ho Farm to Ningsiang Town

Being typical farm people, the Ho family were all up shortly after sunrise in spite of the night's disturbance, so Mao and I decided we should get up too. First we wrote up the events of the previous day in our diaries and I included Mao's comments on the life of Fang Pi-tsung.

After we had greeted the family and eaten breakfast, Old Ho took us on a tour of the farm. Ten pigs in one sty, some black, some white and others black and white, were his most prized possessions. One enormous pig, which was white except for a jet black back, looked like a small cow. Mao asked how much it would weigh and how old it was. "I can see you're no expert," laughed Old Ho. "He weighs about a hundred sixty kilos. When a pig is two years old, we consider the meat old and not good to eat. This one is eleven months old."

"Only eleven months old?" I asked. "And already so big?"

"The size depends upon both the kind of feed they get and the breed. This is a particularly good breed. I'll probably feed him till he gets to about two hundred kilos," explained Old Ho.

Since we had never seen such fine porkers before in our lives, we wandered among the sties for quite a while and Old Ho laughed at us, saying, "Now you've got a good subject for some fine poems!" And afterwards I did actually write a short poem in my diary on "The Fat Pig."

When we walked from the pig sties to the vegetable garden, Old Ho said, "These pigs constitute the family fortune. We couldn't live without the pigs. They cover all our expenses in such things as meat, oil, tea, salt, and so forth, for the whole year, and often a good margin of profit besides. No, we couldn't live without our pigs." Mao and I really understood the importance of these animals to the Hunan farmers. That province is the most important pork producing section of China and at that time, it supplied much of the meat for export.

The extensive kitchen garden was full of excellent vegetables; we especially admired its clean appearance and the complete lack of weeds. When I mentioned this to Old Ho, he was very pleased and tried to reply in a classical literary simile, "The weeds are like low, evil-minded individuals and they must all be got rid of because they are a bad influence on the refined and noble vegetables, the 'gentle-men,' the 'sages'!"

Ho Hu-tzu laughed heartily, "What do you think of Father's classical composition? Not bad, eh? Like father like son!"

Finally we visited the rice fields which were still covered with water, but from which the healthy young plants emerged. Old Ho's second son was working in the field and we were told that the rice would be ready for harvest in two months and this crop would be sufficient to supply the requirements of the family for the whole year. With their pigs, vegetables and rice, they were practically self-sustaining. They had to plant hemp for spinning and they were buying raw cotton.

Ho Hu-tzu, the oldest son, had a good education and was a teacher. His was called a "half-plough, half-study" family. Mao's family as well as mine were in this same category.

For lunch, we had quite a feast: fresh water fish had been netted from the pond, chickens had been killed, and an assortment of tasty smoked meat had been brought out for the occasion. With the

wonderful assortment of delicious vegetables from the garden, there
were more than ten different dishes, each with its own special, individual taste. Both Mao and I cried out in protest when we saw the
sumptuous feast that had been prepared, "You should not have gone
to so much trouble. Remember we are living the life of beggars!"

Ho Hu-tzu was about to speak, but his father interrupted him,
"You are both scholars and Shu-heng's good friends. Now you are
our honored guests. How can you say you are beggars!"

Old Ho was quite incapable of understanding our desire to live
as beggars, and he really felt honored to have us as guests in his
home. Though he did not understand us, we understood him and
we were careful to make no further mention of "beggars," since the
idea was so distasteful to him. From then on we played the role of
honored guests.

Since this role did not fit our plan, we thanked our host profusely
after the meal and said we must be getting on our way. Old Ho was
crestfallen. "But how is this?" he asked. "You walk so far to visit us
and after just one meal you want to go. I thought you would stay
for a week at least. I have killed a pig and so much food has been
prepared and now you talk of going. You have hardly tasted our food.
Please stay a little longer. This afternoon I shall take you up into
the hills to see our woods."

When we saw how deeply offended he would be if we insisted, we
agreed to remain for one day longer as honorable guests. Later we
quietly urged Ho Hu-tzu to persuade his father not to ask us to stay
longer.

After tea Old Ho took us to see his forest, from which they gathered
their firewood. Though most of the trees were pine, we saw many of
species that were unfamiliar to us. One hill side was covered with
bamboo which supplied the delicate young shoots in the spring for
eating and canes for making many household articles. From the top
of the low hill we had a fine view of the broad plain stretching away
into the distance and the four of us sat down under a pine to admire
the scene. Up there where it was pleasantly cool and fresh, Old Ho
told about his early struggles to make ends meet. Ho Hu-tzu listened
quietly and at mention of certain sad episodes he was so moved that
tears welled up into his eyes.

Supper was another sumptuous banquet with a variety of rich plates which made us feel uneasy. This was hardly a good preparation for the life of austerity we had before us! Before we left the table, we announced that we would leave early the next morning. Old Ho was downcast, but said nothing. After we had chatted for a while, we all went to bed.

Next morning after we had eaten breakfast and thanked them all again, we said goodbye. Ho Hu-tzu walked with us for a long way and tried to persuade us to take some money just in case we needed something, but we firmly refused and asked him not to worry. Now we would beg but there was no fear of starving. "You're strange fellows," he remarked unconvinced. "You probably won't die of hunger, but do take care of yourselves." His offer of money reminded us of the money Liu had given us and we asked Ho Hu-tzu to accept it. Since he refused, we put it in our bundles and tried to forget it.

Leaving our friend, we hastened to get back on the wide road which would take us to Ningsiang Town. On the way we talked contentedly of the Ho family and how happy and secure they were. There were numerous such farm families in China at that time.

Toward mid-day when we were hungry, we decided not to stop at roadside eating places. When we came to a large house, we walked resolutely through the gate and into the courtyard. We had armed ourselves with a couple of heavy sticks, but there were no howling dogs, so we knocked at the door. Telling her we were beggars, we asked for rice. Without comment she returned to the house and presently brought us each a small bowl of cold rice without vegetables. Because we were very hungry, we ate quickly and would have asked for more, but she said, "That's the portion we always give to beggars. Isn't it enough?" When Mao told her we would not be begging if we were not hungry, she suggested that we try another house.

Begging for one's food, we realized, was very different from ordering a meal in a restaurant where one could eat his fill, if he had the money to pay for it. A beggar must be content with meager rations and often was obliged to beg from many different homes before his hunger was satisfied. In these country districts the houses were widely scattered, sometimes one or two kilometers apart.

At the next house we did not get a good reception. The master said, "We have no cooked rice. I can give you a little dry grain." That would do us no good; so we walked on.

At the third house, the people were more generous. They gave us a big bowl of cold rice and vegetables which fully satisfied our hunger, even though the food was coarse and hard.

In the district town of Ningsiang we had school friends, but we decided not to visit them lest we have an experience similar to the Ho family and our beggar-life would lose its value if we had such interludes of easy living. In the town itself there was nothing of special interest. On the outskirts there was a broad river called Deep Jade Water, spanned by a picturesque bridge near which were clustered many little boats. In the distance arose a low hill called Shih Ku Shan, Lion Strength Mountain, on the slopes of which grew lovely pines.

Mao and I sat on the bank looking into the deep jade water and admiring the landscape. We wrote a little poem which I found quite pleasing at the time:

Clouds enfold Lion Strength Mountain,
The bridge locks in the boats of the Deep Jade Water.

24

The Journey to Wei Shan

Sitting on the bank of the quiet river, we decided to go to Wei Shan (Mount Wei), which was famous not only for its beautiful scenery but also for the big Buddhist temple built on the mountain side. This temple, or monastery, well-known since the T'ang Dynasty (A.D. 618–905), was very rich and its Abbot, Fang Chang, had won renown as a great scholar. We had two good reasons for visiting the monastery: we wanted to study the organization to see how the monks lived, and we were anxious to make the acquaintance of this famous Fang Chang. Since we were in no hurry, we wandered along, chatting on a variety of subjects and admiring the scenery and changing views which presented themselves.

About twenty miles from Ningsiang we climbed an unknown, not-very-high mountain with a wide rocky front which could be seen from a great distance. On its slope was an ancient spreading pine tree with dense fan-like lower branches opened up on each side like wings forming a shady arbor, and with many large stones strung out like a chain around the trunk. We set down our bundles and umbrellas and sat on this "chain" with our backs firm against the tree. Here we relaxed in a pleasantly cool perfumed atmosphere. Because it reminded me of the happy afternoon we spent with Old Ho, I said, "Old Ho ploughs his fields for a living. He gets up at sunrise and works till sunset. Don't you think he is happy?"

"He often said he was happy," answered Mao. "It's a pity he didn't have a chance to study when he was young. You can see he's not had much education."

"His hard physical work produces a happy mind. That's why he's contented and healthy," I said. "You remember the saying, *wei ku jen tan yu* (why seek useless worry)? If Old Ho had studied, he would probably not be so happy now."

"Yes," agreed Mao, "knowledge is a good thing but sometimes it is better to be without it."

"The only things he has to worry about are the yield of his rice crop and fattening his pigs. When he has enough to eat, he's happy.

But remember, he's a small landowner. He works for himself. That's why he is happy. Farmers who suffer are those who must work for others. They toil from dawn to dark and then they have to hand over the fruit of their labors to the owner of the land!"

"Yes," Mao said, "and still worse are those who want to work on the land but can't find employment. There are many of them in China."

I did not agree. "The majority of those are happy all the same," I said. "The poor are happier than the rich, and healthier, too."

"You're right there," Mao agreed. "We can call that the destiny of the rich and poor."

As we talked, a cool, gentle breeze caressed us and we were so relaxed and comfortable that we fell off to sleep. I slept more than half an hour, but Mao was still sleeping soundly with mouth open when I wakened. Soon he opened his eyes and smiled, "I feel lots better for that sleep."

I suggested, "What do you say to our spending a few days here meditating like Buddha under his Bo tree?"

"If I were to sit here like that, I'm sure I'd fall asleep again," Mao said.

"But quite seriously, would you like to stay here for a few days?" I wanted to know.

"First I want to see the monks in Wei Shan Monastery. Let's see how they meditate and then we can come back here and imitate them," Mao replied.

I agreed and remarked that I was hungry and suggested that we go down and beg for some rice. We were reluctant to leave the shelter of the old pine, but we hitched our bundles on our shoulders, bowed to the tree and to the chain of stones which had served us as a seat, and set off down the hill. Near the foot we saw a big house and hurried toward it.

Everything was quiet. Apparently they had no dogs. As we wondered if the house was empty, a cross-looking old man came out and we concluded that Liu's dogs gave a more cordial welcome. When he heard that we were beggars, not only did he refuse to give us food but he began to rail at us. Annoyed, we answered in the same way.

"We have nothing to give to beggars," he said. "You're wasting your time here."

"What sort of house is it that can't afford to give food to beggars? It's not even worthy of the name of house."

"Shut your mouths and get off with you!" he shouted.

We told him we would not leave till he explained why he should not give us food, and we seated ourselves in the entrance so that he couldn't close the door, but held our bundles tightly lest he try to grab them. When he saw that we would not move, he became furious. His face was almost purple and his neck seemed to swell with the anger he was choking down. "Are you really not going?" he asked unbelieving.

We tried to bargain: if he told us why he gave no food to beggars, or if he fed us, we might go. "We've been all over the world, but we've never come across a house where they refused to give food to beggars," we explained. "What sort of family do you belong to? Begging food is not against the law. Only cruel and unkind persons refuse to give beggars something to eat."

The old man saw that we were not afraid of him, so he tried to conjure up a crooked smile. "I have no cooked rice," he said, "but if I give you some grains will you go away?"

"Only if you promise to treat other beggars who come to your house well and to feed them," Mao insisted.

The old man did not reply. He sat as if he had not heard, but when we repeated our conditions, he finally said, "Yes, yes! All right!"

We picked up our bundles, thanked him with exaggerated politeness and turned away with the words, "When we come back this way in a few days, we'll call again to ask for food."

At the next house, only half a kilometer away, a kind old couple gave us a plentiful supply of rice and vegetables and we had an interesting conversation with them. His name was Wang and he told us, "I have two sons. The older went to Sinkiang ten years ago but we have not heard from him for about five years. The younger has opened a teashop in Ningsiang District. He's not doing too badly and we do have two grandsons. They live in Ningsiang Town."

I commented, "You appear to be a very distinguished person, sir. Are you a scholar?"

"I was very keen on studying," he replied, "but my family was poor and I was able to go to school for only four years. Then I became an apprentice to a tailor, and later I was fortunate enough to obtain a job as concierge in the yamen of a district magistrate. There I picked up quite a bit of money! But you two young fellows? You don't look at all like beggars. How is it that you have to beg for a living?"

"Our families also are very poor," Mao explained, "but we want to travel and the only way we can do it is by begging."

"There's nothing wrong with begging," he said, "beggars are quite different from thieves!"

"Beggars are the most honest of men," I contended. "Much more honest than state officials."

"You're absolutely right there!" he exclaimed. "Those officials are very dishonest. When I was concierge in the yamen, the magistrate thought of nothing but money! When he judged a case, the one who gave him the most money won. It was quite useless to approach him without being prepared to grease his palm generously."

"I suppose, being concierge, you received a lot too?" asked Mao.

"Just a bit of pocket money. Nothing like what the magistrate received!"

"But how did you know when they gave money to the magistrate?" I wanted to know.

"They told me," he said.

"If both the plaintiff and the defendant gave him money," I asked, "what did he do then?"

"It just depended upon which one gave him the most. The more generous one always won the case. The one who lost was very annoyed and he always told me about all the palm-greasing."

"Wasn't the magistrate afraid?" asked Mao.

"Of what?" asked our host.

"The one who lost might lodge an accusation against him with the high court in the capital of the province," explained Mao.

"Little fear of that!" said our old man. "To take a case to the capital takes much more money than in the district, if he were to have any hope of success. And if he couldn't afford to pay the magistrate enough to win in the district, much less would he be able to pay the officials in the capital. Anyway, magistrates and other officials almost always back each other up, as everybody knows."

"What a situation!" exclaimed Mao.

"That doesn't mean that there are not some good officials," the old man hastened to add. "I was concierge for seven or eight years and I worked for three magistrates. The first was grasping; the other two really did their best to be just. But people seem to have no conception of what is right or wrong. There was no justice in the community! You can imagine how the people complained of the magistrate who based his verdicts upon the generosity of his clients; but they complained as bitterly about the two who refused to accept bribes. I told the people it was no good to offer money but they wouldn't believe us. 'What sort of magistrate is he, who won't accept a gift?' they asked. It wasn't worth while trying to be honest. No one believed it and they thought even worse of them than of those who made no bones about what they wanted. Wasn't it better under those circumstances to take the money and have done with it? That's probably why there are so few honest officials."

We agreed that his conclusions were probably correct and after a few minutes of talk, we bade the old couple goodbye and continued on our way, talking further about the deplorable state of affairs. The majority of the lower classes were ignorant and believed whatever they heard, playing into the hands of unscrupulous officials who were supposed to administer justice.

In the distance we could barely make out the Wei Shan, looking like a low cloud, but gradually it took on the form of a mountain as we drew nearer.

25
The Buddhist Monastery on Wei Shan

In the evening we arrived at the Wei Shan and as we approached, the uniform green background gradually resolved itself into trees surrounding the great white Buddhist temple. Soon we arrived at its foot and started up the slope.

At the gate two monks came out to welcome us and to escort us into the building. Presumably they thought we had traveled a great distance to worship Buddha, so to prevent subsequent misunderstanding we told them we had come to beg. They assured us, "Worshiping Buddha and begging are the same thing."

We didn't understand what they meant but we supposed the observation was the fruit of some deep philosophy. Possibly it was a corollary to Buddha's teaching that all men were equal. Without questioning them we followed through the second door and into the inner court where we saw about a hundred monks slowly walking up and down. We were given a room with the suggestion that we leave our bundles and take a bath. This we gratefully accepted.

When we returned, the monks wanted us to burn incense to Buddha, but we told them we had not come to worship. We explained that we had come to see the Fang Chang, the Abbot. They looked askance at our begging attire and said the Fang Chang would not receive just anyone! They added that when he gave one of his famous dissertations, we might see him. We explained that we not only wanted to see him, we wanted to talk with him and that this very night! They were visibly impressed by our insistence, but they dared not disturb him if he did not know us. Finally we persuaded them to take a note which I wrote very carefully and which we both signed.

In about ten minutes they reported that the Fang Chang would be pleased to talk with us at once and invited us to follow them to his room. He was a man of about fifty with a kind, distinguished face. The four walls were lined with books and besides Buddhist scriptures and commentaries, we noticed the Classics of Lao Tzu and Chuang Tzu. On a table in the middle of the large room there was only a tall vase of flowers, a low vase of orchids, and nothing else. We were not able to discuss Buddhist studies with him, but we had a fascinating discussion of the Classics which continued for an hour. The Fang Chang was very pleased and invited us to have supper with him, after which we returned to the big hall where a large number of monks were again gathered.

When they saw us come from the Fang Chang's room where we had dined, they presumed that we were guests of importance and all of them stood to greet us. To be friends of the Fang Chang we must be eminent scholars and as such, first class calligraphers! They all asked us to write a few words on their fans and scrolls for them to keep as souvenirs. That kept us busy till almost midnight.

Next morning when we spoke of leaving, the monks told us the Fang Chang asked that we stay for a few days, that he would like us to visit him that afternoon. Meanwhile they took us to see the vegetable garden, the big kitchen, the refectory, and other parts of the building. The gardeners, cooks, water carrier, all the workers were monks!

When Mao and I went to the Fang Chang's room in the afternoon, he again received us cordially. This time he had apparently decided to talk "business," and in a gentle manner he extolled the virtues of Buddhism in an endeavor to waken our interest in religion. Though we had no desire to discuss religion, we listened politely, careful to give no sign of agreement or disagreement. We just let him talk. Finally when he mentioned Confucius and Lao Tzu, we found ourselves on familiar ground where we could express our opinions. But what really interested us was not Buddhism but the Buddhist organization in China. Now we asked him a series of questions.

When we asked how many monks there were in the monastery, he replied, "About a hundred monks live here permanently. But since there are always visitors here from distant parts, often we have three or four hundred here at one time. Visiting monks usually remain for a few days before going on their way. Years ago they had as many as eight hundred here, which was the record since the foundation of the monastery. But that was before my time."

"How does it happen," Mao asked, "that monks from other provinces several thousand kilometers distant, come to this monastery? What do they do here?"

The Fang Chang explained, "They come here to listen to talks on the scriptures and to receive religious instruction. The Fang Chang of this monastery have always been famous for their explanations and commentaries of the scriptures. The monastery is rich and it is no problem to give travelers board and lodging for a number of days. Monks all know about this place and, as you know,

monks are *ch'u chia jen,* people who have abandoned their homes;
so for them all Buddhist temples and monasteries are their homes
and they visit them in turn to receive instruction in each."

"How many monks are there in China?" I wanted to know.

"There are no exact statistics," Fang Chang continued. "Ex-
cluding Mongolia and Tibet there must be, in China proper, about
ten thousand at least. With Mongolia and Tibet where the ratio
of monks is extremely high, there must be about ten million, maybe
more."

"And how many centers of instruction like this Wei Shan
monastery are there in China?" I asked.

"There must be at least a hundred places like this and, counting
the smaller ones, there are probably a thousand altogether."

"Are there any Buddhist books published?" asked Mao.

"Yes, indeed, a great many, especially in such centers as Shanghai,
Nanking, Hangchow, and Hingpo."

"We are considering visiting the big Buddhist monasteries," I explained. "Could you write some letters of introduction for us?"

"That is not necessary. There is no need for you to have any
letters of introduction, because everywhere you go you will be welcome the same as you are here."

When we had thanked him and told him we wished to leave the
next day, he said that was as we wished, but he wanted to see us
again before we left. We explained that we would like to get started
early in the morning, so we again thanked him and made our
farewells.

When we came into the big room, the monks again stood in
greeting and knowing that we were leaving in the morning, they
asked us to write lines and verses for each as mementos of our visit.
They all crowded around with their respective requests and we did
our best to oblige. Some of the monks themselves wrote beautifully
formed characters and they were obviously surprised and disillusioned
to see Mao Tse-Tung's coarse writing. We had seated ourselves
at two small writing tables and at first there was a big crowd of monks
around each, but before long they all drifted to mine and soon Mao
had no more customers.

Among the monks were five youngsters of about fourteen years, one of whom I remember to this day with deep affection. He was called Fa Yi.

Fa Yi, who was fifteen, had an excellent control of language for his age and his calligraphy was very beautiful. From the moment we arrived he seemed drawn to us and during our stay he lost not a moment's opportunity to talk with us. He was unable to tell us where he had come from and what his name had been before he became a monk. He only knew that someone had told him that he had arrived at the monastery as a year-old baby. We guessed that he was an illegitimate baby who had been brought up by the monks— a very common practice in China. Teasing, I said I could detect a resemblance to Mao Tse-tung, and he retaliated by saying there was no doubt but that he had my features.

Fa Yi was anxious to study books other than Buddhist scriptures, such as those on Confucius and the famous poems of the T'ang Dynasty. Already he could recite several T'ang poems. At first we suggested that he abandon his secluded existence and go out into the everyday life of the world. He was very eager to do this, but at the same time he was a bit afraid, because he knew no other home and he had no possessions. Why shouldn't he live like us, we asked, traveling freely without money and with only one change of clothes. This impressed him but, as he hesitated, we became afraid he might try to escape and follow us and that the Fang Chang would blame us for leading him astray. Also, he was still very young; so we tried to change the conversation and suggested that the best thing for him was to study hard and learn with the monks, many of whom were highly educated and cultured, and that he should not leave the monastery at this time.

That night I wrote him several verses in my very best calligraphy to keep as a souvenir. Next morning, at dawn, Mao and I left the monastery and set off down the mountainside. Fa Yi accompanied us to the foot and there he shed bitter tears as we parted. Poor, delicate Fa Yi! Pitiful Fa Yi!

26
The Road to Anhwa

When we left the little monk Fa Yi at the foot of the Wei Shan, we walked a hundred yards or so before I turned to watch the small figure slowly climbing back to the monastery. Even at that distance he looked lonely and pitiful. I knew how sad he was and I felt sorry for him, but Mao did not share this sentiment. "Jun-chih," I said, "look at little Fa Li. Don't you feel sorry for him?"

Mao glanced back quickly and remarked, "What's the good of looking at him? You're just too sentimental."

We were walking toward the town of Anhwa. Anhwa District was one of the important farming areas of Hunan Province and we figured that it would take us about two days to reach the town. However, we were in no hurry. Since there was beautiful scenery to admire and since we had plenty to talk about, we took our time.

We had many interesting impressions of Buddhist life from the Wei Shan monastery and when we came to a small teashop by the roadside, we decided to rest and write up our diaries. We had written only two or three lines, however, when we put down our brushes and started to talk.

"What a great influence Buddhism has been in China," I remarked. "Even the school of Confucius has been affected by it, especially in the T'ang and the Sung Dynasties."

"Why is it that Buddhism should have become such a great power?" Mao asked.

I explained, "First, because it represents one aspect of the universal truth and provides a satisfying philosophy of life; second, because of the religious instinct or philosophical leanings, whatever you may call it, of the Emperors of China."

"The religious instinct of the Emperors?" asked Mao.

"Yes," I replied, "especially the Emperors of the T'ang Dynasty. You remember, they conferred the posthumous honorary title of 'king' on Confucius and ordered that in every province and in every provincial district throughout China there should be established a

temple to him. This movement started in the T'ang Dynasty and at
about the same time they conferred a similar honor on Lao Tzu,
since his surname, Li, was the same as that of the royal family, and
they proclaimed him the founder of Taoism. Taoist temples were
officially established throughout the country in that dynasty. Then
came Buddhism. Despite its being a foreign religion, it was welcomed,
and temples and monasteries were set up everywhere in the same
way. Thus in the T'ang Dynasty there were three official religions:
Confucianism, Taoism, and Buddhism, all coexisting in harmony. . . ."

"Yes, I know," said Mao. "I remember reading that one of the
Emperors of the T'ang Dynasty conceived the idea of transferring
the mortal remains of Buddha from India to China."

"Then there was the famous scholar-monk Hsüan Tsang who
spent more than ten years in India studying the theory of Buddhism,"
I continued. "He brought back with him more than six hundred and
fifty volumes of Buddhist scriptures of which he and his students
translated seventy-five into Chinese. Everyone has heard of Hsüan
Tsang—that was also in the T'ang Dynasty."

"How very strange!" commented Mao. "It's as if three different
religions sprang up in the T'ang Dynasty at the same time. Though,
of course, Confucius was really a philosopher and not a religious
leader."

"Yes," I agreed. "And Lao Tzu was also a philosopher, though
later the followers of the Taoist movement firmly proclaimed him
as a 'holy man' and the founder of a religion! It is interesting to note
what realists the Chinese are! They may believe in a particular
religion and guide their lives by it, but they seldom if ever become
fanatics. That is why three different doctrines can exist side by side
in perfect harmony."

"Well, it's a good thing for the country that several religions can
co-exist in harmony," Mao contended. "That means there are no
religious wars of the kind you read about in the history of other
countries. Why, some of those struggles between followers of different faiths have lasted over a hundred years! We've never known
anything like that in China."

"Yes, that is very true," I agreed. "But it's much more than that.

It's not only in this country that several religions can live together harmoniously, but also in the minds of individuals; and this has nothing to do with the T'ang Emperors. I know a very good example of this phenomenon in my own home: first, like everyone else, we had the *p'ai wei*, the ancestral tablet, on which was inscribed the order of worship or obedience—Heaven, Earth, Emperor, Parents, Teacher; but my grandmother wished to inculcate in us respect for the Sages, so she put up another tablet to Confucius. Then, as she had a certain weakness for Buddhism, she pasted up a picture of Buddha. Most interesting of all, however, is the fact that when she heard of the teachings of the European and American Christian missionaries, she supposed the doctrine of Christ must be important for people to have come from such distant lands to teach it, so she put up beside the Buddha another picture, of Christ on the Cross. I used to call my grandmother's tablet cabinet 'the religious republic.' This is quite typical of the religious beliefs of many Chinese."

"Not only is that a good example of our religious freedom; it also demonstrates what you said a while ago, that the religious instinct of the Chinese people is weak," said Mao. "Another example of that is the fact that Confucian· philosophy has had more influence and is wider spread in this country than Taoism and Buddhism, which have come to be regarded as religions in the true sense of that word. How is it that the philosophy of Confucius has become such a dominating force? After two thousand years its influence is still as strong as ever. Why? Why did the early Emperors think so highly of Confucius? Was it because of his strong personality?"

"There are two reasons for the persistence of Confucianism," I explained. "It was by chance that the Emperors and indeed all public officials, held Confucius in high esteem. A profound knowledge of the principles taught by him was required to pass the higher examination; so if you hadn't studied and learned his philosophy, you had no possible chance of securing a good position in life! Also, his philosophy serves as a true guide for human relations. He tells exactly what one should or should not do. There are none of the theoretical speculations of Lao Tzu and the Buddhist teachers with their abstract conceptions. Confucius taught us how to live our daily lives with practical and concrete instructions."

"I think we should stop right now and put all this in our diaries," said Mao. "This is very important."

We stopped to write and when we had finished, it was nearly noon. We were beginning to feel hungry, too. We had so much to talk about after our visit to the Wei Shan and so much to write about in our diaries, that we had lost the rhythm of our long walks. Now we thought only of sitting still to talk. We decided to have our lunch in the teashop and then to take to the road.

Mao Tse-tung asked the woman owner if she sold rice. She did, but she had nothing to go with it: no fish, no meat, not even an egg—just some vegetables. We decided that was enough, since now we were accustomed to a frugal vegetarian diet. But did we have any money?

Mao was sure we still had some money in our bundles and suggested we spend all of it to satisfy ourselves with rice and vegetables. "Then we'll see what the future has in store for us," he said, and I agreed that it was an excellent idea.

After eating lunch, it seemed so hot that we could not resist the temptation to waste a bit more time by taking a nap in the shade of the teashop. When we eventually set off slowly along the road, it must have been four o'clock in the afternoon.

27
A Night on the Sandbank

Not far from the teashop the road passed around the foot of a high mountain. Though we did not know the name of the mountain, we did know that now we were in the Anhwa District.

This mountain harbored two industries. Anhwa was famous for its tea, and the slopes were dotted with tea plantations. Also an important industry in fir bark for roofing and other purposes had been developed, and thousands of fir trees with the bark stripped off stood white and strange in their nudity.

We were successful in begging a very satisfactory supper from a little farmhouse, after which we wandered slowly along the bank of an unknown river. Though we continued to walk for several kilometers, the path still followed this broad river which, despite the width of its bed, had only a thread of water trickling through the white sandbanks and the long stretches of well-worn round stones. A few slanting trees grew by the roadside, bending low over the river banks with boughs outstretched, as if begging for a drink of water.

Before long the moon became so bright that it was almost as light as day, and the stars seemed to disappear except for the largest and most luminous which were reduced to mere pin points of light. The sharp outlines of our shadows made it seem at times as if there were four of us walking along that lonely midnight road.

We wondered how long it would be before we got to an inn to spend the night; the countryside was deserted and we had not met a soul to ask the way. The brilliant moon and the clearly defined shadows created a new and strangely attractive landscape; so we seated ourselves on a soft sandbank by the river edge to admire it.

"I wonder how far we'll have to walk to reach an inn," Mao pondered. "Tonight we have no idea where we shall stay. There is no sign of any human habitation in any direction. All four points of the compass are empty."

"Yes, the four points of the compass are empty," I agreed, "but so are we empty. We haven't a cent to our names; so even if we did find an inn, they wouldn't take us in if they knew we couldn't pay."

"Yes, that's true," replied Mao. "I had completely forgotten that we had no money. What do you say to spending the night here? Wouldn't this sandbank make a comfortable bed?"

"Yes," I agreed, "you're quite right. This sandbank will be our bed. We could pick a much worse place than this to sleep and the blue sky will be our canopy."

"This old tree will be our wardrobe," said Mao, as he picked up our bundles. "Let's hang our bundles and umbrellas in the wardrobe tonight."

"Isn't the moon a huge lamp?" I asked. "Let's sleep with the light on tonight, shall we?"

We found two big flat stones for pillows, but since they were too high, we half buried them in the sand. When we lay down to test the bed, we both pronounced it to be most comfortable.

I got up again and announced that I was going down to the stream and wash my feet before I went to sleep.

Mao remonstrated, "Even when you're living as a beggar and sleeping out in the open on a sandbank, you still keep up this bourgeois habit!"

"I always wash my feet before I go to bed," I explained. "It's a habit I got into many years ago and if I don't do it, I don't sleep well."

"Just try for once not washing your feet tonight. You'll see whether or not you can sleep!"

"But why shouldn't I wash my feet?" I asked. "I am even thinking of taking a bath."

"I see you're a gentleman beggar!" chided Mao, as he curled himself up for the night.

I took my towel from my bundle and went down to the water to wash. When I returned, Mao was already sound asleep. I felt clean and refreshed and cool, but unfortunately the cold water had completely wakened me so that I had no taste for sleep. Suddenly I saw a man hurrying along the path. No doubt he was a belated traveler who was not satisfied with a sandbank bed such as ours.

After he had passed, it occurred to me that if we both slept here beside the road, our bundles would hang in the tree by the side of the road in the bright moonlight, and who could say what sort of individuals might pass by before we wakened in the morning. Our possessions had been reduced to the barest essential and we could take no risk of their being stolen. I decided it would be wiser to move over to some other sandbank farther away from the road where we would not be so conspicuous and where our bundles would be safe. I went to waken Mao Tse-tung.

Mao was so sound asleep that he seemed almost dead and shaking him and calling to him made not the slightest impression. I even slapped his face several times until he finally opened his eyes. I quickly explained what I had decided to do and urged him to move. In a sleepy, far-away voice he said, "Don't worry about thieves. Stay here. . . ." Immediately he closed his eyes again and was dead to this world. I thought it would be even more difficult to waken him a second time, and he would probably still refuse to move; but I knew I would be most uneasy if I tried to sleep there.

I thought the problem over and decided to move to another bank alone. I took both bundles and umbrellas and moved to a similar spot about forty meters away. This second bank was sheltered by a group of young trees and it was well away from the road. I prepared my bed and quickly fell asleep.

Some time during the night Mao wakened and missed me. When he saw that the bundles and umbrellas had disappeared from the tree, he got up and called my name at the top of his voice several times, but he got no answer. But this time, I was sound asleep and heard nothing. Mao could not guess where I was because there were dozens of sandbanks along the dry river bed with many groups of trees whose shadows made it impossible to see what lay beneath. He called several times, but when I did not answer, he concluded that I had taken the umbrellas and bundles with me and that all was safe; so he lay down and went to sleep again. Next morning he said, "I thought you must be sound asleep somewhere on the other side of the river. You'd hardly have decided to walk ahead on your own."

Although I had heard nothing of Mao's calls, I had slept but fitfully. I awakened to find myself staring with wide open eyes into the immensity of the deep blue sky at the brilliant circle of the moon. How vast was the universe, and how tiny and insignificant the human being! How many races of mankind had looked wonder-ingly at this same bright moon and at the immeasurable, awe-inspiring night sky above me! . . . Races of ancient peoples passed beyond the ken of modern man? For how long had this silent, celestial com-panion been casting its silvery glow on the dark world of men? The contemplation of its age befogged the imagination. The life of us humans? How ephemeral and insignificant in comparison! Slowly I recited Ch'en Tzu-ang's poem, written during the T'ang Dynasty, over a thousand years ago:

I saw not those who came before me.
Nor shall I know those of future generations;
Disconsolate tears well up from my lonely heart
In contemplation of this eternal and infinite universe.

The emotion evoked by the words of the sad poem and my sad thoughts brought tears to my eyes. I contemplated the insignificance, the meanness, the apparent futility of human life against the grandeur of the heavens. . . .

I do not know when I fell asleep, but I had a frightening dream. A tiger was crouched on the slope of the mound beside the river. It was watching me intently, and was tensing its muscles ready for a spring. At any moment it would come bounding down the slope, baring its savage fangs in a terrifying snarl and would throw itself at my defenseless body! I woke trembling and covered with perspira-tion. The moon had shifted its position but the same calm sky still looked down upon me. I breathed deeply with relief—it had only been a dream after all!

Feeling somewhat recovered, I looked off toward the mound of my dream and my heart leapt into my mouth. A big black animal sat there, looking fixedly at me! This time I was wide awake and it was no dream. This was a real tiger that had scented my presence and was crouched there ready to attack. The guardian spirits or some sixth sense had warned me of my danger by means of the dream so that I would waken and have a chance to escape! But how was

I to get away? I did not dare to move, but lay there watching the tiger out of the corner of my eye.

I must have remained there tense and stiff for ten minutes or more. The tiger had not stirred and I began to wonder, hopefully, if he had really seen me. Perhaps he had taken me for a tree trunk lying on the ground; or perhaps even for the shadow cast by the trees. He might be resting in that spot just by coincidence. However, if I moved, he would surely see me and would spring down upon me in a flash. I lay there still as death, hardly daring to breathe.

Then, all of a sudden, it occurred to me that Mao Tse-tung was asleep and was unaware of the danger. If he woke up and moved or shouted, the tiger would most certainly attack him. I began to imagine that he would awaken at any moment and I wondered desperately what I could do to save him.

It was, I decided, my responsibility to go and warn him and I must take whatever risk was necessary immediately. I must crawl over to where he lay. I reasoned that if I moved very, very slowly, the tiger might not perceive my movements. I started off, an inch at a time, creeping along, or rather dragging myself, at the pace of a snail. At this rate, it took more than a minute to move the first meter and I patiently spent an hour or more getting behind a bunch of trees which finally gave me cover. From this new position I peered back through the branches toward the mound. The tiger had not moved and I felt that my patience had been rewarded. I was safe!

I still had to cover a long stretch of open ground or make a wide detour, and it must have taken another hour to work myself completely out of the animal's view. Then I got up quickly and ran with all speed down to Mao Tse-tung's side. He was in a profound sleep with his mouth open and the saliva running down from the corner. I dared not make a noise even yet. I could not call him and I was afraid that even if I did wake him, he might begin to talk in a loud voice, which would surely bring the tiger down upon us in an instant.

I lay down quietly beside him and tried to sleep. With that nervous tension, that was of course quite useless. Soon the farmers began to appear in the fields and several people passed by on the road quite near to us. Then Mao wakened. With the coming of the new day and with the people moving about, the danger was now almost past and without waiting to tell Mao of the awful fate that we had so narrowly escaped, I ran back to the trees to fetch our bundles and umbrellas. There was now little fear of attack.

I grabbed our things and, ready to run at top speed, I turned quickly to look where the tiger had sat crouched so menacingly. The big black tiger was still there. It had not moved and I looked more carefully in the clearer light. My fierce big black tiger was a natural formation of black rock!

28
After Leaving the Sandbank

Leaving our night's resting place we decided to continue along the bank of the stream, since this river path seemed to be the only road to Anhwa.

Just as we were taking up our bundles to set off for the day, a huge green snake suddenly came out from the grass along the lower bank only a few yards from where Mao had been sleeping a few minutes before. I got quite a scare because this vicious-looking reptile could not have been very far away during the night. If it had seen Mao, would it have bitten him? Had it crossed over to the trees, I also would have been in danger. The tiger had turned out to be the creation of my own too-vivid imagination, but there was no doubt about the reality of this snake. I recalled how people said if you were bitten by a snake, the poisonous venom entered the bloodstream and quickly poisoned the whole body. In this out-of-the-way place it would have been very dangerous to get a snake bite because it would be impossible to find a doctor or to obtain any treatment. I told Mao what I had been thinking and we decided that we would sleep no more out in the open.

Our walk was monotonous and the river seemed to be interminable. Along the bank at frequent intervals were low straight trees which made one think of a line of soldiers standing at attention as we passed. We seemed to be holding review and I imagined the troops saluting us as we passed by.

After an hour of this we came to a bridge with a stone sign bearing the words, "Anhwa City: Right." We crossed the bridge and turned on the road to the right, which parted company with the river and led to a group of hills. At the foot of one of the hills was a small pavilion by the roadside—a square pointed roof like those of the pagodas, supported by four columns and with the sides open to the air, and containing only a long wooden bench for travelers to rest upon.

We sat on this bench to rest, and looking around, I saw a path leading up to the top of the hill on which appeared to be a small temple. Telling Mao to wait there for me, I walked quickly to the top and found it was, in fact, a relatively small temple, only four or five meters wide and about seven meters high. In the center stood a small stone statue. The walls were white and bore no inscriptions. There was a fine view and from this point one could look out into the far distance from all four sides. I descended the hill, took my brush and ink from my bundle and returned to the temple where I wrote just two words on the white wall: *yuan ta* (far and great).

When I returned to Mao, another traveler had arrived and they were talking. He asked me the name of the temple and I said, "I don't know its name but I have just written the words, *'yuan ta'* on

the wall. You remember how Professor Yang Huai-chung, of the First Normal School taught us that there are five principles in cultivating one's character and the first of these was *yuan ta*. He explained that this meant that one's conduct and thoughts should be far-seeing and one's purpose should be high. One should always aspire for something above the ordinary. I have never forgotten that lesson, those words immediately came into my mind. They seemed to me to be symbolical."

Mao understood immediately and said, "Very good. Very good, indeed."

Only a short distance from the pavilion we came to a little tea-shop where we begged for our breakfast. The owner as usual was a young woman of about twenty years. She seemed very kind and understanding and immediately gave us each a big bowl of rice. I wondered if she knew the story of the little temple, so I asked if she knew its name.

"It's called the Liu Pang Temple," she answered.

"The Liu Pang?" asked Mao. "How do you write that name?"

"I don't know how to write. I only know that the temple is called the Liu Pang," she replied.

"Is there a person called Liu Pang who lives near here?" continued Mao.

"That I wouldn't know," replied the girl. "I was born in Anhwa City; I was married there and came here to live only two years ago. I know very little really about the history of this place."

Mao was thoughtful for a moment, then he said, "Liu Pang was the name of the first Emperor of the Han Dynasty. He didn't come from here and I doubt if he ever visited this part of China. I wonder how it is that this temple should bear his name?"

"Really I don't know," the girl answered. "I didn't know that Liu Pang was the first Emperor of the Han Dynasty."

"Do you know why this temple was built on this mountain top?" persisted Mao.

"No, I have no idea at all," replied the girl patiently.

At this moment a man came in who looked as if he might be her husband; so we turned to him with our questions about the temple, and this is what he told us: "We're not quite sure how the name Liu Pang came to be given to the temple. Some people say that Liu Pang was an Emperor; others that he was someone with the same name as the Emperor. I don't know. There is an interesting story told about this temple: Years ago there was a man who fell sick. He was desperately ill, on the point of death. Everyone thought there was no hope for his recovery. Then one day he had a dream and in his dream a man named Liu Pang appeared. This Liu Pang gave him a prescription for some medicine which would cure his illness. When he wakened, he sent his son to have the medicine made up and when he took it, he was immediately cured. That, they say, is why he built this temple to the memory of the Liu Pang who appeared to him in his miraculous dream."

"Was he the Liu Pang who was the Emperor?" I asked.

"That I don't know," replied the husband. "Some say he was, others say no. I don't know."

"How long ago was the temple built?" asked Mao.

"I really don't know. I remember seeing it when I was quite a little boy and now I am twenty-six years old. There are people around here who say it is an ancient temple. But I don't know about that."

We thanked these two, picked up our bundles, and set off again down the road. As we walked, I pondered over the possible origin of this dream temple. Who was this unknown Liu Pang? But did it really matter? However, the name Liu Pang had awakened a train of thought, and as we walked, we talked of the Emperor whose life interested Mao so much.

"Why was Liu Pang called Liu Chi?" he wanted to know.

I explained that Liu was his family name and that Chi was his second name, or his private name, just as his was Jun-chih and mine Tzu-cheng.

"Liu Pang was the first commoner in history to become Emperor," he continued thoughtfully. "I think he should be considered to be a great hero!"

"Oh no," I remonstrated. "Liu Pang was a bad man! But lots of bad men are called heroes," I conceded.

"He was a commoner who gathered together an army to depose the despot of the Ch'in Dynasty," argued Mao, hotly. "He was founder of the Han Dynasty. How can you call him a bad man?"

"He was a bad man. He was too selfish, too self-centered to be an emperor," I explained, "that's why I call him a bad man. He was really nothing more than a man with political ambitions who was successful. Perhaps he was not at heart a bad man, but political ambition tends to grow and become a vice. Ideals become obscured and one's character begins to degenerate. Then he's a bad man."

"At least Liu Pang was a successful revolutionist who succeeded in overthrowing the Ch'in despot," Mao countered.

"Yes, he got rid of one despot only to become another himself. Ch'in went out and Han took his place. What's the difference? Both were bad."

"I suppose," Mao suggested, "that you think that after his revolutionary forces had gained control of the country, he should have established a democratic republic. Two thousand years ago democratic republics had never been thought of! People had never heard of such a form of government! It was impossible for him to visualize a democratic system in those days."

"Yes, I know," I said. "But even if he couldn't visualize a democratic republic, he could at least have avoided being a cruel despot!"

But Mao persisted, "You can't really call him cruel, if you take into account the age in which he lived and compare him with other Emperors of his time."

I still disagreed, "He was treacherous and absolutely devoid of human sentiment. Remember the friends and generals who risked their lives fighting for him? When his armies were successful, these men became famous leaders and he became afraid that one or another of them might try to usurp his throne; so he had them all killed. Some of them, you remember, were literally cut to pieces, and he had whole families and all near relatives of others exterminated! He bore a knife in his breast in the place where his heart should have been. He was a very cruel bad man."

"But if he hadn't killed them, his throne would have been insecure and he probably wouldn't have lasted long as Emperor," said Mao.

"So in order to be successful in politics, one must kill one's friends?" I asked. "Politics seems to be a lottery. Many people buy lottery tickets and, of course, someone gets the first prize. Political success is nothing more than that. Liu Pang was not only cruel, bad, and treacherous, he was also uncultured, low-minded, and nothing but a vulgar boaster!"

"Just what do you mean by that?" asked Mao.

"Well, a very good example of his mentality is the proclamation he wrote when he returned to his native province after becoming Emperor. Do you remember how it ran? 'The strong wind blows and the clouds fly. The all-powerful ruler returns to his place of birth. How can brave men be found to stand guard?' The first line shows his spirit of boastfulness and conceit; the second is written to awe or frighten the simple country people; and the third shows clearly that he realizes that his throne will be difficult to preserve and, at the same time, that it will be no easy matter to find faithful guards who can be trusted not to revolt."

"And that is why you call him uncultured and low?" asked Mao.

"Yes, but there's another episode. Did you know that he made his nephew the Marquis of Soup?"

"The Marquis of Soup? No, I haven't heard that one."

"Well, once when he was very poor, he asked his sister-in-law for a bowl of soup. She refused him. He never forgave her, nor forgot the incident. When he became Emperor, he conferred on her son the title, Marquis of Soup, to make him the laughing stock of the court and of his friends."

"I think that's very funny!" laughed Mao. "But now I remember something else. He was very kind to your family. He made your ancestor Siao Ho his first Prime Minister!"

"Yes," I agreed. "But that was because my ancestor was no soldier. If he had been a soldier, he too would have been cut to pieces like the rest long before he could reach such a high position. Siao Ho was interested only in his books and culture; so he was no threat to the Emperor's position."

"He didn't treat Chang Liang badly," persisted Mao, determined to find some good and to prove that Liu Pang was not a bad man.

"And why did Chang Liang become a Taoist?" I asked. "Wasn't it so that he would have a good excuse for going on a pilgrimage when he realized that Liu Pang might at any time accuse him of unfaithfulness and have him killed? No, believe me, politics is the most degrading profession that exists! Can you tell me of just one person who has been successful in politics who can still be regarded as basically honest? No. Take Ch'in Shih Huang. Han Kao Ts'u, T'ang T'ai Tsung, Sung T'ai Tsu, Chen Ch'i Szu Han, Chu Yüan-chang, and others; were any of these good, honest men? No. From the most ancient times in China, those who have worshiped power have been mean in spirit. The two things seem to go hand in hand. To struggle for a high position by the use of force indicates meanness of spirit."

I knew quite well that Mao Tse-tung would not wish to continue the argument further lest I might criticize him directly. We both knew that he was identifying himself with Liu Pang in his ambition and I knew that he would not admit that he was himself *hsiao jen,* mean of spirit.

29
Difficulties in a Distant City

After we left the Liu Pang Temple, we took things easier than we had before. We paid more attention to our discussions than to the speed of our progress; so it took us several days to reach Anhwa City, the district capital. On entering this city, we really felt that we were a long way from home. The people spoke with a different accent; their habits were strange to us; and it really seemed as if we were in a foreign country.

Though we knew that some schoolmates lived here, we decided not to visit them because we were afraid they might wish to entertain us lavishly, as had been done on the Ho farm. However, we had no idea what we would do here, since our last money had been spent long ago. We were truly beggars who had to live by their wits.

When we arrived, it was about ten in the morning and we were very hungry, since we had eaten no breakfast. When we came to a teashop, we hesitated a moment; then, throwing caution to the four winds, we walked resolutely in. We sat down at a square table in front of a window with umbrellas and bundles beside us, and we ordered breakfast with tea to drink.

After our hunger was somewhat appeased, we discussed how we were going to pay the bill. We would have to beg or earn the money somehow, somewhere. There was no doubt about that. I suggested that Mao stay at the table to write up his diary, while I went out into the town to see what I could do.

It took but little time to discover that the shopkeepers of Anhwa had no time for beggars. I was refused time after time: "We've nothing for beggars here!" "Don't stand there in the customers' way!" On several occasions I was not even allowed to enter the shop. Someone barred my way saying, "There's nothing here for you! Be on your way!" Their talk was very coarse and the faces seemed cold and cruel. A few people condescended to give me one or two *wen*, a practically worthless coin, but in an hour and a half, after calling at all the shops along two streets, I had only twenty-one *wen*. I gave it up as a bad job and returned to the teashop.

I told Mao how difficult it was to beg in that city, that I had collected less than half enough for our bill after begging along two long streets. How could we pay our bill? How could we get out of the teashop? Mao suggested that he try another street while I wrote my diary, but I knew that was no good. Finally I thought of a plan. I suggested that I take the money I had collected and with it buy some paper. Then I would write out a number of scrolls to present to shop owners, like the *sung hsien sheng*. They are a sort of intellectual beggar who does not beg directly, but presents a written scroll, usually containing a verse of his own composition. The recipient then gives him a small sum of money.

"Maybe I can get a bit more money that way," I suggested. "You stay here and prepare the ink while I buy the paper."

Mao welcomed this suggestion enthusiastically and immediately prepared to rub up some ink. When I went to buy the paper, I copied down the names of the most important shops that I passed. Each paper was about a meter and a half long and thirty centimeters wide; so we cut each one into two pieces.

In my best calligraphy I very carefully wrote out the name of one of the big shops at the top of each sheet. This was a most important point, since each scroll was to be written exclusively for

a single shop; so it would not be easy for them to refuse to accept it.
I hoped, too, that they would feel honored to received a personal
scroll. I had selected only big shops which presumably would have lots
of money.

At the first shop, my scroll was accepted by a young employee who
gave it to three older men. They opened it and smiled in apprecia-
tion as they read. Though it was doubtful if they could really appreciate the calligraphy, they did realize that they could not write so
well. They looked at me and again at the scroll, repeating time after
time, "Very good writing. Very good writing indeed!" They whis-
pered among themselves and I knew they were discussing how much
they should give me. If they gave too much, the owners might be
angry with them; if they gave too little, they were afraid they would
offend a scholar! They could not decide, so finally one of them took
the paper into the office of the owner. Instantly a gentleman with
a smiling face came out and handed me four *t'ung yuan*, each of
which was equivalent to ten *wen*.

He asked me where I came from; how it was that I was so poor,
and similar questions which I was about to answer when another
well-dressed man came out of the office. He was about forty years
of age and very fat. Apparently he was the owner, since the other
five immediately scattered, leaving me alone with the newcomer.
He asked me some questions in a very polite manner and then he
called the young man who had come out first. He had given me
some money? Four *t'ung yuan*. "Give him four more!" said the fat man.
I thanked him and left the shop. I had received eight *t'ung yuan*,
four times the amount I had collected after toiling through two long
streets shortly before! I meditated on the cold, cruel looks which
greeted my empty hands and on the smiles with which the printed
word was welcomed. I found comfort, thinking how learning was
respected and I walked to the next shop with greater confidence.

However, the flower does not bloom forever; the moon is not
always round; and man is not always happy. Hope was great, and
disappointment was also great. In the second shop the owner impatiently waved me away: "What use are words to me? Take your
calligraphy away and give it to someone else!" he shouted.

"But the scroll is of no use to anyone else," I protested. "It is written just for your shop. See, your name is written on it. Please accept it even though you don't want to pay me for it?" I asked.

The man looked at the calligraphy now for the first time and read the name of his shop. Grudgingly he accepted the scroll and thrust two *t'ung yuan* toward me. I thanked him politely and left.

Back in the street I thought of Mao waiting for me in the teashop. If he was to wait for me to distribute all the scrolls, he'd have a very long wait; so I decided to go back. We paid our bill and discussed the next move. Though we did not need more money immediately, it seemed a pity and a waste not to utilize the scrolls; so we divided them between us and agreed to meet again in the teashop after we had distributed all of them. I gave Mao only the scrolls for the smaller shops since I knew that the larger ones often employed private teachers for the children of the proprietors and they might ask him to write something on the spot. If that happened, he might find himself in a very difficult and embarrassing position, since calligraphy was not his strong point and no one could possibly confuse his large clumsily written words with the writing on the scrolls.

At my first call the writing was accepted politely when the name of the shop was seen to be at the head. Next was a tea store. The owner was a learned man who wrote calligraphy. After admiring my writing, he invited me into his study where I was introduced to his children's tutor. The two of them studied my scroll and the owner sent for some paper and asked me to write a *tui tzu*, the famous antithetical sentences, for him and the tutor. I did as they requested and then asked them to write something. They smiled but the owner pointed to a *tui tzu* hanging on the wall, which had been written by the tutor. The calligraphy was not bad, but I thought mine was better.

I was invited to have tea with them and we three had an interesting talk. "Learning and calligraphy are difficult things," he said, "and they constitute valuable possessions. It is indeed unfortunate that the scholar is so little appreciated in our modern society. I studied for over ten years, but I was unable to find a good job; so I finally decided to open this tea store. If I had continued to study, I should have starved to death years ago!"

"If you had not opened the tea store, I should have been out of a job, too," added the tutor, "and that would have made one more learned person starving to death."

"And if you had not opened the tea store," I added, "I should not have had the pleasure of meeting you two learned persons, and I would probably have died of hunger in this city of Anhwa!"

The owner laughed loudly at this and said, "It's a pity the store is so small; otherwise I should like to have both of you as tutors in my home!"

"If one studies, he takes the risk of dying of hunger; but if one doesn't study, he does not attain culture. What is one to do?" asked the tutor.

"It seems to me our host has chosen the best plan," I replied. "Study first and then go into business."

"Since I have changed my profession, I cannot be called a scholar," said our host. "But I do have three sons. Two of them I'll put into business and the third will devote his time to study. That way we shall maintain an element of learning in the family and I hope no one will need to die of hunger."

"That's all very well for you because you are fortunate in having three sons," the tutor said, "but what of those who have only one child?"

"This is a father's scheme," I suggested, "a plan for the family as a unit. But, you must remember, a son does not exist merely to support the family. He should be allowed to plan for his own future. He must realize that he's a member of society and he should plan for the ultimate good of that society."

Obviously they didn't understand this idea; but we had already talked for such a long time that I judged it best not to go into further explanations. I had other shops to visit and I said I must get on my way. The owner went to his office and when he returned, he presented me with an envelope. Thanking him, I bade them goodbye and went out into the street. When I opened the envelope, I found it contained twenty *t'ung yuan!*

After I made several other calls with moderate success, I returned to the teashop to pick up Mao.

The next point on our itinerary was to be the district city of Yiyang.

30
The Road to Yiyang District City

Leaving Anhwa, we set off along the main road and soon came to a stone signpost on which was carved: "To the right for Yiyang District City." This was to be our next destination, since from the start, we had decided to be guided only for the broadest road, take us where it would.

We had no idea how far Yiyang might be and since we were not especially interested in distance, we asked no questions. It was all the same to us. Our feet walked on, one step after another with regular monotony, like a ruler measuring the road; but the movement was purely mechanical, since our interest was completely concentrated on our conversation and we were oblivious to everything else.

After we left Anhwa, we discussed the conversation I had had with the tea store owner who had set one of his sons to study, but since learning could not be relied upon to bring in an income, had arranged for the other two sons to go into businesses. Each was to have a separate business, so that, if one failed, the other could be depended upon to carry on. I criticized the father's decision as one that was selfish, since he contemplated only the welfare of the family unit, without taking into consideration the wishes of sons or what might be more beneficial to society as a whole. This led to a long discussion of the family system in general. I held that this store owner was a typical Chinese father, but that his ideas were antiquated and out-of-date.

Mao replied, "You know the old saying which speaks of bringing up children to care for their parents in their old age! That's been the Chinese system for countless generations. The chief function of the son is to take care of the father and mother when they are old. They depend upon him entirely."

"It's strange that I should never have shared this selfish conception of the family," I stated. "Naturally if I had a son, I'd be very fond of him; but I should never regard him as my own private property to dispose of as I thought fit. He should be a member of society and

137

it would be my responsibility to bring him up and train him. His attitude toward me later in life would depend upon his own sentiments. I would not for a moment expect him to support me in my old age! My father has always had similar ideas and, even though he belongs to a previous generation, he has always been against selfishness with children."

"I think it is because the idea of family is so strong in China that the people are so lacking in nationalistic sentiments," Mao suggested.

"The son doesn't belong exclusively to the family," I added, "but neither does he belong to the State! An exaggerated nationalistic idea is just as bad as an exaggerated family system."

"Your ideas of children are new and strange even to me," said Mao, surprised.

I explained, "The truth of the matter is this: a person comes into the world as a member of the family into which he happens to be born; at the same time he is an integral part or unit in the country or nation; and also, he is a citizen of the whole world. He has responsibilities to his family, to his country, and to the world as a whole. In a word, he is responsible to society."

Mao did not agree. "I believe that the State comes before everything else," he said.

I explained further, "My idea is that if an individual is confronted with a line of conduct which would be beneficial to himself but harmful to his family, he would not follow it. If it would benefit his family but harm his country, he should not follow it. And most important of all, if it would benefit his country but be harmful for world society, he should turn aside from such conduct. The ultimate good of society is the final test of conduct."

"But the State protects the people," Mao argued, "and therefore the people are under obligation to protect their State. The people are the sons of the State. In the ideal State of the future, children will be taken from their parents and they will be brought up and educated at public expense."

"Then there would have to be two systems," I said, "one for bringing up the children and another for taking care of the old people. If you take away the support of the aged to which they have become accustomed by tradition, you will have to care for them in some other way."

"The first and foremost need," stated Mao positively, "is for a strong and powerful government! Once that is established, the people could be organized!"

"But when the government becomes too strong and powerful, it means the curtailment of the freedom of the people. It would be as if the population were a flock of sheep and the government were the shepherd. That's not the way it should be," I countered. "The people should be the master and the government should be their servant! However, all governments do inevitably want to become shepherds or masters!"

"But I do regard the people as a flock of sheep," insisted Mao, "and it is obvious that the government must play the part of the shepherd. If there is no shepherd, who will guide the sheep?"

"There's another way of looking at this problem," I stated. "If people are a flock of sheep, the government must also be sheep, and that's the worst type, those who scheme for power, who want to be masters. The members of a sheep government will say they are the most intelligent, the most capable. They will never admit that they are the bandits of the group!"

"Following your idea," said Mao, "if you don't want sheep to form the government, who will be the shepherd?"

"If the sheep are looked after by a shepherd, it means they have lost their freedom. They are at the mercy of the shepherd. They have no individual security. The shepherd can kill them at will. The only thing left for them is to eat, work, and sleep. Why must they have a shepherd?"

At this point in our discussion, we observed some cows peacefully munching grass on the plain some distance from the road. Apparently no one was looking after them. "See, Jun-chih," I said. "Look at the cows. Aren't they quite happy and content? What better organization do they need?" Mao did not answer and we walked on in silence, watching the cows. Before we got level with them, suddenly a man, carrying a long whip, appeared. The cows seemed to associate the whip with painful beatings, because, as the man approached, they scattered quickly in all directions. Those lying down chewing their cud jumped up, and those that were standing started to run. Instantly the whole herd became disorderly. They were too frightened to think of eating more grass.

I looked at Mao significantly. "You see the effect the shepherd has upon the cattle? When he's around, they live in terror!"

Mao Tse-tung answered stubbornly, "The cows have to be kept in order! The man has a whip and he must use it to beat them. It really seems that this particular 'shepherd' is too weak with them and is incapable!"

"What a pity that the cattle cannot understand your excellent explanation!" I ejaculated.

"It's because they cannot understand what the man says that they have to be beaten and that they have to have someone to look after them," Mao replied.

As Mao spoke, a big fawn-colored cow in front of all the others stopped suddenly, raised its head, and bellowed loudly! It seemed to be protesting. I said, "If they are continually bullied and domineered, even cows and sheep may revolt one day."

31
Arrival in Yiyang City

We arrived in Yiyang District City at about three o'clock one afternoon. There was nothing out of the ordinary to distinguish Yiyang from any other city of its size. There were many shops and crowds of people on the streets but that was not unusual. Suddenly, however, I did see something that was very interesting to me. "Jun-chih, look!" I exclaimed. "Have you noticed the District Magistrate's proclamations pasted on the walls?"

"Yes, I've seen them," replied Mao. "But I didn't bother to read them. Why are you so excited? Why do you ask?"

"Here's another one," I said, stopping. "Just look at it carefully."

Mao looked and turned to me, "All cities have proclamations like this pasted on their walls," he said. "I see nothing unusual about this one."

"But look at the Magistrate's signature," I suggested. "Who is he?"

"The words are very clearly written," replied Mao. "His name is Chang Kang-feng."

"But don't you know who Chang Kang-feng is?" I asked.

"No, I don't," Mao answered. "Am I supposed to know him? Who is he?"

"Why he's the head chemistry professor at First Normal School," I explained.

"Oh, he taught only the higher classes, so I don't know him," said Mao. "Our chemistry teacher was Mr. Wang. Are you sure this Chang Kang-feng is the same person? There must be many people with that same name."

"Yes, I'm sure this is he. He comes from Yiyang City. Not only do I remember his strong Yiyang accent, but he left school two months before summer vacation. Mr. Liu took over his classes. Now I realize that he came back here to be District Magistrate."

"Are you and he good friends?" Mao wanted to know.

"Oh yes, he liked me a lot. He used to give me a hundred in every examination. We had some very interesting talks together and he

141

always discussed politics with great enjoyment."

"If that's the case," Mao suggested, "you must go and see him."

I laughed at the suggestion. "Don't forget," I said, "in this community government officers and beggars are the two extremes. They represent the highest and lowest in society. No one looks down on beggars so much as government officers. We came from Changsha as beggars and we have had some very interesting experiences. But we have never called on a government officer. I think you are right. What do you say to our taking this opportunity to make a new experiment?"

"After all, he does know you, and he won't treat us as beggars," said Mao confidently.

"The biggest problem," I pointed out, "will be to get past the doorkeepers and the other servants of the yamen. Mr. Chang Kang-feng himself will not treat us as beggars, but his attendants will. Our problem is to get past the attendants. Come on, let's go and try. We'll see what happens."

Mao was enthusiastic. "Good!" he exclaimed. "This is another unique episode in our adventure: 'The Beggars Visit the Mandarin!' I suppose we will go just as we are? Straw shoes and all?"

"Of course. We're going to visit District Magistrate Chang as beggars!" I exclaimed.

The District Magistrate, who held one of the most important government executive posts in the district and who wielded the most power, was highly respected by the people. His position was far more important than that of mayors in other countries and his yamen, or official residence, was palatial and imposing—very different from local government offices in most western countries.

Mao Tse-tung and I had to ask the way several times, but eventually we arrived at the magnificent yamen. In front was a broad square, the center of which was exactly opposite the middle gate in the outer wall and one could look through to two similar gates beyond. These gave access to the large public hall where justice was administered. The private rooms of the Magistrate would be beyond this. Inside the big main gate and to the right stood the doorkeeper. He was also a very important person because it was his function to act as a screen, allowing only those who had legitimate business with the Magistrate to pass through.

We walked across the wide square and up to the big gate, where we were immediately halted by the guards who barred our passage. We insisted upon entering and, finally, after a brief hesitation, he let us pass on to the gatekeeper's office so that we could argue with him. The guards gave us the impression of being too lazy to take any responsibility upon themselves and they thus seemed to be more in the nature of a neutral element.

The doorkeeper, a very tall and coarse individual, came striding out, shouting as he came, "Get out! Get out of here quickly! What are beggars doing in the yamen?" He paused to stare at our shorts, straw shoes, umbrellas, and bundles, and then he started off again, even louder than before, "Get out, I tell you! What have you come in here for?"

"We've come to visit the District Magistrate," I said, taking one of my visiting cards from my pocket and writing Mao's name on it. "Will you please announce us?" I handed him the card quietly.

He stood there stupefied! "Beggars with visiting cards! What's the name? Siao Shu-tung and Mao Tse-tung! Why do you give me this card?" he asked.

"Please give it to the District Magistrate and tell him we would like to see him," I replied.

"Why do you come to see him? Do you want to accuse someone? Don't you know that you have to send in a petition first?"

"But we have not come here to accuse anyone," I said. "We were passing through the city and we want to pay him a visit."

The poor man stood and stared at us as if he could not believe his own ears. One could imagine that he suspected we were a pair of lunatics. In a puzzled voice he asked, "What business can beggars have with the District Magistrate?"

"Your District Magistrate is an excellent official and a very kind man. I am quite sure he will be willing to talk to a couple of beggars. Please go and see. Just take the visiting card to him and ask him!"

The doorkeeper shouted, "You're mad! If I go and tell the Magistrate that a couple of beggars want to see him, he'll think I've lost my reason and he would probably fire me on the spot! You get out of here! And don't bother me again! If you don't want to go of your own free will, we'll have the guards kick you out. Come on, get going!"

"No," I remonstrated. "We must see the District Magistrate."

Mao added, "We are beggars, yes, but we must see the Magistrate!"

The doorkeeper lost his patience and shouted, "Well, if you won't be reasonable, I'll have to have you removed by force! Guards! Guards! Guards! Come quickly!"

It looked as if the doorkeeper really meant business. The two soldiers who stood guard at the gate came walking over.

"Who dares to use force on a guest of the Magistrate?" I asked. "Aren't you afraid of being dismissed from your post?"

"We only want to see the District Magistrate," added Mao. "We have done nothing against the law. Let's see who dares to compel us to leave!"

Sitting down on one of the stone benches inside the gate, I said, "We two beggars are not going to leave the yamen till we have seen the District Magistrate." Mao took a place by my side.

Now three men had come out of the gatekeeper's office and another soldier had joined the group. Some of these individuals were very coarse featured, but others looked at us more kindly. They all stood in a semicircle staring at us and telling us we had to go, but not one attempted to lay hands on us.

Presently an older man in the group spoke to the gatekeeper, "Why don't you go and tell the Magistrate that there are a couple of fools here who say they want to see him, and that they are annoying us because they refuse to leave?"

"How can I do that?" asked the doorkeeper. "Only last week a poor relative came to beg money. I went in to announce him without suspecting. After he had gone, the Magistrate scolded me because after I'd announced him, he couldn't refuse to see him and he had to give him money. He said then that my very first duty was to distinguish among the visitors and to announce only those whom I thought he ought to see. If I thought they were undesirable, I was to turn them away without bothering him. How can I announce a couple of beggars after that? Even if they are mad, I'm not!"

The old man agreed that he was right and said, "Let me try. I'll go in and tell him they are bothering me and that we tried to get them to leave, but they refuse to go. I'll ask him what we are to do. I won't show him the visiting card, unless he asks for it. That way he can decide what should be done, and we are not responsible."

The old man went inside, put on a long gown, and combed his hair. Then he took my card, put it in his pocket, and walked slowly toward the inner gate. The younger gatekeeper with the coarse manners shouted after him loudly, "You get an order from the Magistrate to have these two fools tied up and sent to prison for a couple of days. That will teach them not to go around bothering honest citizens!"

We knew this admonition was meant for us and not for the old man, so we pretended not to hear. We just sat there quietly; but we could not help smiling to ourselves.

The old gatekeeper was not away very long. Suddenly he appeared through the second gate, walking much faster than on his outward journey. He was smiling to himself. He walked straight to the younger man and said, "The Magistrate says to take these two gentlemen to his private study as quickly as possible!"

We still sat quietly on our bench, pretending not to hear, but we were amused to see the astonished expressions on the faces of the soldiers and the others as they looked at one another when they received this unexpected order. The coarse-looking gatekeeper asked the older man very earnestly in a low voice if he was quite sure he had understood the Magistrate correctly. Did he really say to take them to his private study?

"Oh, yes," the old man replied. "I heard him clearly and correctly. He told me twice that they were to be shown immediately to his private study!"

After this brief aside, he came over to us, bowed low and said politely, "The Magistrate will receive you immediately. Will you please follow me?"

When we picked up our bundles and umbrellas, the old man wanted to carry them for us, but we said, "No, thank you. Beggars carry their own bundles, you know." We followed him through the second and third gates, then through a garden and to the Magistrate's private rooms. Mr. Chang Kang-feng was in his study waiting for us.

When the gatekeeper had departed, he asked in a surprised voice, "Mr. Siao, what has happened? Where have you come from? You look as if you have had trouble!"

"We have come from Changsha," I replied. "This is Mr. Mao

Tse-tung, my First Normal schoolmate of Class Fourteen."

Mr. Chang shook hands with Mao and asked, "Have you both come from Changsha directly to Yiyang?"

"We started from Changsha and passed through Ningsiang and Anhwa Districts on foot," I replied.

"And how is it that you came to see me here in Yiyang?" he asked.

"It was just by chance," I explained. "When we entered the city, we saw the proclamations pasted up on the walls and when we realized that you were the District Magistrate, we decided to pay you a visit. From here we plan to go on to Yuankiang."

"I see," Mr. Chang said. "And where will you go from Yuankiang?"

"We'll just follow the main road and let it lead us wherever it will," I replied enigmatically.

"But where is it you really want to go? What are you trying to do?" he asked, puzzled by my reply.

I knew that Mr. Chang was at a complete loss to understand this strange situation; so I explained in detail our idea of the "beggar holiday" and told him of some of our experiences on the road. He was clearly astonished, but he said he admired our courage in trying such an experiment. "Most people would not be able to understand," he commented. "That's why the gatekeeper came in a while ago to tell me that there were a couple of fool beggars who insisted on seeing me and that they would not be sent away! When I asked who they were, he gave me your visiting card and I realized it was you. But, to tell the truth, I can fully appreciate the man's attitude when I look at your dress and at your straw shoes! Now you go and have a good wash and then we can have a good long chat."

We talked with Mr. Chang for several hours and had supper with him. At the table he told us that one of our former schoolmates was now chairman of the local board of education; another was director of the high school; and another director of the primary school. Altogether six graduates from my former college now held important positions in the local educational circles. He wanted to send them messages to come to the yamen the following morning to have a welcome party for us.

We protested that we did not really want such a welcome party, but Mr. Chang insisted. "How can I keep your visit a secret?" he asked. "They will all be delighted to see you!" Finally we consented, but we went to visit each one of them first.

Thus the two beggars were again transformed into honorable guests. We remained in Yiyang for three days before continuing our journey to Yuankiang. When we left, Mr. Chang insisted upon our accepting four dollars for emergency expenses and he ordered the gatekeeper to accompany us as far as the city wall. We assured him that we did not need the company, but Mr. Chang would not hear of our going alone.

When we were out on the road, I said to the gatekeeper, "Your master is a very good man! He would not hear of beggars being tied up and sent to prison. Instead he has entertained us charmingly!" The gatekeeper lowered his head, but spoke not a word.

32
The Yuankiang Flood

The gatekeeper from Mr. Chang's yamen left us near the Yuankiang signpost just outside the city gate, indicating that the main road led to the district city of Yuankiang. The District of Yuankiang is one of the largest in Hunan. Once we were alone, we began to discuss this latest experience.

Mao criticized our host, Mr. Chang, "Although that doorkeeper was hateful and intolerant, his master, Mr. Chang was really worse. After all, the doorkeeper was only obeying the orders and Mr. Chang had positively given him instructions not to let poor people come in! Mr. Chang is what you call a *shih li hsiao jen,* a person whose chief aim in life is the obtaining of personal influence and money, and whose mind seems to be incapable of rising to higher thoughts. As for the gatekeeper, I've seen many better types! They're not all like that!"

"No, and not all the district magistrates are like that either," I replied. "There's an old saying, 'The doors of the yamen are wide open like a figure *pa* (eight); but however good your case, it is useless to go in for justice if you have no money!' Money is Justice!"

"Yes," agreed Mao. "There are very few people in the community who do not share that attitude. Money is one of the most powerful influences in human affairs. Money gives power."

"Power is a bad thing," I exclaimed. "All power is bad! And to use one's personal influence to tread one's fellow men underfoot is a crime!"

"Just a minute," protested Mao. "You talk about 'all power.' Just what power are you referring to?"

I explained, "First, in the primitive world, power was won only by physical strength which enables the owner to kill wild animals for food and to fight successfully other members of the tribe. Then there's the power of the soldiers, of armed forces. Then there's money power and of course, political power."

"So you say there are four kinds of power that are bad?" asked Mao.

"Power in itself is neither good nor bad," I explained, "it all depends upon the way it is used. To force people to do things against their will is a crime. Power is like a knife, which in itself is neither good nor bad, but if it is used to kill a person, it has made possible a crime."

"Do you mean that political power is like a knife?" asked Mao. "Surely you don't mean to say that since a knife may be used to kill, it should not have been made? Knives can also be used to make fine sculptures and carvings. In the same way, political power can be employed to organize and develop a country."

"You cannot compare politics with artistic creations," I protested. "If you analyze history, both Chinese and foreign, you will find that there are no politics in which the partisans do not seek to kill their opponents. Even the best of politicians tend to kill or to harm the people, and I cannot accept that as something good."

"I think political power is better than money power," said Mao. "The money power of the capitalist is nothing more than the accumulated blood and sweat of the workers. A person may be completely unprincipled, a thoroughly bad fellow, with no culture or education; yet if he has wealth, he will be a respected and honored member of the community. He can openly commit acts of wickedness, but if he has wealth, people will fawn upon him and kow-tow before him, telling him what a fine fellow he is! It's exactly like you said, 'Money is Justice!' Money is the father and the grandfather of the mean of spirit! Why, if you and I had been wearing fine clothes when we went to call on Mr. Chang, wouldn't the gatekeeper have met us with a smile of welcome? If we had given him some money as a tip, would he not have kow-towed before us? They are all mean of spirit! They all worship the god of money!"

"You say that political power is better than money power," I said. "I cannot agree with that. Money power is bad, but political power is even worse! You must remember one important fact: political power includes within itself both money power and military power. The person who has political power also has the other two! Money power is one force for evil, but political power is several forces for evil all combined. When an uneducated individual without conscience succeeds in obtaining political power, he may rise to the very highest position in the country. He may come to be called king, or emperor, or president, and then he can have others killed or punished to his heart's desire. However, he may say that he loves the people, that he is working for their good. He is the keystone of the country and the people's guiding star.

"It is for this reason that in Chinese history, there have been many scholars, pure of spirit and of exceptionally fine character, who have refused offers of posts as government officials. Some scholars have been invited by their Emperor three or four times to take important positions, but they have refused because they were unwilling to kow-tow to a person without education or culture. These scholars did not feel that political power added to the intrinsic value of an individual. They knew that political power was the crystallization of several potentially evil forces and that more often than not the Emperor himself was no more than a very successful bandit. These men who voluntarily renounced power were called superior beings or superior intellectuals.

"During the Chin Dynasty," I continued, "Huang-fu Mi wrote a book which he called 'Biography of the Superior Intellectuals' and in it he lists nearly a hundred old-time scholars who had refused to kow-tow to their so-called social superiors, and who preferred to maintain their own self-respect rather than to accept privileges and lucrative positions. That book was written two thousand years ago, and who knows how many thousands, or perhaps millions, have chosen this same path since then."

To this rather long interpretation, Mao replied, "Is it your theory that political power is a combination of evil powers? That's all very well. It's very interesting but it's much too deep for most people to understand and appreciate. You seem to be far above us common folks; you seem, in fact, to be speaking from the sky, and unless you speak in a voice of thunder, the people on earth will not be able to hear you. I speak from a somewhat lower level. I agree that the mean-spirited power-worshiper is hateful but what does it all boil down to? It seems to me the situation is like this: if you have money, or if you are a high official, all these people will greet you with smiling faces and will kow-tow to you; if, however, you do not have money, or if you are not an official, they just don't recognize you. That's what happened to us with the gatekeeper and it's typical!"

"The expression *shih li hsiao jen*, mean-spirited power-worshiper, is very ancient and is the accepted antithesis of the other expression *tao yi chun tze*, high-minded sage. This would seem to imply that all the *hsiao jen*, the mean-spirited, are worshipers of power, which is disdained by the sages. This was accepted by Chinese scholars as long ago as three or four thousand years back. Confucius said, 'For the sage, moral development always comes before thoughts of food or material possessions,' and Mencius commented, 'With moral sufficiency money has no attractions'; Tung Chung-shu, in the Han Dynasty, wrote similarly, 'One's aim must always be the following of high principles of living, never the search after material gain.' Humanity's standard of conduct should be based on these teachings, but the power of money and politics has been too much of a disrupting influence," I argued.

To which Mao answered, "That sounds very good, but it is often very difficult to stick to such high principles in real life. When people are starving to death, they are not going to meditate on their moral development. As for myself, I prefer what Kuang Chung said, 'After one is satisfactorily clothed and has eaten his fill, then should one give thought to the ceremonies.' That is just the opposite of what Confucius said, 'First follow the doctrine, then consider the material needs of the body.' "

I countered with, "You know the old saying, 'If the moral doctrine is one foot high, then the devil will be ten feet high.' The moral progress of humanity is very slow, but material progress is very rapid. This saying can be interpreted to mean that for every ten per cent of material progress, there will only be one per cent of moral progress. Great headway has been made with airplanes and military equipment. Guns and cannons grow ever larger so that more people can be killed, which of itself proves what meager progress has been made in the advance of morality. The Chinese sages always emphasized moral rectitude, but it will always be a difficult task to persuade people to act against their lower instincts."

Mao replied impatiently, "All this talk of doctrine and morality is very fine and good in principle, but it won't stop people from starving to death!"

"But if you leave out doctrine and morality," I insisted, "and insure only that everyone will have plenty to eat, then the people will just grow physically to be like so many fat pigs. I think that would be just as bad as to be lions or tigers."

We walked along the Yuankiang road for several days, talking in this fashion most of the time. One evening we stopped at an inn to have our supper and then decided to remain there over night. Since there were no other travelers, the owner, a very pretty young woman of about twenty, came over to our table to talk with us. "Where do you two gentlemen come from?" she asked.

When Mao told her we came from the Yiyang district, she commented, "You don't have much of a Yiyang accent."

"We are from Siangtan and Siangsiang," Mao added.

"Oh my," she said, surprised, "those districts are a very long way from here!"

When Mao told her they were about a thousand *li*, or four hundred kilometers from there, she wanted to know where we were going. She couldn't believe us when we told her we had no fixed destination, that we were just traveling across Hunan Province with no destination in mind; so I told her that we were beggars, which was the reason for our not having any purpose.

She was astonished to hear this and she laughed heartily, showing her fine white teeth. "You're beggars? You can't be! You look so refined! Are you really beggars?" she asked incredulously.

"We are not trying to deceive you," I replied. "We have walked all the way from Changsha to this inn, always as beggars."

She still could not believe it. She was completely bewildered. "But why don't you believe us?" asked Mao.

"Simply because neither of you looks a bit like a beggar!" she insisted vehemently.

"Do beggars have special looks?" I asked. "How do you find us different?"

She looked at us carefully a moment then said, "I can see that both of you are great men!"

"What is a great man?" I asked. "Can you, by chance, read faces?"

She nodded her head, "Yes, I know a little about physiognomy and the art of word conversion in foretelling the future. My grandfather taught me. He was a poet who published a collection of works called, 'The Shepherd Songs of the Peach Orchard.' My father also was a great scholar, but both of them died within the space of three years, leaving my mother and me alone in the world. Since we could not make ends meet, we finally opened this little inn."

"So you are still unmarried?" I asked the young lady from a scholarly family. "I wonder if you would loan me your grandfather's collection of poems to look at? You must be a learned person also?"

"Oh, I studied for seven or eight years with my father and I was just beginning to learn to write poetry when he died," she answered. "My grandfather's collection, 'The Shepherd Songs of the Peach Orchard,' are stored away in a coffer. I'll be glad to find them for you tomorrow."

"If you know how to read faces, please will you read ours?" asked Mao.

She hesitated a moment before replying, "Yes, if you like. But you must promise not to be angry if I say something wrong."

When she said this, her mother must have heard her, because she called out to her from the back room, "Yü-ying, stop that nonsense. Aren't you afraid of offending our guests? Talk about something else!"

But Mao protested, "No, no, we don't mind at all. Please speak quite frankly; just tell us everything that occurs to you. We will certainly not be angry!"

"Well, first, I must ask you both to tell me your family names," she said.

Mao replied for both of us, "Mine is Mao and my friend's is Siao."

"Oh, Mr. Mao," she cried, "your name is not good! Hung Hsiu-

ch'uan was called Ch'ang Mao. Yüan Shih-k'ai is called Mao Hou-tzu. (*Yuan* and *hou* have the same meaning: monkey.) It's really a pity that your name should also be Mao!"

Mao squirmed and asked, "What's my name got to do with my physiognomy? You look at my face and then you criticize my name!"

She answered quietly, "Your name is a very important aspect. Your physiognomy indicates that you can become a great officer, a prime minister, or a great bandit chief. With your name, you can probably become a person like Ch'ang Mao or Mao Hou-tzu. You are very audacious and have great ambition, but you have no senti-ment at all! You could kill ten thousand or even a hundred thousand people without turning a single hair! But you are very patient. If you have not been killed by your enemies when you are thirty-five, you can consider yourself safe by the time you reach fifty, and you will be lucky day by day. Around fifty-five, you will be even more fortunate. You will have at least six wives, but not many children. I see that you and your family do not get along well together. You will never live in your home town, and I see that you will have no fixed home."

Mao and I both listened to her somewhat amusedly and without paying a great deal of attention to the things she said. Mao was not the least bit annoyed because we treated the whole thing as a big joke. When she had finished with Mao, he suggested, "Now, how about Mr. Siao?"

She turned to look at me and said, "Mr. Siao, your physiognomy is entirely different from your friend's. You make me think of Taoism, and somehow you have the air of a sage. You really look as if you had descended from the sky—more like a spirit than a human being! You are really very sentimental. I could well compare Mr. Mao to a cup of very strong brandy and you to a cup of pure, clear water. I see that you will travel far during your lifetime, and the farther you go. . . ."

I interrupted her to ask, "Shall I have six wives, too?"

"No," she replied, "I see that you will marry twice but that you will have only a 'half' son, because a spirit wants neither family nor son. . . ."

After she finished, she again asked us about being beggars, and we told her frankly and honestly what we were doing and why. She was extremely interested in our ideas and she told us that if it were not for her old mother, she also would like to make a similar experiment by living like a beggar.

Next morning after breakfast, we wanted to leave, but she begged us to stay another day. When we tried to pay her for our room and board, she refused to take any of our money. When we asked, she told us her name was Miss Hu Yü-ying, and I said, "When Mr. Mao becomes Prime Minister at some future date, or a big bad bandit chief, he will write to you and invite you to become his adviser!"

She laughed loudly at my joke and replied, "But he is a person without sentiments! At that time he will have completely forgotten me; he will not even remember a bit of my shadow!"

Although I kept her address for many years, I never wrote to her. But her beautiful face, her kindness, and her refined character still remain very clear in my memory after all these years.

After we left the beautiful Yü-ying, we walked on about three hours before we saw that we were approaching Yuankiang City. We saw water everywhere around the city and this puzzled us until the owner of an inn explained that this was the *Hsi Shui*, the west water, which appeared every summer. The source of the Yangtze River is in a very mountainous country, and when the snow and ice melt in the summer, an enormous volume of water is released and flows downstream from the west. This water very quickly fills the streets of the city and after four or five days, it gets so high that all road communication with the outside world is cut off, because the land in this area is very low.

We soon realized that we could not possibly live as beggars under such conditions; so, our adventure having been brought to a sudden close by these circumstances, we decided to take a river steamer back to Changsha.

33
We Return to Changsha

When Mao Tse-tung and I got on the boat, it seemed to us that the waters were so high that they reached the sky. The whole landscape was completely transformed, with numerous houses and trees almost inundated or with their tops barely visible above the swirling flood. The boat, as you can imagine, was overcrowded and exceedingly noisy with mothers shouting to their children and the children crying or shouting back.

Since we wanted to write up our diaries, we found ourselves a seat in one corner, but we had barely begun to write when two men started a fight just in front of us. Both of them seemed to be about fifty years of age; one was clean-shaven with glasses, while the other had a moustache and no glasses. Both were well dressed and gave one the impression of being persons of some social position. When they fought, we could not understand what they were saying, but the one with the moustache pulled off the glasses of the other man and threw them onto the deck, then kicked them into the river. The man who had lost his glasses retaliated by tearing his opponent's gown, pulling it with such force that it was torn completely in two. A crowd quickly gathered and Mao and I walked over to see how it would end. We were curious to know what the fight was about, but we could not understand their native dialect, and we did not want to ask any of the other bystanders.

Finally things quieted down. The man with the moustache wrapped his torn gown around himself, picked up his bundle, and looked for somewhere to sit. He came over to the corner where we had left our things, so I took the opportunity to satisfy my curiosity.

"Tell me," I said, "why did that man tear your gown? He was certainly a ruffian!"

"The scoundrel!" he exclaimed angrily. "He was very lucky that he didn't get thrown into the river!"

"But what did he do to you?" I persisted.

"What a rascal he is!" he repeated vehemently. "The fellow came along looking for a place to sit and I moved over so that he could sit at my right side. He seemed to be quite pleasant and he introduced himself as the secretary of the Magistrate of the Chang Te District. Meanwhile I put two packets of cigarettes which I had bought down beside me on my right side. A few moments later I looked for the cigarettes, but they had disappeared. He had one packet in his hand just ready to take out a cigarette, and the other packet was in his pocket. I could see it quite distinctly because his pocket was not deep. When he had sat down, he had nothing either in his hands nor in his pocket. What is more, the brand I smoke is rather uncommon. There was no doubt at all about it, he had stolen my two packets of cigarettes. When I asked him what happened to my cigarettes, he began to shout at me and then we started to fight. He didn't know that I am an officer in the Yuankiang City police; but anyway it's not very difficult to catch thieves like that!"

"Oh well, it's no good being angry any more," I said, trying to pacify him. "It's all over and done with now."

During this exchange Mao Tse-tung had sat without saying a word, just looking, and showing his surprise when the man said he was a police officer. He gave me a rather cool smile and I said, "Jun-chih, you said that 'one should have sufficient to eat and clothe him-self well, and that he should study courteous manners.' Here is an illustration. How do you explain the fight between these two men? A police officer of this one's stature and a yamen secretary are hardly the sort of people who go hungry, and you can see that they are very well-dressed."

Mao sighed but said nothing. I had not realized that the police officer could hear me, but apparently he had caught some words with-out getting their context.

"Did you say that I was hungry?" he asked. "Yes, that is true. I was in such a hurry to catch the boat that I had no time to eat. I think I'll go now and get myself some lunch. I wonder if you will just keep this seat for me, please. I'll be back very soon."

I laughed to myself as he departed and Mao did not miss this opportunity to pull my leg. "You see," he said, "he had not had any-thing to eat! That is why he started the fight!"

By this time we were completely surrounded by water. Everywhere one looked there was nothing but an endless sea, and it almost seemed as if we were floating in the sky. From dawn to dusk it was almost impossible to tell where the sky began and the water ended, since the misty horizon merged perfectly into the river. This was an excellent opportunity for us to talk of everything under the sun and we took full advantage of it. We even discussed the dialects of the motley crowd of passengers and the actions of the various individuals. Suddenly someone shouted that the boat was due to arrive in Changsha within half an hour!

I turned to Mao and suggested, "Jun-chih, in half an hour we shall be back in Changsha. Let's have a general summing-up of everything that has happened since we left here. What do you say?"

Mao agreed, saying, "That's a very good idea. First, we know that it is not impossible to overcome all difficulties, since we were able to realize our aim fully and completely. It was not easy to live without a cent in our pockets, but we did manage to do it. Up to now we have begged our way and we have never been in danger of starving to death. We managed to solve quite a few difficulties and overcome many obstacles along the way, too. But there are other points."

"Yes," I agreed, "there are other things. Hunger was the worst experience; it is very painful to have an empty stomach for a long time—one's hands and feet even lose their strength when one is hungry. In this world there are many people who spend most of their lives enduring hunger like that. But there is still more."

Mao added, "We found that almost every member of the community is a *shih li hsiao jen*, a mean-spirited money-worshiper! They think of and recognize only money! We left Changsha without any money in our pockets and as a result we had to accept many harsh words and very unpleasant treatment. Beggars are considered to be low and disgusting people because they have no money!"

"Don't forget that pretty girl," I reminded him. "The one who was so expert at physiognomy and told you your fortune! She was not a money-worshiper!"

"Yes, in all our travels," Mao agreed, "she was the only one who did not worship money."

"But there are still other things," I persisted. "Don't forget that police official and the magistrate's secretary who had enough to eat, and yet they stole things and then fought over it. That proves that money does not tend to improve morals; only greater knowledge will do that."

"What else?" asked Mao.

"Well, you must not forget the cows without the cowherd, eating their grass so very contentedly and peacefully; but when the cowherd appeared with his whip, only confusion resulted."

"Anything more?" inquired Mao.

"Only that now we can vouch for the truth of that old Chinese saying, 'After begging for three years, the beggar would not accept even a post as mandarin.' And why is that? Because the beggar's life is a life of complete freedom."

Now the other passengers were making such a noise that we could hardly hear ourselves speak. All were very busy arranging their packages and bundles, shouting to each other, so that it was quite impossible to continue our conversation. Soon the boat drew in toward the bank and there was a grand rush for the gangway, everyone trying to squeeze past the others in order to be the first to get off.

Soon we found ourselves again at the West Gate and I stopped and said, "Jun-chih, let's go down and find that ferryman with whom we quarreled. Let's see if he's down there yet."

"But why should we go and look for him?" asked Mao.

"Now we have money and we could pay him what we owe him," I said.

"I don't agree!" answered Mao.

"You don't? Why not?" I wanted to know.

"Because we did suggest to him that we would pay him on our return, but he refused to accept our offer. Now we have no obligation to pay him because we promised him nothing," he answered.

"But I feel sorry for him," I continued. "Now that we have some money, why not give him some? After all, we did take his boat without paying the regular fare!"

"But that is all past and finished now," Mao insisted. "There's no need to drag that matter up again." So saying, he turned and set off, walking in front of me for the first time since we had set out. He seemed so determined that I decided to let him have his own way and I followed him into the city.

Just inside the gate we had a picture taken, with our umbrellas on our right shoulders and the bundles hanging close to our backs, exactly as we had carried them on our travels. I remember that Mao stood at my left. We really made an interesting picture with our short-cropped hair, shorts, and straw shoes, all much the worse for wear. This photograph was left in the house where I was born in Hunan. No doubt the Communists failed to recognize their leader when the house was confiscated several years ago and I suppose it was burned as one of those "capitalist things."

After we had the photograph taken, we returned to the Ch'u Yi School where we both had a bath, ate a meal, and then sat down to open our bundles. We finished writing our diaries and then proceeded to count our money. We had two dollars and forty cents left, which we divided equally between us as beggars' property. Then I said to Mao, "I'm going back home now. My father and mother will be expecting me. What will you do?"

"I also shall go back home," he replied. "They were making two pairs of shoes for me and they will be waiting for me."

34

How the Movement for Study Abroad Developed

I taught in the Ch'u Yi for more than two years. During this time, Mao Tse-tung came frequently to see me—often several times a week. All my students got to know him as a close friend of mine, and, since they respected me, they also treated him with respect.

It is impossible to tell here all the various subjects we discussed during this time, but one day the following important conversation took place. Mao Tse-tung was again interrogating me about a teacher's life, when he said, "You seem very enthusiastic about your teaching. Will you be able to stay here long?"

I told him I really did not want to teach much longer. He was visibly surprised and asked, "Isn't your work here in Ch'u Yi less tiring than it was in the Hsiu Yeh School?"

"Well," I said, "I do repetition for the students after classes, and often I have them with me up to ten o'clock in the evening. And apart from the classes, I have to grade their essays, calligraphy, and notebooks. I figure that I work at least twelve hours a day; but I enjoy the work and I don't usually feel at all tired. I don't want to continue with teaching, however, because I have other plans."

"What other plans do you have? I just took for granted that you would continue teaching."

"No," I explained, "I'm thinking of going abroad to study."

"Oh yes?" asked Mao. "To what country, may I ask, are you thinking of going?"

"I don't know yet. To France, America, England, or Japan. I don't know which."

"How are you going to get the money to go abroad?" asked Mao, incredulously.

"The money? I shouldn't have to worry about getting the money. That's a problem for the Hsin Min Study Association. You know, all of us should go abroad to study!" I said.

"Yes, that's very true," agreed Mao, "but we have to work out some practical plan to make it possible."

"The first step should be for us to call a meeting of a dozen or so members to discuss ways and means."

"Very well," said Mao, "you're the secretary. You send out the notices. We'll have a meeting and see what can be done."

Mao Tse-tung and I continued to discuss the problem of how the members of the Hsin Min Study Association could go abroad for study. The first and most difficult problem was how we could raise the necessary funds.

"If we wait until we have enough money to go abroad," I contended, "we shall never get there. First, we must resolve that we are going abroad, and then we can start to talk about the money problem."

Mao Tse-tung insisted that we should call together all the members of the Association to talk it over together. I countered by suggesting that it would be advisable first to talk the question over personally with each member who would be asked to attend the meeting, in order to work up their enthusiasm. Finally Mao agreed to this; so I had a talk with Hsiung Kuang-ch'u and Ch'en Chang.

These two both felt that the plan was good in principle, but Ch'en Chang was an only child and he had no one to look after his family if he went away. He was sorry, but he himself would never be able to go abroad. Hsiung Kuang-ch'u and I advised him to sell his land and to take his wife and child with him, but he said he would not have sufficient money to pay the expenses of all of them. He did not see how it would be possible for him to go abroad! Hsiung Kuang-ch'u, who was one of the oldest members of the Association, was very keen on study, and he would be delighted to go abroad. He said he could get his brother to take care of his wife and son.

Next, I had quite a long talk with Ts'ai Ho-shen, who was also delighted with the scheme. He said it was an ideal which must be put into practice soon. He was all for it and enthusiastically inquired, "What country do you prefer?"

I replied, "My first choice would be France and then America, but I don't think I would care so much for England or Japan."

He said he would like to go to France also, but then he asked, "Where can we get the money?"

"I have heard that there is an organization called the Franco-Chinese Educational Association," I replied, "whose president is the

Rector of Peking University, Mr. Ts'ai Yüan-p'ei. I'm planning to have a talk with him to find out more about it."

"Good!" said Ts'ai, "You and I will work together on this scheme. France is at war now and there are more than a hundred thousand Chinese laborers working there. Many of them have left their wives and children here at home. We could write letters for them. We could also teach the children that are in France. I think we could live that way. If we can just earn our living, we can study."

"Apart from teaching the children," I said, "we ought to get the Chinese laborers together and encourage them to learn French, to study a trade, and to get some knowledge of French social and political organizations. Then when they return to China, they can form the nucleus of a reform movement among the lower classes. We should be able to find many colleagues among these workers for our task of reforming China."

Ts'ai thought this was all very interesting and that we should proceed with our plan to get to France without loss of time. I told him that I was about to send out notices to members of the Hsin Min Study Association to call a meeting for the next Sunday afternoon, for the express purpose of discussing how we were to go about it. I asked him to be sure to come and bring his suggestions.

When the meeting was opened, I told those present, "The purpose of this meeting today is to discuss ways and means of giving members an opportunity to study abroad. We would like all the members of the Association to be able to go abroad, and we would like to know, first of all, what country each individual member would prefer. We will then discuss how the plan can be realized. From now on 'Study Abroad' must be our watch-word. It is our call to arms! We must help every member to go abroad to study!" At this meeting I also added that I had heard said that there was a Mr. C. K. Chang* (Chang Ching-kiang) who had a tea business in Paris and later a very large business in rare Chinese antiques. After having made a

---

* Mr. C. K. Chang (1877–1950), one of the founders of the Chinese Republic, was a great economist. After having contributed enormously to Dr. Sun Yat-sen and President Chiang Kai-shek, he retired to New York where he died. Ten years after this meeting at which I spoke of him he became one of my great friends. I have much respect and admiration for him.

fortune, he gave freely to Dr. Sun Yat-sen to aid him in the Revolution. "I like this man very much," I told them, "and when I see him, I shall urge him to aid education, to give to the best but poor students as a more fundamental reform of China."

Mao Tse-tung then spoke, "First we must decide on the country, and then on how to get there. We must have everything well organized. I think it is best if our colleagues study abroad in different countries. The chief ones should be America, England, France and Japan."

Ts'ai Ho-shen added, "Mr. Siao and I have decided to go to France. Let us ask Mr. Siao to tell us the details of his plan to go to France."

To which Hsiung Kuang-ch'u said, "I think Mr. Siao's scheme for studying in France is very good. It seems quite practical and many students can go. I have decided to go to France also."

"Several of the members are not aware of all the details of Mr. Siao's plan," Mao Tse-tung interrupted. "I suggest that we ask him to explain."

I told them about the Franco-Chinese Educational Association and about the Chinese laborers, who were working in France during the war. Everybody thought the plan, as I outlined it, was sound and practicable, and, if it proved to be so, they were willing to go to France. Only one member, Chou Ming-ti, said he preferred to go to Japan. Ch'en Chang again said that he had no one to look after his wife and son, so he could not go. However, he said he would stay in Changsha and would help us from there in whatever way he could.

After further discussion, I said, "Professor Yang Huai-chung has gone to Peking where he has accepted a post in the Peking National University. I shall write to him, telling of our desire to study in France and ask him to find out about the Franco-Chinese Education Association from the Rector, Ts'ai Yüan-p'ei. As soon as I receive his answer, I shall call another meeting."

35
The Student-Worker Movement

The meeting of our Association which took place in June, 1918, just before the summer vacation, marked the practical beginning of the student-workers' movement in France. During the first year alone there were more than two thousand student-workers who took advantage of this scheme, and among them were about twenty of the chief actors in the Peking scene today, such as Li Wei-han, Li Fu-ch'un, Li Li-san, Chou En-lai, Ch'en Yi, Yao Su-shih, Hsu T'e-li, and Ts'ai Ch'ang.

About a week after the meeting, I received "Confucius" Yang Huai-chung's reply to my letter. It was a postcard addressed to me personally. He was very fond of writing postcards. The text was brief and to the point. He said, "Yesterday I received your letter and today I went to see Rector Ts'ai Yüan-p'ei. He said he was President of the Franco-Chinese Educational Association and that there were student-workers in France now grouped together in an association. Your plan to go to France on a work-study basis can be realized. . . ."(26)

I was naturally very happy to get this news and immediately went off to see Mao Tse-tung. He, too, was delighted, and he laughed and smiled for a long time with pleasure after reading the card. Next I went to see Ts'ai Ho-shen across the river.

I gave him the card to read and he exclaimed, "You see, your plan is successful! The student-workers' organization is the solution! Mother (his mother and sister sat there beside us), do you and Sister want to go to France with us? There are now no unsurmountable difficulties! This is excellent news!"

Miss Hsiang Ching-yu, his sweetheart, was there also when I arrived, and now a happy smile disclosed her beautiful, even, white teeth, as she said quietly, "Mr. Siao, I have also decided to go to France." I told them not to be late for the meeting which we would hold next day in the First Normal School at three o'clock.

At the meeting, everyone read Mr. Yang's postcard. It could not have aroused more enthusiasm if it had been a winning lottery ticket! All of them were concentrating their every thought on the idea of going to France, thinking that very soon we should all be together in Paris! I said, "First, we must go to Peking to see Mr. Yang and Rector Ts'ai. I have to return home next week, but when I get back to Changsha, I shall be able to leave almost immediately for Peking. Who wants to go with me? Who needs train fare?" I asked, because I knew that I was the only one teaching and the only member with a fixed income. I knew that Ts'ai Ho-shen and Mao Tse-tung, who would want to go, had no means of paying train fare to Peking.

Before he left to teach in Peking, Mr. Yang Huai-chung had unconsciously influenced us in many ways into conceiving this plan to study abroad, not only by his remarks, but also by his own trip overseas. He had taught in Changsha for six years and the post he had accepted in Peking represented quite a considerable advancement. We attributed his success to his studies abroad, and this was one big reason for our desire to emulate him. Not only that, but it was largely as a result of his assistance that we were finally able to put the plan into practice. We did indeed have every reason to be grateful to him.

That summer, the end of July or the first of August, ten of us went to Peking.(27) Mr. Yang kindly allowed Mao Tse-tung, Hsiung Kuang-ch'u, Ch'ang K'ung-ti and me, who arrived first, to live for a time in his house outside the back gate in Tou Fu Ch'ih Hutung. Afterwards we rented a two-room house in Three Eyes Well Street quite near the University.

One room in this house we used as a study and the other as a bedroom. The bed was a k'ang, a Manchurian-type stove bed, made of bricks and heated by a fire underneath. In the icy winter weather, seven of us slept on this big bed, huddled together to keep warm, because we had no fire underneath. We had a very small stove in the room on which we cooked our meals. We did everything cooperatively. In winter, the Peking climate is extremely cold, but the seven of us had only one coat among us; so we took turns going out during the spells of particularly low temperature. By the end of the year, the one coat had increased to three, but Mao Tse-tung never did manage to buy a coat for himself.(28)

Ts'ai Yüan-p'ei, the Rector of Peking National University, held the highest educational degree obtainable, the *Han Ning*, conferred by the Emperor. He had also studied philosophy in Germany. Later, he took part in the revolution and with the establishment of the Republic, he became the first Minister of Education. Later, he again took a trip abroad, this time to France, for educational research, and on his return, he was nominated Rector of the National University in Peking. He was the recognized leader in educational circles at that time and he was both wise and erudite. During our visit we were struck especially by his modesty. He was truly a great scholar and sage, and he made a very deep and lasting impression on me.

At two o'clock on the day following our visit, I went to call on Mr. Li Yü-ying, with a letter of introduction furnished by Rector Ts'ai. Mr. Li lived in the Sui An Po Hutung. He was not at home, but the doorkeeper said he would return by five. I called again at five o'clock, but he had not returned; so the servant asked me to wait. Soon Mr. Li arrived. He was around forty years of age and had a moustache. I asked him many questions about our plan to study in France. He told me that some time previously they had encouraged students to save money to go to France and, since the expenses were naturally much greater than for Japan, to learn to live as cheaply as possible. More than a hundred had gone and they had achieved very satisfactory results.

"More recently," he continued, "Rector Ts'ai, Mr. Wu Che-fei and I organized a student-worker group to go to France to study. We have all the details written out, but there are very few members and the student-worker system has to be developed and put into practice. You people from Hunan are noted for your perseverance and your endurance; so I think you might be able to make a success of the scheme. I advise you to start learning French right away. Also, learn some trade or handicraft—drawing, for example, or a general idea of foundry work. The war will soon be over and then you will be able to go. You should get yourselves well organized and I'm sure your project will be a success."

As soon as I returned to our rooms, I told my companions all that Mr. Li had said and they were delighted with the optimistic opinion he had expressed. When they asked what sort of impression he had made upon me, I said he seemed to be a shrewd type of person, who thought things over very carefully before expressing an opinion. He was quite different from Ts'ai Yüan-p'ei, since the Rector was a typical Chinese gentleman, while Li Yü-ying gave one the impression of being a Chinese who had studied a long time in foreign countries. Again, Rector Ts'ai looked like a professor, but Mr. Li looked like a revolutionist. He promoted liberal thought and internationalism and I agreed with his principles.

Ts'ai Ho-shen, Hsiung Kuang-ch'u and I set about organizing classes for students to study French and to learn a trade. All the members for the Hsin Min Study Association were expected to attend.

One day, discussing our plans with Ts'ai Ho-shen, I remarked, "The World War will soon be over and France will be victorious. Then there will be an enormous amount of reconstruction work to be done and there is certain to be a shortage of workers in France. Not only the members of our Study Association, but many others, could go on a half-day work, half-day study basis. This movement could spread and I think many young people should be encouraged to go. Why, just think how many students there are who are anxious to go abroad, but cannot for lack of funds. This way they could all go! A thousand—ten thousand—of them can go! And China will reap the benefit of the knowledge they will bring back!"

My enthusiasm was contagious and Ho-shen said, "Yes, I agree with you entirely. From now on we will do all we can to spread our movement so that more people can go to France!"

Before we started, however, there were still two important problems to solve. First, the cost of the voyage from China to France must be greatly reduced, and, second, after our arrival in France, there would be a preliminary period in practically all cases during which the students would need money to pay for board and lodging until remunerative work was found. The Franco-Chinese Educational Association would have to help at the start. I talked these two problems over with Rector Ts'ai and Mr. Li at great length several different times, and eventually we worked out a satisfactory solution. The French steamship company agreed to grant us special rates: we would be referred to as fourth class passengers and we would pay only one hundred *yuan* (Chinese dollars) as compared with the normal third-class rate of more than three hundred *yuan*. On arrival in France, the Franco-Chinese Educational Association would look after us until we became acclimatized. They would arrange for students to attend schools in the provinces to learn French and they would help them to find suitable jobs. Their expenses and the fees for attendance at the schools would be paid by the Association.

Once we had this assurance, we set to work on intensive propaganda to arouse wider interest in the scheme. But a great deal of our time was still taken up with the details of organization. In the beginning, only forty students were taking preparatory French classes in Peking, but soon a second and then a third class had to be started, until eventually there were over four hundred pupils.

In November the World War ended and all of us thought that we would very soon be sailing to France! I was engaged by the Franco-Chinese Educational Association as a secretary, and in 1919, I went with Mr. Li to Shanghai and from there, we left for Paris. At that time Ts'ai Yüan-p'ei was Chinese co-President of the Association and Mr. Li was Head Secretary. They asked me to help them not only with the affairs of the student-workers, but also with the education of the Chinese laborers who had been working in France during the war. Of these, there were more than one hundred thousand.

In China the Association was not very well organized. The students who were going to France were grouped by provinces, so that the groups varied in size. For example, one group would have fifty persons, while another would number one hundred and twenty. The students were given no preparatory training in China, nor did they have enough money to sustain them after reaching their destination. The Association, therefore, had a very busy and difficult time trying to look after all of the students. Many of the things we did at first proved to be most unsatisfactory, but that was inevitable.

The student-worker plan had got so well under way that within a year more than two thousand students had arrived in France. My Province of Hunan was best represented with more than five hundred, then came Canton and Szechwan, each with about three hundred, and Chekiang and Kiangsu with more than two hundred each. Other provinces were represented, but in lesser numbers. All these people were distributed to schools in various parts of France and factory work was found for many of them.

A big percentage of these young people whose studies were organized by our office later assumed posts of considerable importance back in China, such as ministers, ambassadors, regional governors, professors, artists, heads of industry, and a good many now hold high positions under the Communists as political leaders, army generals, and the like. Of the early members of our Hsin Min Study Association, Ts'ai Ho-shen, his mother, his sister, Ts'ai Ch'ang, and his sweetheart, Hsiang Ching-yu, were sent to Montargis Middle School, which developed into a center of Communist propaganda for Chinese students.

36
Mao Tse-tung Remains Behind

While Ts'ai Ho-shen, Hsiung Kuang-ch'u, and others worked with me to organize the student-workers' preparatory classes, Mao Tse-tung was helping, but after several discussions with Ho-shen and me, Mao finally decided not to go to France, saying he preferred to remain behind in Peking.

He gave four good reasons for this decision. First was the problem of passage money. Mao had no money at all and despite the appreciably reduced fare, a couple hundred *yuan* represented a very large sum for him, and he knew no one who might lend him that much. Second, he was by no means proficient in languages. At school he had not been able to manage even the very simplest forms of English pronunciation. Third, in Peking, he could carry on with his studies and would at the same time be able to recruit new members for our Hsin Min Study Association, and, of course, we who went to France would need a reliable contact in Peking. Fourth, he had always remembered the almost prophetic words of Tan Wu-pien that day in the Tien Hsin Ko, "the building which reaches the heart of Heaven." Tan had said that to be successful in politics, study or learning was of itself not too much help, that the essential thing was one's ability to organize a party and to gather together a great number of faithful followers. Fundamentally, Mao was a man of action who was not cut out to be a scholar. In a word, he was not interested in going abroad for the sake of study. Study was simply a means to an end, and it was without doubt Tan Wu-pien's formula for success in politics that influenced Mao more than anything else to make his decision. The seeds had fallen into fertile soil.

Ts'ai Ho-shen and I agreed that Mao should remain in Peking to carry out the same work-study program there as we would in France. This brought up the inevitable problem of work for Mao to support himself, and the three of us had several discussions of this problem. At that time we were recruiting members for our Association in Peking National University and we told Mao that in our judgment the best thing he could do would be to get a job in the University itself. We thought of a classroom-cleaner job because he could listen to the lectures, even as he carried out his simple tasks. It was the practice of the University to employ a person to clean the blackboards and sweep the classrooms after each class. It was light work and had the added advantage of enabling the person who did it to be in constant contact with the professors and students of the several classrooms under his care. We all agreed that this arrangement would be ideal for Mao.

How to obtain the job was the immediate problem. We discovered that the person whose responsibility it was to engage people for such tasks was a very highly placed professor who had at the same time many more important responsibilities, and we did not know quite how to approach him about such an insignificant job. When we finally thought of our friend Rector Ts'ai, who had already been so very kind and generous to us, we wrote a letter directly to him asking if it would be possible for him to give the order for one of our colleagues to be employed as a classroom cleaner. The Rector was an admirable person who understood our problem immediately. However, he had a better idea: rather than ask for a job as classroom-cleaner, he suggested that Mao work in the library. He therefore sent a note to Mr. Li Ta-chao, Director of the University Library, "Mao Tse-tung requires employment in the University in pursuance of a work-study program. Please find a job for him in the library. . . ." The Rector made no mention of the fact that Mao came from Changsha, nor that he was a "youth leader." Li Ta-chao obediently gave

Mao the task of cleaning the library and keeping the books tidy, really a very simple job. This was all accomplished through an intermediary, since Li was a very highly placed person and had no direct contacts with hiring of menial workers.

In 1921, Li Ta-chao with Ch'en Tu-hsiu also became the secret Communist leader in Peking, while Mao Tse-tung occupied a similar position in Hunan. I had several long talks with Li in 1921 before I went to France the second time, and when I returned, we worked together from 1924 to 1926 for the revolution against Generalissimo Chang Tso-lin. Often we had to hide from military authorities and we were obliged to meet in secret. We discussed Mao Tse-tung and once he said, "When I gave Mao that job of cleaning the library, I was merely obeying the Rector's orders. Naturally I did not know your good friend and I hope you will forgive me." In 1926, Li Ta-chao was arrested in the Russian Legation in Peking by Generalissimo Chang Tso-lin and was hanged.

Mao was always very grateful to Rector Ts'ai. Every letter to him started, *Fu tze ta jen* (My Respected Master). He considered himself the Rector's student and never failed to show great politeness and respect for him. In 1938, about twelve months before Ts'ai's death, when he was hiding in Kowloon (Hong Kong), I often called at his house for an intimate chat, and we talked of Mao on several different occasions. In his old age the Rector had forgotten many details and, while he could still remember Mao's letters to him, he could not recall either his face or his voice.

Mao's activities in the library did not prove to be successful.(29) As we had planned, he endeavored to talk to the students who came in for books, but the results of his efforts to enlist new members for the Hsin Min Study Association were not good. Nor did he make much success with his studies. He wrote me saying that he felt deceived by the students of the National University of Peking, such as Fu, Toen, Lo and the others, as he had heard at Changsha that they were the best students.

In 1919, Mao returned to Changsha and participated in the movement to overthrow General Chang Ching-yao, the tyrannical Governor of Hunan. The only way to get rid of Chang appeared to be to persuade the army, stationed on the Hunan-Kwangtung border, to march to Changsha to help in the revolution and then it was decided to ask Tan Yen-k'ai, the former governor, to take over again. The principal instigator of the revolutionary movement which developed in educational circles was Professor Yi Pei-chi, who had been Mao's Chinese language teacher in the First Normal School. Practically the whole of the teaching profession was involved, and Chang Ching-yao was declared an enemy of the people of Hunan. Yi Pei-chi, with Mao Tse-tung amongst the students, worked hard planning the uprising to which they referred as their "struggle against evil powers."

As background for understanding Mao's departure from Peking, mention should here be made of the radical leaders in the University: Ch'en Tu-hsiu, who was Dean of Literature, and Li Ta-chao, Director of the Library. Both these men had written articles in praise of the October 1917 Revolution in Russia, and later they were secretly contacted by the Russians who suggested that they assume responsibility for organizing a Communist Party in China, and money was given to them to cover the expenses of such an undertaking. Since they could not openly organize Communist groups, they started a "Marxist Study Association" and also "Socialist Youth Associations," with headquarters in Peking University. Another important step was the starting of a "foreign language institute," the sole object of which was to teach the people Russian. Neither of these leaders considered Mao Tse-tung in his plans, since at that time Mao was merely a servant in the library, and not even registered at the University. Since they did not even notice his existence, Mao realized that in his present status it would be impossible for him to achieve a position of any importance in their eyes. Also, since he had really not been successful at his own enterprise in the University, after only a few months, he decided to return to Changsha in his native province, and there to start all over again. He still had the Hsin Min Study Association as a nucleus on which he hoped to build a strong organization.

Through the revolution against Chang, Mao Tse-tung came into close contact with a large number of young, impractical idealists and he spared no efforts in his attempt to gain their sympathy, which proved not to be too difficult. The majority of them were desperately earnest, impractical and idealistic, full of enthusiasm and ambition. Their primary aim was to rid the Province of Hunan of its tyrannical ruler and, more vaguely, to reform society. They had, however, no definite, long-range plan and no specific political tendencies nor allegiance, and no recognized, trusted leader. Mao had a blind faith in Russian-style Communism and he compared these youngsters to a sheet of blank white paper on which he imagined himself working out his own design in bold, strong red lines. In his mind's eye he drew from left to right and up and down to his heart's desire. In his mind's eye, Mao was their leader and they were as clay in his dexterous hands.

Such was the situation in 1919, shortly after Ts'ai Ho-shen and I arrived in France. We three, Mao, Ts'ai, and I, were still the principal organizers of the Hsin Min Study Association, and while Ts'ai and I recruited thirty or forty new members in France, Mao enlisted over a hundred in Changsha. He had, however, abandoned the restrictive selection to which we adhered and he chose members on the basis of their ideas only. He published a journal, *Correspondence of the Hsin Min Study Association,* consisting of letters and commentaries, and in which members might express their own particular opinions. But this publication appeared only three times.

Outside the Association, while he was preparing for the provincial revolution, Mao published a weekly paper which he called the *Hsiang Kiang P'ing Lun (The Hunan Critic)*.(30) The articles in this paper were very radical and greatly pleased his student following. Many of the younger students even volunteered to sell copies of the *Critic* in the streets. Often the letters which I wrote from Paris were published in this weekly for propaganda purposes. It was about this time that he opened the cultural bookstore for the sale of new-thought publications. This shop was managed by his first sweetheart, Tao Szu-yung, our oldest and most respected woman colleague about whom mention has already been made.

The provincial revolution was successful.(31) Chang escaped and Tan Yen-k'ai was returned as governor. Yi Pei-chi, the prime instigator and mover in the uprising, himself took over the tasks of five cabinet members in the new Provincial Government: First Secretary to the Governor, First Secretary of the Military Commander, President of the Hunan Educational Association, Director of the Provincial Library, and Director of the First Normal School. The First

Normal School was the intellectual center of Changsha, and Yi appointed Mao Tse-tung as Director of the Primary School Section.

At this time, our old and respected Hsin Min colleague, Ho Shu-heng, or Ho Hu-tzu (Moustache-Ho) as we called him, was made Director of the *P'ing Min Chao Yu Jih Pao*, the *Popular Education Daily News*, which was an excellent medium through which to influence the lower classes, since it was widely read. Ho Hu-tzu worked hard in his new position and did a good job. He secured several very good editors, one of whom, Hsieh Chüeh-ts'ai later became Minister of Justice, and then Minister of the Interior in the Peking Communist Government. Hsieh and Ho came from the same town and were good friends. Later Ho introduced Hsieh to us and we became friends, calling him "Hu-tzu" in intimate fashion. These two colleagues were the oldest members of our Association, being about thirty-five, while most of us averaged abount ten years younger. Ho was already an intimate friend of mine, since we had taught together in the Ch'u Yi School. Although I did not know Hsieh Hu-tzu so well, I liked him because he was such a good friend of Ho.

The Hsin Min Study Association therefore had now two bases in Changsha: the *Popular Education Daily News* and the Primary Section of the First Normal School. I myself directed the third base in France, assisted by Ts'ai Ho-shen, Hsiung Kuang-ch'u, Hsiang Ching-yu, Li Wei-han, Ch'en Shao-hsiu, and several other new members. Back in Hunan, with Yi Pei-chi and Tan Yen-k'ai running the province, Mao enjoyed a greatly increased freedom of action and as a result he became even more enthusiastic and articulate in his political ambitions.

There was at this time no Chinese Communist organization and all our activities centered in the Hsin Min Study Association, even though many of its members had a blind faith in Russian Communism as the magic wand which could suddenly reform China.

However, two years later, in 1921, the mother association broke up into two separate groups. The larger which was one hundred per cent Communist became the Communist Party in Hunan under the leadership of Mao Tse-tung.

37

The Germ of Chinese Communism in France

On November 11, 1918, the Armistice was signed.(32) Early in January the following year, the year of the Versailles Peace Conference, I followed Mr. Li Yü-ying to Paris, where we set to work for the Franco-Chinese Educational Association, helping the student-workers and at the same time, organizing the Chinese "combatants" or war-workers.

First, a house was purchased in the Paris suburb of La Garenne Colombes, where we established a "Federation Chinoise" which became a center for both students and war-workers. The greater part of our time, and the time of the many colleagues who were assisting, was of necessity taken up by the student-workers arriving from China. But apart from my work with the students, I was editor-in-chief of a magazine, published for the war-workers, the *Chinese Labor Monthly*. When he was in France, Rector Ts'ai wrote many articles for this publication which was the only Chinese-language magazine available for our one hundred thousand fellow countrymen living in France. It was really quite an attractive publication since at that time there was a Chinese printing house at Tours.

A few days after my arrival in Paris, I wrote about our activities to Mao Tse-tung, so that he could report to our friends at home. I quote an excerpt from that letter:

The student-workers' and laborers' organization seems quite effective and we could handle at least a thousand more students. From that thousand we should be able to select one or two hundred new members for our Hsin Min Study Association. As for the war-workers, there are already more than one hundred thousand of them and I don't think it should be too difficult to pick at least ten thousand from among them. In this manner we can build up our Association to form a really practical basis for the reform of our country. Up to this time I have been concentrating all my efforts on the workers because I want to wait for Ts'ai Ho-shen to arrive before starting the recruitment of the students. When he arrives, we can get down to work in real earnest.

When Mao Tse-tung's reply came, he seemed very enthusiastic. He wrote, "We are laying the foundations for the reform of China! Of course I should be doing my best to spread the movement here in Changsha, but now it seems that it will be much easier for you over there in France. . . ."

At that time we were both adhering strictly to the original principles of the Association as regards to moral and ethical qualifications of its members, and our main aim was the growth of the Association as a sort of cultural and intellectual leaven.

Many active and intelligent students came to France from China under the part-time employment scheme. However, since we did not know them, we could hardly invite them to join the Hsin Min Study Association, and this created jealousies. At times, of course, this situation was inevitable.

Another difficulty which it was practically impossible to avoid was created by the fact that the funds of the Franco-Chinese Educational Association were inadequate to cope in a satisfactory manner with the ever-increasing numbers of student-workers. Many arrived with little or no knowledge of French, and to look after all these young people and to find them suitable jobs was by no means an easy task. We had to put up with much criticism and grumbling from those whose economic situation was insecure.

Few of these thousands of Chinese in France, war-workers and students, knew very much about Communism. Many of them, however, had anarchistic tendencies in varying degrees and quite naturally this created a propitious atmosphere for Communist propaganda work. They could see with their own eyes the outward appearances of success attained by the lower classes in the Russian Revolution, and while few if any of them had time or ability to study the abstract underlying theories, the majority had learned the word Marxist and what it stood for in a practical, everyday sense. They were not in a position to analyze and to criticize the new Russian doctrine, but a number of them regarded it in the light of a new religion under which one had to have a blind faith in Karl Marx and his precepts in exactly the same way as Christians believe in their Christ. Some had already adopted just such an attitude and belief, but it was their own private, blind, almost religious conviction, since there was as yet no organized propaganda work among them.

In the spring of 1919, Ts'ai Ho-shen arrived in France and whenever the opportunity for such a declaration arose, he told his fellow countrymen what a good thing Communism was. He had no organization for them to join at this time, nor had he studied the Marxist or any other theory of revolution. Long before this, however, Ho-shen had adopted on his own initiative, the slogan, "Down with the Capitalists!" He told me, "I wrote a long letter to Jun-chih (Mao) saying that the Russians must have sent someone to China in secret to organize a Communist Party there. I said that we should follow Russia's example in this matter. We should not delay. There's no need to study all the details first!"

Well do I remember our subsequent conversation on the subject when I insisted, "But we *must* study the matter carefully before making any decision! I agree in principle that capitalism should be overthrown but I am not prepared to follow blindly the principles of Russian Communism!"

"What does it matter what type of Communism it is?" asked Ts'ai. "The more we study the longer we have to put off making our decision. We've got the Russian plan all worked out for us. It's all ready-made. Tell me why we should go looking around for some other type? Their whole scheme is all ready, it's written out on paper for us to read, and they themselves are carrying it out in practice. Why should we waste our time in further experimentation?"

"But," I asked, "why should China be the son of Russia?"

He was adamant. He was furious. He wanted action. "Because Russia was the Father of Communism!" he replied. "We should follow the Russian lead. First, simply because it is much easier. Second, the revolution in China, when it comes, could then depend upon Russian aid, both clandestine and openly, in supplying funds and arms. Geographically, Russia and China are destined to be allies. Transport between the two countries is easy. In a word, if the Chinese Communist revolution is to be successful, we must follow Russia unconditionally. I am telling you the truth. That is exactly how I feel!"

"I do understand how you feel," I continued. "But, my friend, we must think first of all about the welfare of our country and about our own people. The problem is by no means so simple as you make it sound! This is not our own personal affair! How can we allow China to become a vassal state? How can we as loyal citizens be a party to such a plan?" I asked.

Ts'ai insisted, "To carry out the revolution we must choose the most expedient course. I have already written to Jun-chih to tell him what I think about this idea and I am sure he agrees with me. You're much too idealistic, sentimental, theoretical, and easy-going!"

"Even though Jun-chih does agree with you entirely, I do *not* agree!" I exclaimed. "I can't help being sincere and I cannot go against my conscience. I want my conscience to be clear. I simply could not be a party to making China a vassal of Russia."

"Yes, I know," Ts'ai agreed quietly. "We both understand your personality and we all admire you very much. That's why I want to study this matter with you very carefully."

"But," I pointed out, "you are not studying it! You have already decided upon a course of action and now you are trying to convert me to your idea. You are asking me to accept your principles unconditionally. You are exactly like a preacher, trying to persuade an old friend to believe in his religion!"

"Oh no, I wouldn't dare to do that!" Ts'ai declared. "I have a very great respect for you, your character, and your opinion, quite apart from our personal friendship. We are just having a friendly discussion now."

This conversation took place just two days after Ts'ai Ho-shen arrived in Paris. Fifty or sixty students had come in the same boat with him and the Franco-Chinese Educational Association decided to send them to the College de Montargis where they could spend their time studying French while they were waiting for suitable jobs to be found for them. Montargis is a four-hour train journey from Paris. After Ts'ai left, we wrote to each other frequently. Sometimes he wrote me letters twice a day. But our respective opinions did not change.

Ts'ai Ho-shen talked about Communism to his companions in Montargis and at the same time wrote persuasive letters to students in other parts of France. He had little talent for speaking but he expressed himself well on paper, even better than Mao Tse-tung.

The others all found his letters inspiring and his enthusiasm was contagious. His mother, who was about fifty at that time, and his young sister, Ch'ang, had come to France with him and they both listened respectfully to his ideas. His first real convert, however, was his sweetheart, Hsiang Ching-yu, who was also one of the best members of our Hsin Min Study Association. Miss Hsiang not only wrote well, she was also a very good speaker. Her character was particularly sincere and at the same time she was attractive and very gentle. She became China's first woman Communist and Ts'ai Ho-shen's medium for propaganda. She influenced both sexes and converted many people to her way of thinking, but the women especially listened to her attentively and were moved by her earnest sincerity. She wrote me many long letters discussing our perennial problem.

Another old friend who came to France at this time was Li Wei-han. His second name was also Ho-shen and we called him Li Ho-shen or sometimes Lao Li (Old Li). He too was one of the earliest members of the Association and we were very fond of him. I had known him in Changsha where we attended the First Normal together, and I liked him very much. His father was old and very poor but, though Li loved him dearly, he was not able to help him and we all felt very sorry for both of them. Li Wei-han was a very modest, quiet person who spoke slowly and carefully. He always took great pains to understand the other person's point of view in any discussion. He had no Chinese books to read and he could not read French; so in Montargis he spent much of his time talking with Ts'ai Ho-shen. The two Ho-shens usually agreed, and it was quite natural that Li Wei-han should accept Ts'ai's ideas and opinions. During the war between China and Japan the Communists sent Li and Chou En-lai as delegates to talk peace with the Government in Chungking and later in Nanking. Afterwards, I saw from the newspapers that he was the chief secretary of a seemingly very important political conference in Peking and at the present time, he must have a high position in the Government. When I see or hear news of his "play-acting," I cannot help thinking of the talks we used to have in Montargis, and how he stuttered at that time. Li Wei-han, Ts'ai Ho-shen, and Hsiang Ching-yu were the three most enthusiastic evangelists who worked to spread the Communist doctrine!

But in 1919, though the potentialities of the group had apparently been considered by the French Communists who had carried out a little propaganda work on a very small scale, there was no Communist organization among the more than one hundred thousand Chinese workers and students in France. The established Chinese colonies in that country had a pro-Communist organization. In 1920 and 1921 already quite a number of members had been enlisted. The inspiration for this organization came directly from Peking and indirectly from Moscow.

First, the Russians had sent a secret agent (whose name is not important here) to Peking to contact the Dean of Literature at the University, Ch'en Tu-hsiu, who was a very aggressive type of person, and the Director of the University Library, Li Ta-chao, in an endeavor to persuade them to prepare the way for the organization of a Communist Party in China. Why prepare for the organization? The Chinese Government would not permit any open organization of Communist elements; so it was decided to create an association of young people whose aims were declared as "socialistic." This association was known simply as CY. That is, the two separate letters pronounced as in English, but which in fact stood for "Communist Youth." To those who were not initiated it meant nothing at all.

In a similar manner and for the same reasons of security, the incipient Communist Party itself was known to its members as the CP. Only the best and most promising elements of the CY were chosen to make up the CP. At the same time, outside the CY, a number of *Ma Ke Sze Yen Chiu Hui,* or Karl Marx Study Groups, were formed and an official Foreign Language School was opened, the primary object of which was to create the facilities necessary for teaching Russian without giving rise to suspicion. The Marx Study Groups even had their signs hanging in the University quite openly for a time.

As the reader has gathered from the foregoing, Ch'en Tu-hsiu accepted the suggestion emanating from Moscow, and what is even more important, he accepted the Russian money, paid to him in dollars, to cover the expense of forming these groups and organizing the nucleus of the Communist Party. Several organizations and subsidiary branches came directly under his control.

Ch'en Tu-hsiu had two sons, Ch'en Yen-nien and Ch'en Ch'iao-nien, both of whom entered the CY. Near the end of 1920, these two boys were sent to France with instructions from their father Ch'en Tu-hsiu and their "grandfather" Moscow, to start a Communist organization in that country. In Paris, they were known as "the two Ch'ens." The work which they had been entrusted to do proved to be beyond their capabilities and they were recalled to China and two others were appointed to take over.

These were Chao Shih-yen and Jen Cho-hsuan, two Szechwan students who were living in France at the time. Chao and Jen were both very capable and responsible young men and they did a great deal to further the cause of Chinese Communism in their positions as head secretaries of the CY in France. In the secret registers which they kept were listed several hundred names of those under their orders, but not all of these were members of the original Chinese colony.

Later when Jen Cho-hsuan returned to China, he was made head of the CY and the CP in Changsha in Hunan Province. Eventually he was arrested by the Government, and condemned to death and shot. His body was left lying on the ground where it fell and the next morning someone passing by heard his breathing and removed him to a hospital where his life was saved. Public opinion, through the press, was so strongly in his favor that the Government took no further action against him. When he had fully recovered from this unusual experience, he declared that his work for the Communist Party had been a success, but that in this, his second life, he did not wish to be a Communist! In due course he was elected to the Central Committee of the Kuomintang and is now in Formosa. He became Dr. Sun Yat-sen's best theoretician, but I have not seen him for about forty years.

Among the Communists of that time whom I knew well, Ts'ai Ho-shen and Hsiang Ching-yu are dead. Hsu T'e-li is nearly eighty years old. He was my professor of pedagogy and later that of Mao Tse-tung. He went to France with Ts'ai Ho-shen as a student-worker with the title of "old" student. It was he who chose me to go as professor to the Hsiu Yeh, though I was still a student at the First Normal School. Though he was not a very good theoretician, the Chinese Communist

Party took him to "decorate" their party as an old combatant. Ts'ai Ch'ang, Li Wei-han, Chou En-lai, Li Li-san, Li Fu-ch'un, Ch'en Yi, Jao Su-shih, and many others also were among the several hundred whose names were on the secret registers of Chao and Jen.

Thus did those first germs of Communism spread among the Chinese in France.

38
The Meeting in the Forest

By October of 1920 the activities of the Franco-Chinese Educational Association had increased to such an extent that it became necessary to send a delegate back to China. It was decided that I should return to discuss certain matters with Rector Ts'ai and Mr. Li Yü-ying. When I knew I was going, I wrote letters to both Ts'ai Ho-shen and to Mao Tse-tung. In his reply, Ts'ai said that before my departure we should call a general meeting of Hsin Min Study Association. He suggested that it should be a sort of farewell or *bon voyage* party for me, and that we should discuss together what methods should be adopted to carry out the revolution in China, and finally whether or not Russian-style Communism was a practical system for China.

As yet the power of the Moscow-controlled CY was not strongly felt among the Chinese in France; so we considered ourselves quite free to discuss whether or not Russian Communism was suitable for China.

The majority of the Hsin Min members lived in Montargis; so the date was set for the meeting to be held in that town. I left Paris at four o'clock on the day before the meeting and even before the train entered the Montargis station, I made out Ts'ai Ho-shen with his mother, Aunty, and Hsiang Ching-yu, and many others who were waiting for me on the platform—about twenty of them altogether. I shook hands with all of them, and then Ts'ai and Hsiang Ching-yu invited me to a café near the station. I suggested that I would prefer to find a hotel first and then we could go there to talk where it would be much quieter. However, Hsiang Ching-yu said, "Ho-shen and I have already found you a room. It's in a hotel quite close to our school."

As we set off for the hotel, I asked, "Where are we having the meeting of the Association tomorrow?"

"We really haven't decided yet," Ts'ai Ho-shen replied. "As you know, there are more than thirty members here in France, but some of them live too far away from here to be able to come. However, there will probably be about twenty of us here. We can't use the classrooms in the school, because there are classes all day long, and besides there are fifty or sixty Chinese students living there who are not members."

Hsiang Ching-yu suggested, "Can't we hold the meeting in Mr. Siao's hotel?"

To which Ts'ai replied quickly, "If a large group of yellow-skinned Orientals suddenly descended upon the hotel for a couple of days, the French people would think it was very strange. Also, the proprietor would probably not allow it, or if he did, he might present us with a bill for our stay. And you know we have no money to pay any such bills!"

"How about the Municipal Park?" I asked.

But Hsiang pointed out, "This park is not very big and all the seats are often occupied. Besides, our own Chinese schoolmates spend quite a lot of their free time there."

Then Ts'ai's face brightened. "When you mentioned the park just now, I had an idea. There is a big forest just outside the town. Why shouldn't we go there and sit on the grass for our meeting? Don't you think that's the solution?"

"That's an excellent idea," Hsiang agreed. "But if it rains, the Hsin Min Study Association's big meeting in France will never be held!"

"If it rains, it will be an omen that the gods do not wish for us to reform China! I'm sure it will be a fine day," I declared.

Hsiang smiled, "Very good, Mr. Siao. If it is raining tomorrow, that will mean that the gods do not agree with our plans. If the sun is shining, we will take it to mean that they do want us to reform China!"

The next morning when I awakened, the bright sunbeam was playing directly on my bed. I bounded up and dressed hurriedly, and very soon Ts'ai Ho-shen, his sweetheart, Hsiang Ching-yu, and about ten others came to my room. Hsiang Ching-yu greeted me delightedly, "Come on, Mr. Siao! Let's go at once and reform China! We have had no sunshine for several days and suddenly it is shining brightly. How good it is!" We all left the hotel together and in about ten minutes we were in the forest.

Thinking back on that moment, I seem to smell again the delightfully exhilarating perfume of that early morning forest glade. We chose a low grassy bank, so soft and green that it seemed we were seated on a velvet sofa. But it was still quite damp and chilly; so we decided to take a short walk before opening the meeting. As soon as the sun shone on the grass and all the members had arrived, we sat down in a circle and I declared the meeting open. Hsiang Ching-yu stood up and said, "First we want to say goodbye to Mr. Siao and wish him a pleasant trip back home. Then we will ask him to talk to us. We all have great hopes for Mr. Siao's trip to China."

Then Ts'ai Ho-shen said, "I saw Mr. Siao's agenda for this meeting. The first item was a discussion of what is the most suitable plan for the revolution; second, the introduction of new members; and third, his own report of his duty and his plans on his return to China. I want to suggest at this time that we give the third item first place, since all of us are anxious to hear from him and to know what he plans to do. Also, the first item will require much more time and it should be last."

Since everyone agreed to this plan, I told them a bit about my plans and what I intended to do in China. Then Ts'ai Ho-shen introduced the new members. The first two were Li Fu-ch'un and Li Li-san. Li Fu-ch'un was small and quite young. We all knew him and had a very good opinion of him. He was an excellent speaker, with clear, considered diction and a good voice. Later he was to become Vice Governor of Manchuria and Vice President of the National Council in Peking, of which Chou En-lai is President. Li Li-san was a very different type of person. He was large, coarse, and loud-speaking. He had a habit of making jokes which were not always in good taste. At one time during the meeting, he yelled out, "Li-san Road!" at the top of his voice, indicating presumably that we should all follow his lead. Many of us considered this childish and in very poor taste. Several other new members were also introduced, the men by Ts'ai Ho-shen and the women by Hsiang Ching-yu. Among the women was Ts'ai's young sister, Ch'ang who is now the President of the Communist Women's Association. At the same meeting Liao Yi-nan and Chou

En-lai were proposed as new members by Ts'ai.

After the lunch period we all gathered again on the grassy slope and now the subject for discussion was the question of adopting Russian Communism as the political system for the new China. Ts'ai Ho-shen maintained that Russian Communism should be adopted unreservedly. On the other hand, I stated that though I agreed fully with the principles of Communism, I did not favor the Russian type for China. The members were divided in their opinions. Some agreed with Ts'ai, others took their stand with me. Ideas and opinions were expressed and discussed calmly and quite dispassionately. At five-thirty we had to stop for the day so that those who lived in the school would not miss their evening meal, and it was decided that we would meet again the next day at eight-thirty in the morning to resume our discussion.

After dinner a large group came over to my hotel room to chat informally. Most of them left by ten o'clock, but Ts'ai Ho-shen, Hsiang Ching-yu, and Ch'en Shao-hsiu stayed to continue the discussion of Russian Communism and whether it was good or bad! Before we realized it, we had talked till two o'clock in the morning. It was too late for them to return to the school and we didn't want to bother the proprietor to get in the hotel; so we finally decided that we could all sleep cross-wise on the bed. It did not even enter our minds that Hsiang Ching-yu was a girl and I am sure that she herself did not at the time think of the fact that she was of the opposite sex. It was not till later that I was impressed by the purity of mind and the high idealism which we demonstrated on that day.

The whole of the next day's sessions were spent in discussion, but the fundamental problem remained unsolved. Finally it was decided that after my return to China I would have further talks with the members there, and that I should write to Mao Tse-tung, giving him full details of the two-day meeting so that he could circulate it among our friends. Afterward my letter was published by Mao Tse-tung in the *Hsin Min Study Association Journal*, Number 3.

39
Our Long Talk in Changsha

In the winter of 1920 I returned from Paris to Peking. Mao Tse-tung had already been back in Changsha a long time. And, although we wrote to each other frequently, it was not until March of 1921 that I was able to go to Changsha to see him. He was Director of the Primary Section of the First Normal School, but most of his activities were secretly directed toward the organization of the CY (Communist Youth).

From March to July we spent most of our free time discussing the Socialist revolution, but the more we talked, the further apart we seemed to grow. However, the same spirit of intimate friendship characterized our relations and we sincerely tried to understand each other's point of view.

Mao's lack of interest in the old Hsin Min Study Association was significant. It was not a political organization and though the members had not studied Socialism or other political systems, many of them attended secret meetings of the CY, and they began to believe blindly all that was told them there. The birth of the CY entailed the death of the Hsin Min Study Association. When I arrived in Changsha, I had the impression that I had been invited to attend its funeral service.

Nevertheless the members welcomed me warmly and, when I had many intimate talks with numerous members, it was quite obvious that Mao did not like it. He was afraid that some of them might be influenced by my ideas and as a result they might lose their present blind faith in Communism as inculcated by CY. I found that he quietly asked older members to persuade me to return to France and he even suggested the same to me himself! He knew I was to return to Paris and he was anxious for me to leave as soon as possible. His great hope, however, was that I accept his faith in Russian Communism and collaborate with him in spreading this doctrine throughout China, and put it into practice.(34)

In Changsha was a large building called the Ch'uan Shan Study Institute, so named in honor of a scholar called Wang Ch'uan Shan

(1619–1692). A group of fifty or more converts to Communism had taken over this building, and since Mao Tse-tung was a member, I was invited to live there. The enthusiasm of this group was probably due to the hope that age and experience would secure them posts of leadership if the Communists came into power.

Since one of the main purposes of my return to China was to arrange for the establishment of Franco-Chinese Institutes in Lyon and in Charleroi, Belgium, I was interviewed by reporters of the leading newspaper, *Shih Shih Hsin Pao (Current Affairs)* as soon as I arrived in Shanghai and my remarks were printed on the first page. Naturally the article was read by our old friends in Changsha and when I visited the city, they came to talk with me about the plan. Mao was quick to take advantage of the atmosphere of enthusiasm in order to group them together for his own purposes, and he and I introduced a proposition that the Ch'uan Shan Study Institute be converted into a "self-study" university. All agreed and I was asked to be chief organizer.

To me the "self-study" university plan has always seemed an ideal system because it emphasizes free study and resembles the old-time Academy of China without fixed hours for work and with no teachers. Only abundant reference books and a good laboratory are necessary, and also someone to arrange meetings and discussions among the students. I gave some talks about the system and aroused enthusiasm. I consulted with intellectual and educational circles in Peking and Shanghai about the system and received some favorable comments. The Rector of Peking University, Ts'ai Yüan-p'ei, and Chang T'ai-yen, the leading Chinese language scholar, wrote long essays in their own beautiful handwriting expressing their approval of the plan. I also received a long letter from Wu Chih-hui, a famous savant and reformer, one of the founders of the Chinese Republic, analyzing the possibilities of the self-study system. I had these manuscripts bound into a book, but they were left behind in China and I have no idea who has them now. Soon afterwards I returned to Paris and the Changsha Self-study University remained a dream.

After my preliminary discussions with Mao Tse-tung, I considered trying to revive the Hsin Min Study Association, but Mao and I found it impossible to agree.

Discussing the problem with Ho Hu-tzu, he told me, "Siao Hu-tzu, if you stay in Changsha and don't return to France, the old Hsin Min Study Association members will rally around you, but if you are not here, they will inevitably follow Jun-chih (Mao). It's like that with me, also!"

My old friend, Ch'en Chang spoke in similar manner, "All our friends," he said, "have secretly become members of CY and it would be very difficult to bring them back. You know that the Association aimed at reforming China in a sort of abstract way. It had no political views and no fixed plan of action. They now think the only way to attain practical results is to follow Russia's lead and to go all out to propagate the Russian doctrine. No one is looking for any other way to bring about the reforms. Why? First, because they have Russia's model to follow. Second, by playing up to Russia they hope to get economic support as well as help in other ways. Third, everyone is enthusiastic about the secret movement. The very mystery of the secret meetings proves an attraction and I doubt if anything would induce them to turn back. I know that you have your own 'anarchistic' ideas of freedom, but everyone could not be expected to agree with Communism. I think you and Mao Jun-chih will walk different roads in the future, but both of you will remain my very good friends. Personally, I think it is good for people to differ. There are many aspects of truth, and they are all precious."

When I told Mao what Ch'en Chang had said, he commented, "It's quite true! Many people are not satisfied with the present situation. If we want to bring about reforms, we must have a revolution! If we want the revolution to be successful, the best thing we can do is to learn from Russia! Russian Communism is the most suitable system for us and the easiest to follow. There is only one road for us to walk and I hope sincerely that you will walk this road with us."

40
A Chain of Problems

Mao Tse-tung and I indeed had a whole chain of problems to discuss. Often during this period we talked all night forgetting about sleep. Sometimes our talks made us very sad, even to the point of shedding tears, since we were unable to find a basis for mutual cooperation. I was unable to accept Mao's reasoning, but neither did my answers satisfy him. During the months consumed by these fruitless discussions, we never expressed a word of anger; rather it was a cause of genuine disappointment and sadness to both of us that we were unable to work out a common plan of action. Although our major premises were poles apart, our friendship was very precious to us. However, I could not overcome my presentiment that a revolution on the lines Mao wished would have unhappy results for the people of China.

After each period of intense sorrow, we encouraged each other to renew the discussion which only led to further sorrow and disappointment, and so on in cycles, from laughing to crying and from crying to laughing, a never-ending spiral. Such patience and untiring effort to convince each other were a great tribute to the deep bonds of friendship which united us. Mao realized that I was not arguing for my own selfish interest, but right or wrong, that I was motivated by a sincere love for the people of China and indeed for humanity itself.

The pith of our discussions may be summarized briefly. Once I started out with a simile: "Two wheels or one wheel?"

"Humanity," I said, "could be compared to a rickshaw which runs on two wheels. With two good wheels it will run smoothly, but if one wheel is taken away, it will fall over and become quite useless and incapable of movement. The only way to make it move on one wheel is to hold up the other side by hand, to lift it by brute force. This force must be maintained constantly and evenly to keep the vehicle in movement. Now the two wheels of humanity," I pointed out, "are Freedom and Communism." I was against capitalism and agreed entirely with the principle of Communism, but if people were to be governed by Russian Communism, the rickshaw would lack the wheel of freedom and would therefore require superhuman pressure to maintain its equilibrium. Communist leaders could perhaps maintain this pressure on the people for many years but when it ceased, the vehicle would fall over. I said that the principle involved was fundamentally wrong.

Mao understood quite well what I meant but he answered without hesitation that he was entirely in agreement with the application of pressure.

"Pressure," he said, "is the very essence of politics. If you are successful in keeping up the pressure, that means that your politics are good. In the final analysis political influence is quite simply the constant maintenance of pressure."

"If you are right," I said, "then I want nothing more to do with politics."

Another time I suggested that we look at Freedom and Communism as two roads.

"Now we are at a fork or at the crossroads," I said. "After the struggles and bloodshed of the past few centuries, man has finally gained a certain degree of freedom and that freedom is a very precious treasure to be guarded jealously. Both roads lead to death, the inevitable end awaiting each individual. Why then should we choose the path of Communism over Freedom? Mankind has two primary or basic desires, to exist and to be free, and only with freedom can civilization flourish."

Again Mao Tse-tung's answer was simple, "The implantation of Communism did not mean that the people would not be free."

I said, "There are several kinds of freedom, the freedom which can be enjoyed by human beings, and that which is accorded to domestic animals such as pigs and chickens. Pigs are free, but only within the boundaries of their sty. Chickens are free only within their run. It is true that the Communist State grants freedom to people, but it is the freedom of chickens and pigs. Russian Communism is like a religion: one must believe blindly in its doctrine and never discuss whether it is right or wrong. There is in that sort of religion no freedom of thought. Communists say they believe in freedom, but they do not allow people to live freely. There is no freedom for gatherings, for

organized associations, for the making and publishing of free speeches.
Is that the 'freedom of the people'?"

Mao replied in general terms to the effect that the public must be controlled by laws, even if they are arbitrary. The individual must obey the State and, if necessary, he must make sacrifices for the good of the country.

When we discussed the relation between the State and the individual under Communism, I said, "The power of the State is too great. It is omnipotent as the gods, while the individuals in the State are like flies and ants. If the State orders certain people to kill others, they must kill them. If the State wishes persons to be burned at the stake, they must be burned. If the State wants people to eat less food, they must eat less food. If the State wishes people to die, they die. Compared with the State the individual is nothing. People laughed when Louis XIV proudly proclaimed, 'I am the Nation!' because they thought the nation was something superior. I say you can also laugh at this because it is just as fallacious! Since the advent of democratic systems the power of the State has greatly decreased, and the individual, conversely, has increased in importance. However, today, Russian Communism, under the guise of Socialism, has returned the power to the State, which controls absolutely the daily life of its people."

In answer to this, Mao maintained that Communist countries must practice a "new democracy."

Continuing, I proposed a fifth point for discussion: new democracy or new despotism? In my opinion the Russian Communist system came much nearer to a "new despotism" than to a "new democracy."

"In our country," I said, "from ancient times, the Emperor has represented the old-fashioned despot. The Russian Communist Party, however, has now put into practice a new scientific form of absolute despotism! In the early history of China there were many emperor-despots who were excellent rulers, practicing the principle of 'loving the people as their own children.' They ruled much better than the majority of the monarchs in smaller kingdoms. Today the leader of Russian Communists is vested with a thousand times more arbitrary power than the worst of the *bad* Chinese emperor-despots!"

To which Mao replied, "If the leaders have no power, it is impossible to carry out plans, to obtain prompt action. The more power the leader has, the easier it is to get things done. In order to reform a country one must be hard with one's self and it is necessary to victimize a part of the people."

Next we discussed the sixth problem, victimizing the people for the good of the State. I told Mao quite plainly that I did not agree with the principle of victimizing one sector to help others, nor with the idea of victimizing everyone to a greater or lesser extent for the hypothetical good of future generations. He answered that if we were to be sentimental about such matters, the ideals of the social revolution could not be attained in a thousand years! And so to the seventh point of discussion: a thousand years or ten thousand years?

"If we are able to achieve the ideal social structure within a thousand years," I said, "that could be considered very satisfactory. Even if it took ten thousand years, it would still be satisfactory. For the individual a hundred years, or a thousand years is a very long time—it seems endless; but for a country, or a nation, it is not long; and in the whole history of mankind it is a very short time. Communism, in theory, is an excellent principle and it should certainly be put into practice. But this must take time. The Russian revolutionary method was an artificial forced growth. It was, to use a Chinese saying, like "possessing a beautiful woman on sight.""

Mao said, "I admire your patience in being willing to wait a hundred or a thousand years. I cannot wait even ten years. I want us to achieve our aims tomorrow!"

The eighth point we considered was, should we be guided by individual standards or by those of society? I contended that if he wanted to see the Communist principles put into practice tomorrow, he was being guided by his own individual standards.

"This is the principle of doing apparently fine things for the present with no regard for its effect on the future," I said. "It is like the deeds of the so-called heroes of history. The heroes were fond of interfering with the business of others and were, in the final analysis, undesirable persons. The hero idea is out of date and should be eliminated. We have proof of the ill-bestowed glory accorded to these heroes in such material symbols as the Arc de Triomphe. Only symbols of eternal ideals, such as the temple of Confucius, should be preserved. If the aims of reforming society are sincere, then they must be carried out always with an eye to the future. Permanent improvements must be brought about through better education, freely available to each individual, and by a continual increase of culture. But all this will take a long time."

To this Mao replied that the reformation of society must really be carried out through military power and political action.

The ninth problem was: education or politics?

I maintained, "Changes brought about through the use of military power can only result in tyranny; while reforms through education, in the widest sense of the word, are peaceful and enduring. They are 'silent changes' and of course, for visible, immediate results, cannot be compared with those enforced by the power of arms."

Mao said, "I like to see things happen before my very eyes. Frankly, your ideas do not appeal to me at all!"

Next was a discussion of the interests of the individual. I contended, "If you follow the lead of the Russian Communists, after a struggle lasting ten years, or twenty years, you may one day be successful in imposing the system upon the country. Such success may not even be particularly difficult to achieve. But neither will it be a valuable achievement. If Russian Communism is eventually established, it will be a very sorry day for China! *Your* ideas do not appeal to *me!* In accepting them, I would have no further peace of mind. You remember Mencius: 'There are three things capable of rendering the sage very happy, and being an Emperor is not one of them.' He was speaking from his heart when he said that. Think also that mighty struggles such as that of Liu Pang and Hsiang Yü* are, in the eyes of Christ and Buddha, like two street urchins fighting for an apple."

Mao commented, "What a pity that you disagree with the theory of Karl Marx!" to which I replied, "What a pity that you do not agree with Prudhon's theory!"

We talked of idealism and materialism. We discussed topics without stopping, but the more we talked, the more unanswerable questions popped up. Mao was emphatic in his belief that answers were not necessary. Only action was necessary to achieve success. To this I

* Two rival war-lords at the beginning of the Han Dynasty.

would counter that with such a disastrous success as the aim, it was preferable not to act!

We talked along these lines, always in an atmosphere of intimate friendship, until the day of the formal establishment of the Chinese Communist Party. That last night we slept together in the same bed, talking till dawn, and Mao still begged me to attend the meeting at which the fateful decision was to be made.

41
The Chinese Communist Party Is Born

In the spring of 1921, I lived in Changsha for about three months because I had many things to do before I returned to Peking. As I was returning to Peking, I went to Shanghai, visiting on the way the President of the Educational Association of Hupeh and the Governor of Kiangsi Province. Some days before I was to leave Changsha, Mao Tse-tung suggested that he would accompany me, saying, "I want to tell you, in the very strictest confidence, that in Peking, Kwangtung, Shanghai, and in fact everywhere, Communist groups have been formed and over a dozen delegates are due to gather in Shanghai for a secret meeting. The purpose of this meeting is formally to establish the Chinese Communist Party. I am the delegate for Changsha and I would very much like to have you go with me to this meeting."

I told him, "We can go to Shanghai on the same boat, but I do not want to attend your meeting."

He insisted, "Go on! You go there and meet these colleagues. Listen to their ideas. Talk with them!"

However I asked, "What's the good? Your meeting is not a discussion group. Everything has already been decided and now the Chinese Communist Party is to be established. If I were to attend that meeting, I should be one of the founders of Chinese Communism! I should then be responsible in the eyes of the Chinese people for a hundred, a thousand years, and I should be responsible before humanity for ten thousand years. I tell you, I am not prepared to have any part in the formation of the Communist Party!"

Mao replied, "If we work hard, in about thirty to fifty years' time the Communist Party may be able to rule China."

"That all depends upon how you go about it," I said. "I also believe that after a long period of struggle, it may be possible for the Communists to dominate China. But it will not be for the good of the Chinese people; and their domination cannot last forever."

"But if we manage to become the rulers of our country, don't you think that's a great achievement?" Mao asked.

"No, I don't," I replied. "I can best answer your question with a quotation from Lao Tzu: 'Ruling a big country is like cooking a small fish.' "

Mao laughed loudly at that. He thought I was joking. He did not know, and he never will be able to realize, that I was speaking very seriously. As a matter of fact, I wholeheartedly agree with Lao Tzu's philosophy, so aptly expressed in the sentence I had quoted.

That afternoon Mao and I left Changsha by the West Gate on the river boat. We occupied the same cabin; I took the upper berth and he the lower. Many friends came down to see me off, as they knew I would soon be returning to France; so we were very busy talking with them all afternoon. In the evening, when the boat sailed, we had a sound sleep. When we entered Lake Tungting, it seemed as if we were on the ocean with a boundless expanse of water all around us. Mao was up first and went to sit on deck. Later I joined him and noticed a small thin book in his pocket. When I asked what it was, he took it out to show me the title, *An Outline of the Capitalist System*. I said jokingly, "Do you have to study capitalism to be able to form a Communist Party?" Mao smiled a little and said nothing. To break the silence, I continued, "I understand you didn't have to study to be a Communist; so you shouldn't need to read books like that. The most important thing is to believe. That's why Communism is like a religion." Mao just smiled again and still did not answer. Finally to break the spell, I asked if he had eaten his breakfast. "No," he replied, "I was waiting for you, so we could eat together."

Soon the boat reached Hankow and we parted. I went ashore while Mao went on to Shanghai, where we arranged to meet. He gave me the secret address where I could find him after I had completed my business in Hupeh and Kiangsi.

When I arrived in Shanghai, I went directly to Valon Street in the French Concession and found the house the number of which he had given me. In the room were two beds, one of which was undoubtedly for me, but Mao was not there. In the evening when he returned, he told me they had had trouble with the secret police who had held them for some lengthy interrogations. Since the schools were on holiday, they had, after some difficulty, obtained the use of a classroom in a girls' college. Although they had locked all the doors for the meeting, the police had traced them and now it would be impossible to meet there again. These French Concession secret police were very smart and now they followed the delegates wherever they went; so they dared not meet again as a whole group. Though they scattered widely and maintained contact only by means of one or two delegates who acted as messengers, after several days' inactivity the police still maintained a close vigilance.(35)

"We've hit on a new plan," Mao announced one day, looking a bit happier than usual. "One of the delegates has a girl friend from Chiahsing in Chekiang Province and she says that on the way from Shanghai to West Lake you pass through Chiahsing. Just outside that city is another lake called Nan Hu (South Lake) and we are going to visit it as if we were tourists and have our meeting on the boat. We shall try to avoid the police, but to make doubly sure, we shall buy train tickets to Hangchow as if we were going to West Lake. There will be lots of tourists on the train and when we get to Chiahsing, we shall get off as if we were going to walk up and down the platform. We shall mix with the crowd till the train leaves. If the police follow us from Shanghai, they will not think of this. Besides, they are not so particular about what happens outside of Shanghai City. I want you to come to Chiahsing with me and after the meeting we'll go and visit West Lake. Since I was a very small boy I have been told about the beautiful scenery there and now, thanks to the Shanghai secret police, I'll see it."

"Very well," I consented. "Tomorrow we shall go and visit West Lake."

Next morning at seven, Mao and I left our room for the station where we bought third-class tickets for Hangchow. As we entered the station about nine o'clock, we saw the name "Chiahsing" in large characters on a big white signboard. When the train stopped, we jumped down and mixed with the crowd on the platform. After a time, as un-obtrusively as possible, we made our way out onto the road. As I looked at the waters of the lake so close to the town, I mused that these placid waters were so shortly to give birth to a monster, the Chinese Communist Party. The other delegates had also left the train but, when they met, they gave no outward sign of recognition. Mao and I kept a sharp lookout as we walked, but no one was following us. We found a little hotel on a side street where we engaged a small room for the night.

In the room was one bed and a tiny table. The bed was quite large and occupied a good two-thirds of the floor, leaving barely enough room to move about. The mosquito net was white and clean, so I decided to stay. In the hot summer, a good net is a very important consideration in choosing a room. As soon as we were settled, Mao set off for the meeting place. He took my arm and said, "I would like you to go with me to visit South Lake!"

"No, I'll wait here for you to come back and we will visit West Lake together," I replied. "What time do you expect to return?"

"It is really too bad that you don't want to see South Lake with me," Mao continued. "I expect to return late in the evening. We shall eat on the boat, so don't wait for me for supper."

After saying that, he looked hard at me for several minutes and then left without another word. After writing a few letters, I strolled slowly along the bank of South Lake, watching the boats sailing slowly past. It was a good idea to hold the secret meeting on the boat and I wondered which craft was destined to give birth to the Chinese Communist Party. The muddy waters of the lake made me think of the Deluge, the New Flood which would sweep away old China if the Communists were to dominate the country—turbid, murky, *huo shui* (evil waters).(36)

After supper there was still no sign of Mao Tse-tung; so I took a bath and spent some time looking out of the little window. Lights showed everywhere even though, on the horizon, the sky was still not quite dark. I switched off the room light and got into bed. When Mao arrived two or three hours later, he held open the net and asked, "Mr. Siao, are you asleep already?"

"Yes," I replied, "I was asleep. But please don't hold open the net. The mosquitoes are terrible here and they'll come in! Are you satisfied with the day's work?"

"Yes, very satisfied," Mao replied. "We were able to talk quite freely in the boat, at long last! It's too bad you didn't go."

I answered quickly, "You see you appreciated the 'Freedom'! In Shanghai you were not free to talk with your colleagues. You were not free to hold your meeting. The police followed you everywhere. You didn't like that, yet that situation lasted only a few days; whereas in Russia it's like that night and day, every day, wherever one goes! Where could a group find a 'South Lake' in Russia? How is it that you like your freedom so much and yet you deliberately decide to destroy the freedom of your fellow countrymen, to make China a second Russia? What did you decide at the meeting? What action are you planning to take?"

Mao replied quietly, "We decided that we must make China into a second Russia! We must organize ourselves and fight to the end."

"How are you going to organize?" I asked.

"The delegates are not a bad lot," Mao explained. "Some of them are very well educated and they can read either Japanese or English. We decided that we must first form a nucleus. This nucleus is to be the Chinese Communist Party. Afterwards we shall arrange details of the propaganda to be carried out and the specific plan of action. The main idea is to start off by converting the laboring classes and the younger students to Communism. Then, too, we must be certain to have a sound economic basis. That explains why we must belong to the Third International."

"But," I protested, "the Third International is Russian. Why don't you organize the Fourth International?"

"What is that?" asked Mao.

"The Fourth International," I explained, "is the idealist part of Communism. It is a combination of the ideals of Karl Marx and Prudhon. It is *free* Communism. You remember what I said about the two wheels of the rickshaw? The rickshaw of *free* Communism has both wheels; it needs no force to support it! If you agree to organize your movement along the lines of the Fourth International, I shall dedicate my whole life to it!"

"Let's talk about that again in a thousand years," said Mao sadly, as he opened the mosquito net and got into bed.

What a smell of hot, sweaty, unwashed flesh! I had nevertheless become used to this strong odor. As the Chinese saying goes, "If you stay in the fish market long enough, you don't notice the smell." But I felt obliged to suggest, "Wouldn't you like to have a bath? You can in this hotel. I've just had one."

To which Mao replied, "I feel too lazy to get washed. Let's sleep now and we'll get up early tomorrow and visit West Lake." So saying, he lay down and made himself comfortable, but inevitably, the eternal discussion of Communism and freedom, state or individual, commenced again and it was almost dawn before we stopped talking. Mao was a sound sleeper, never restless, and in the big bed, I did not feel his presence.

The sky was bright and clear when I awakened. Mao was still sleeping; so I lay quite still. After a time, he opened his eyes and I called him, "Jun-chih, it's broad daylight. Let's get up!"

"What time is it?" he asked. "Can't I sleep just a little longer?"

I told him he could and I got up as quietly as possible. Half an hour later he awakened and got up immediately, saying, "What time is it? Have we missed the train?"

"No, don't worry," I told him, "it is still early. There are many trains to West Lake each day from here."

The weather was beautiful and a gentle breeze wafted the sweet perfume of summer flowers from the banks of South Lake. I stood looking at the lake for a long time. There were no tourist boats yet and all was peaceful; but I thought of what had taken place on those serene waters the day before—waters of bitterness, poison juice. I turned away sadly.

Since there were few people on the train, we had another long talk of several hours, but it was rather disorderly, without going deeply into any topic. Mostly we criticized Ch'en Tu-hsiu, the leader of the Communist movement, because he was too much of a scholarly type and rather bourgeois in outlook. Li Ta-chao seemed to us a more appropriate choice, but apparently the Russians favored Ch'en Tu-hsiu and he had been the chief organizer in the South Lake meeting.

In the afternoon we arrived at Hangchow, capital of Chekiang

Province, and the houses, roads, and gardens along the lake shore formed a scene of indescribable beauty. I thought of the saying that Hangchow was one of the earthly paradises, and realized that it was no exaggeration: "Above there is Heaven, below there is Soo and Hang" (Soochow and Hangchow). *Shang yu tien tang, hsia yu su hang.*

Mao and I visited many famous spots but despite the splendor of the outer world, we were not happy. At one time I said, "Look at these marvelous gardens. How could they have been made, and how could people come here to enjoy them without money?"

Mao Tse-tung replied, "This is a criminal production. Many people use their money for criminal purposes!"

"Well, we shall be two temporary little criminals today," I smiled.

"Tomorrow we must get away from here quickly!" said Mao.

Next day we took the train back to Shanghai and soon Mao returned to Changsha. I remained for a week to finish my business and then returned to Peking.

42
"Before the World Comes to an End."

Up to this time Mao had kept no secrets from me as regards his Communist activities; indeed, he had told me many things in confidence of which I had breathed not a word to anyone! After we separated in Shanghai, we wrote to each other frequently, sometimes using secret language which only we could understand. When I returned to France several months later, our letters took ten to twelve weeks to reach their destination, since there was no air mail service then. It was fortunate for Mao's pocket that air service was not available, because his writing was so big and clumsy and his letters were always so long, that he would have had to spend a fortune on stamps!

When I returned to China late in 1924, I lived in Peking. Since I could not go to Changsha to meet with Mao Tse-tung and the other members of the Hsin Min Study Association, we exchanged letters frequently. At this time Dr. Sun Yat-sen decided to collaborate with the Communist Party and, as a result, the Communists became simultaneously members of the Kuomintang. In reality, however, the Communists simply put on the cloak of the Kuomintang, while they continued to work secretly for their own Party. This collaboration misled the militarists who often accused members of the Kuomintang of being Communists.

During this period both the Kuomintang, to which I belonged, and the Communist Party had the same primary aim—to attack and destroy militarism. I participated actively in this movement of the Revolution. Mao Tse-tung, my other friends of the Hsin Min Study Association and I all shared this same focal purpose.

Although I had direct communication with Li Ta-chao, the leader of the Communists, and with other active Communists, naturally I knew nothing at all of the secret discussions or plans within the Chinese Communist Party. Mao Tse-tung continued to write me long and intimate letters. Although he could not discuss openly the actions of his Party, we carried on our theoretical discussions as frankly as we had done in the past.

In Peking, the members of the two parties worked well together. For example, when I was named General Editor of the *Ming Pao* (*People's News*), the only newspaper of any importance in the north, we held an editor's conference every day after midnight. We sat around a large table: opposite me was my secretary, to my left were three Kuomintang members, and to my right, three Communists. One of the Communists was Fan Hung-chi, who later was hanged with Li Ta-chao. I smile now to think that it was in reality a miniature Deputies' meeting and that we were in complete agreement.

Both the Communists and the Kuomintang felt that there was a great need to print articles and pamphlets against militarism, but the business houses did not dare to print them. The Communist leader, Li Ta-chao, proposed at one of these conferences that we organize a publishing house at Peking in the name of the Kuomintang. I was named Director General, and the Treasurer of the Kuomintang gave me a considerable sum of money for the project. I proposed Hiong King-ting to come from Changsha to Peking as my Executive Editor. (Hiong was a professor with me at the Ch'u Yi School and later a member of the Hsin Min Study Association. Now he is working in Peking with other old members of this Association.) I had worked at the project for only four or five months before the police began to watch me in a suspicious manner. Finally I returned the balance of the money to Ku Mong-yu, who was Professor and Director of Studies of the National University at Peking and later Minister of Railways for the Republic of China. This incident illustrates again the close collaboration between the Chinese Communist Party and the Kuomintang.

In 1925 I was constantly under police surveillance and I lost my freedom. Often it was necessary for me to hide in the Foreign Concession in Peking or Tientsin in order to escape capture. In 1926, when Li Ta-chao and many other Communists were hanged by the Military Government, we Revolutionists worked even more actively, though more dangerously. Our homes were often thoroughly searched by police and soldiers. Once when I was hiding in a Foreign Concession, my family burned a whole suitcase full of letters which Mao Tse-tung and other friends in the Hsin Min Study Association had written to me. Periodically I received some short verbal messages brought by friends traveling between Changsha and Peking, but gradually even these messages were stopped.

I remember very vividly one of the last letters I wrote to my friend Mao Tse-tung. In it I made the following points: we are faced with two great problems and choices, liberty or totalitarianism, the supremacy of the state or of the individual. . . . No politics are entirely good. Any political power may be bad and political power usually is bad. Comparatively speaking, democracy is better by far than other forms of government. . . . You should read "La Philosophie de la Misère," not "La Misère de la Philosophie." . . . *Tao kao yi che, mo kao yi chang* (Goodness grows slowly; badness grows quickly) is as true in government as in other human relationships. In the evolution of humanity, material progress always greatly exceeds our moral and social progress. . . . Confucius said, "The commander of the forces of a large state may be carried off, but the will of even a common man cannot be taken from him." * A nation is not a machine which can be

---

* From a translation by James Legge (1861).

set in motion at will by the operator. It is neither just nor is it intelligent to attempt to bind the thoughts and will of a people. Our
great philosopher said, "Do not unto others that which you do not
want done unto you." He did not say to do to others what you want
for yourself. . . . The driver with a whip thinks he is more intelligent
than his beasts which he brings into subjection. I am sure that driver
is very bad for his animals and I doubt that he has more intelligence.
. . . I hope we have an opportunity to conclude our discussion before
the world comes to an end.

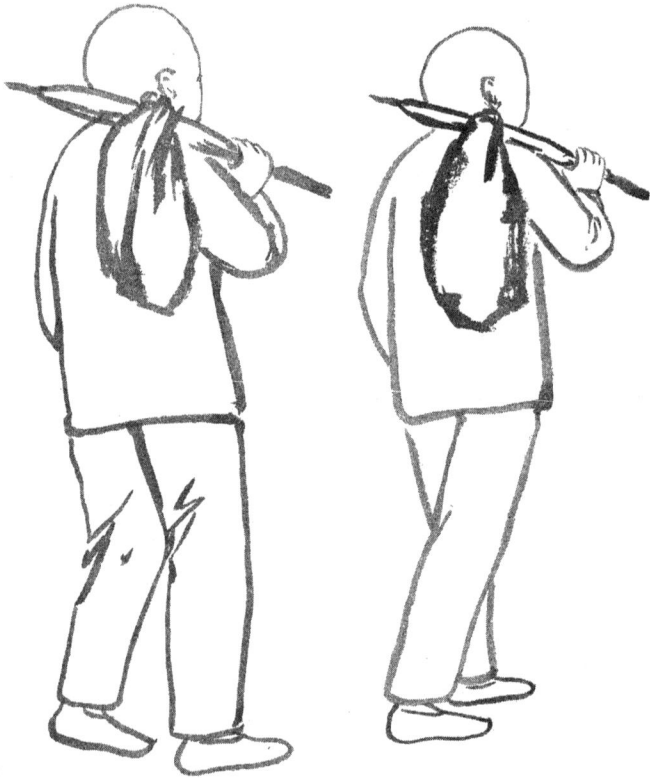

Illustrations

Mao Tse-tung's birthplace in the village of Shao Shan.

Leaving home
He said goodbye to his mother, but did not call his father.
Shouldering his parcel,
He walked like a duck.

Alas,
I see everywhere the continent entangled.
On looking back,
For what reason did he go to school?

Note: The author has signed, "The best student of Mrs. Siao-ying" (Mrs. Siao-yu) as Mrs. Siao-yu called the author. The two small square seals bear the name and pseudonym of the author, and the lower right-hand seal signifies the Ling-Siao studio. Ling Siao is the name of a flower, and as the pronunciation is the same as their combined surnames, it was taken as a symbol of the studio of Dr. and Mrs. Siao-yu.

家出去拜年 娘不叫爷 挑鬼去

走路似鸭爬

噎口頭七亂似麻 回頭看

上学做甚麼

七八分令妈闹题 毛澤東難家

初上小学面远當

元宵節字為三女

者陰夫人真是为子孟战

A primary school of fifty years ago
Is called Tungshan, in the district Siangsiang.
Coming out of the city, crossing the river, walking two or three li,
One sees from afar a tall house above the round wall.
Inside the wall runs a deep moat,
A round moat resembling a belt around the body.
From the stone bridge I liked to watch my reflection;
I knew the fish in the water were content, and they too knew my joy.
More than a year after I left this school
I heard it said, one day there came a madman
Wearing old clothes, his bags on his shoulders.
The children, hurrying to see him on the square, jostled one another,
Their babbling and questioning mixed with laughter.
An adult with an obsession wished to enter primary school.
At first the porter did not want to let him pass.
Since he entered that door to study,
The results of his studies make a "false red" with "violet." *
The source was the same,
Which, as it ran, divided into the clear and the troubled.

---

*A true revolution can be called a red one; the Russian and Chinese Revolutions are here called "violet." The color violet resembles red, but because its colors are mixed, it is called "false" red. Confucius said, "I hate the manner in which purple takes away the luster of vermilion (red)." (Translation by James Legge.)

东山小学即我母校亦即人皆知的
湘乡县立东山高等小学堂

一九五八年在南宁毛泽东入小学

Dreams are seldom realized in life.
Sadly I think of things of forty years ago.
I showed no sign, but she had this thought.
*To fly side by side with touching wings was impossible.**
The thoughts remained uncommunicated.
How can I hang my beautiful sword on her tomb?†
With pain I see that person (Mao) with heart of stone,
Intent solely on power,
Allow her unhappily to pass into another world.‡

*The author was already married.

†In Chinese history there was a high official who stopped to visit a dear friend while returning from a mission. On learning of his friend's death, the official visited the tomb, hanging on a nearby tree his sword which had been greatly admired by his friend.

‡The author refers here to the death of Mao's wife, Yang K'ai-hui, who was shot because she was a Communist.

人生好夢最難圓往事

悲惡の十年未挑琴心竟有

犀曾未通肯次霸劍何

意偕飛比翼早無緣靈

由掛基前太息無情貪

霸業害妻飲恨在黃泉

楊開慧女士欲嫁余余於二

十年後始得知之時因毛澤東

故已慘死宛六七年矣與其夫隱夫

人敘述往事相與太息不置

感賦一律良潛路也

一九五二年左右春季某某

寫並題

All night until sunrise
On the Miao Kao Feng
We fully discussed the problem,
The transformation of China.

改造中國縱談方案妙
高學上圍宵達旦

長沙南門外乃一小山坡名妙高峯在第一師範校後
為當日余與毛澤東縱談地凡六年在校與暑假時期
思齊遠寫

甯薆齋

Umbrella and bundle supported by the shoulders,
Without hat on the head, without a cent in the hand,
We started out to see a million li of rivers and mountains,
To find if we could manage with an empty fist.

Note: The seal on the lower right-hand corner signifies a Chinese proverb which says, "Be a beggar for three years, then you would not be even a mandarin."

雨華行囊荷一肩歌舞無冠戴手二雲錢去首海山千萬里

呂伯糠頹仗空拳

一九三五年暑假余作元兩周
遊於中毛澤東偕行生藐目
余於日記上題行吟省考也
一九三六年去美展觀田
慎連寫

舞蕭瑜並識

迄今人多發毛澤東心
圖春詞品為誇大者不去
其病不在誇大而在行之不由道也

孝隱夫人高足弟子再題

Crossing over with the ferry,
The way takes us to the district of Ningsiang,
Walking a hundred li
Along high mountains and long rivers.
The house of "Moustache" Ho
Was in the district.
Very late in the night we went to visit him,
Knocking on the door and banging on the wall.
First frightened, then pleased, he shouted excitedly,
"Old Mao, Old Siao!"
He lit the candle and warmed the wine;
All the family was in a busy confusion.
The old father took us to see the pigs and sheep,
The cultivated fields and vegetable patch,
A valley of bamboos and a hill of pines.
They lived from their own efforts,
Their food cultivated with their own hands.
With small property, modest bourgeois he,
Was he not happy?
That day he gave us a sumptuous feast
Of chicken, rice and wine.
The beggars change suddenly
And sit grandly in the beautiful hall.
This only happens in the theater;
Our beggar's life does not often permit such luxury.
Insisting on leaving them,
We hurried to make our bundles.
After saying goodbye
We were again with empty pockets.

何朔子家古宴之好
烏酒口道生蓴鄉五里餘
山為水下必何苦上家日在此方且
准探汤彩門本墙寰多飛呼乎心
兩郎勇收漁全姑鮮世老夫牛
飲有猪首禾稻出菜圍竹花松岡
貝食其子昼雜生攘毛生小座堂
此每東田旧日大會雜麥松柏松之好一
雖沒辭別意拾行世幾従此揮手又是空畫
獨有生辜畫俚出本作就不多爭
些決辞別意拾行世幾従此揮手又是空畫
元五全毛隅昨事随我作之马旅行心所影調子家元五六年柱南事
吾為同接連寫
俚辞子家大安叫子化子掠月一変上了金鑾殿作我自在人寰栽本
此面金鑾殿叫化子不慕不羨沈

齊白石題

The pig was as big as a cow,
The pig was as fat as a balloon,
Depending on his body
To provide salt and oil for his owners.
The weak become the meat the strong eat,
But the pig is not concerned with that.
Men show no justice;
The pig has no liberty.
For that reason it is called a pig.
Men are no better than pigs when they have lost their liberty.

豬大如牛猶肥如球全伏此身豪壯
油勿肉煤食豬不知愁人無公道豬
亦有自由此之謂豬人未必優
於牛矣毛澤東渡我作之乃為旅行入寧鄉
縣境訪韶山毛子家何名瞻岵號叔衡為吳東屯
長沙林怡學校信主任敦頁早已深此豈當享尊
深炭昆其家田其尊翁執煉別導首先夢
觀為怕之一豬圈有豬最大者約重二百公斤似
下牛欣然告曰此一家鹽油耶自此也余謂人
殺豬無公道人失自由等於豬矣因思惜畫
之一九五八年在南美孟若

舜羹藩藍澤

Clouds enfold Lion Strength Mountain,
The bridge locks in the boats of the Deep Jade Water.

The poor farmer treads the wheel,
Tread once, kneel once,
A thousand treads, ten thousand treads,
To save the dying crop.
The sun is like fire,
It rises burning and is difficult to escape.
With a cup of water one cannot save a load of firewood in flames.
This is no small calamity.
The farmer perspires profusely,
With deep sighs and small grunts.
His sweat is more than the water he raises up.
The work is so hard, I cannot bear to look at it.

勞農車水圖

勞農車水一踏一蹺
千跪千踄搶救禾薑
炎陽似火烧未雖杯
水車新笑紅小可苦苦
大汗圭哼歌汗比雨涔
若不忍看
乞与旅逅聖信連寓一
作我吞者毛澤东せ一
无亟之圣运南之叟

韓羽草筒

In summer all the earth burns in the sun.
Two mad people wander aimlessly.
Under the shadows of the Aleurite Cordata,
They wake up after a deep sleep.
They converse intimately on the rise and fall of nations.

"A cup of pure water,
A bowl of water of life." *
Two joking phrases
Come from a cherry mouth.
That night she lit a candle,
Read our faces and read our hands.
Now one can judge her predictions
After forty years have passed by.
She could be called "Chih Ki," †
She could be a good friend.
That young girl, a lovely person,
Is she still there today?

*Strong wine.

†A word meaning "a friend to me as my own self."

一杯清水一碗烧酒雪子笑
話出櫻桃口当日剪烛相面
樜手合谊音繰の才後み谓知
己也為良友り女奶人今尚在
否

乙己　旅画田怕逵宇之一

一九五二

Knowing that my return journey to China draws near,
They are happy,
And say goodbye with much sentiment.
I was at Montargis for three days to meet with dear friends.
All were intimate and sincere.

Taking the earth for a seat and the sky for a tent,
We have opened a meeting.
The trees are allowed to listen,
On the branches the birds are applauding.
From time to time they cry out to us.

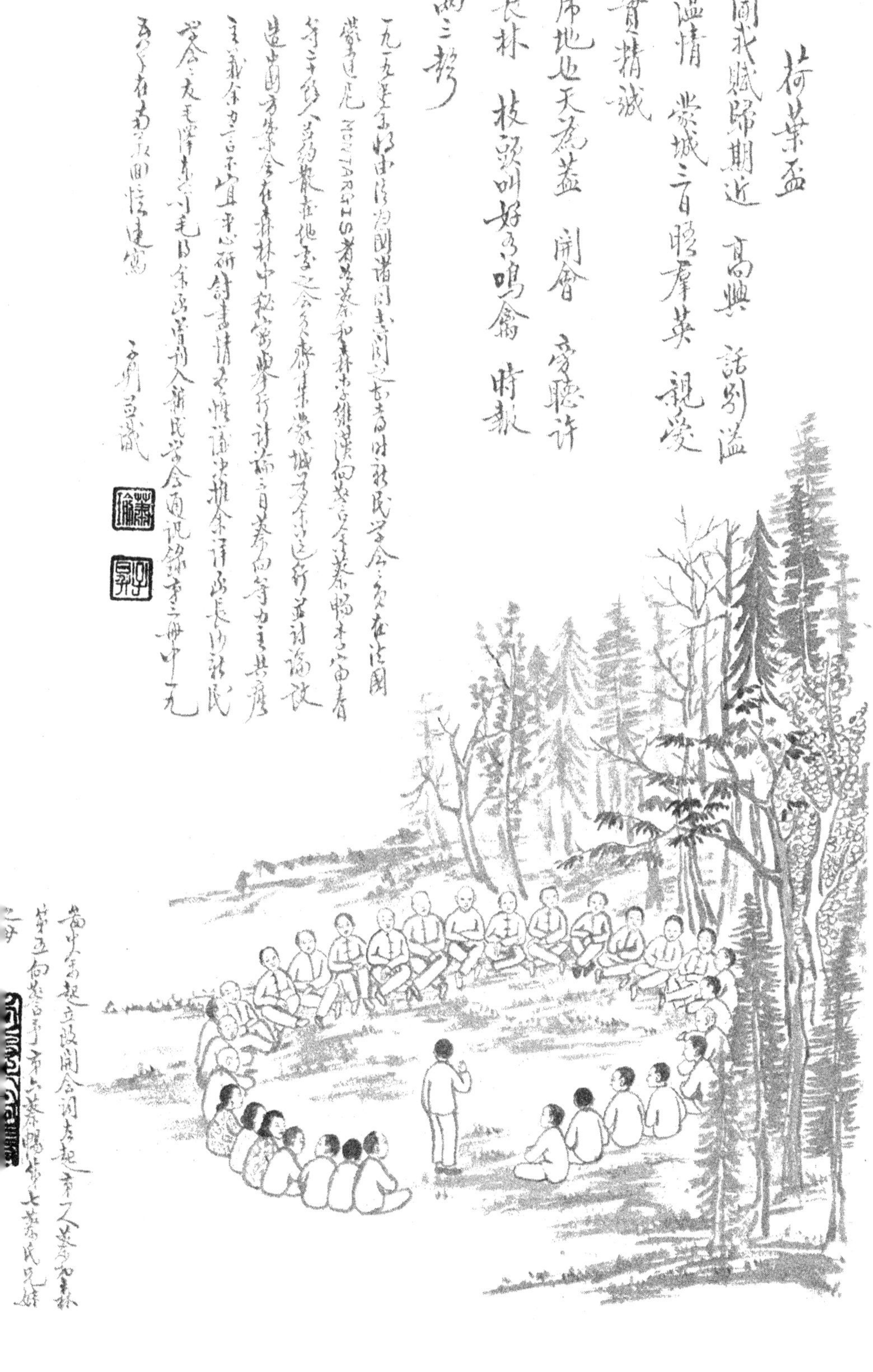

荷葉盃

闢永賦歸期近　高興　話別溫
溫情　蒙城三日照群英　親爰
資精誠

席地坐天為盖　開會　爭聽許
長林　枝頭叫好多鳴禽　時報
兩三聲

一九五五年五月由法國蒙圖爾市赴巴黎途中社民學會分會在法國
蒙達尼城MONTARGIS森林中集和森林中雖渓何人多人茶暢不富者
宇宙三多為費在地上一人多多者牛在蒙城三日每力這行討論議
進上開方集合在森林中就當時史行勘勒三日葑力等力主要
主我会在吾是此革力史其雇月是新句情在棋於牛諸汝當長的社民
常念左毛澤東汉人毛日多多道刊入新民學會通訊録第二冊中元

右在南京用憶追寫

廋景凱〔印〕〔印〕

當中富起立設開會同志起立為人蒙如集林
第五句葉白白有七蒙暢修作七蒙民兄妹

Going boating like this
Seems to be without precedence.
A lake of dead water,
But the red waves reach the sky itself.
That day by the lake
I was already sorrowful!
Now I paint a secret history
With my brush feeling as heavy as a log.

中國共產黨之誕生

一九二二年七月中國共產黨在
地組織人開第一次代表大會於
共黨成立會於上海法租界團
迷薄尾跟偵探晝夜要道諸
後集議乃由一代表之女友提
議謂其故鄉嘉興縣之南
湖距上海不甚遠可借遊湖
以避耳目毛澤東與余二人
同自滬出發忘其地城下車
投宿旅店主顛我車我未
上岸僅見其船之開放監二
至湖行會畢乃返當晚揮寢
翌日同車興余同遊西湖
子升丹記

此是遊船似屋空高一沼池水來浪
淄天尝日在旁我已戚發备付秘
史大筆如椽
蕭瑜逢德並題

Playing the chin* before the cow —
Before this, there was never a painting on this subject.
I tried to paint it.
This phrase, is it really true?

Playing the chin futilely but with patience before the cow,†
I spoke of the correct doctrine of the revolution.
The laws of heaven and earth decree there shall be communism.
The laws of earth and heaven decree there must be liberty.

---

* Ancient Chinese musical instrument.

† "Playing the chin before the cow" is a Chinese phrase comparable to the expression "throwing pearls before swine."

對牛彈琴
自古無畫
竊試為之
豈其然乎

考隆夫人畜兔事子遼寫并題

不惜強琴對華生山
宗夏介說源法子經
地義須共產物義天
強要自由

與羣謂肯進份子設社會革命
理源後加作

此畫仲弗畫之竟
子肖草畜

Historical Commentary and Notes

Historical Commentary and Notes

While working on a Chinese leadership study some years back I was struck with the fact that it is often extraordinarily difficult to find material about the early lives of important political figures—even those like Mao Tse-tung who are still alive. Once such men are dead, and as year after year folds over them, the problem becomes increasingly difficult. Legends about a great man's youth are soon elaborated upon, and even his enemies may join in making a good story of it.

With Communist leaders the task of the biographer or the historian is further complicated by the demands of ideology: if the hero was not born a worker or a peasant, his early life is often retailored by official record keepers to make him one—the poorer and more exploited the better.

What the biographer and historian never give up hoping to find, of course, is "hard" documentation such as village records, family papers, and other archives. Materials of this sort seldom provide more than the barest elements of the story, however, and in the case of a revolutionary leader even these may be wholly unavailable. Sooner or later, therefore, the scholar begins looking for other data—anything at all that will help him to reconstruct the details of a birth and a period of growing up that took place many years before. With such material, much of it unreliable, he does the best he can.

In the case of Mao Tse-tung's origins there is not much documentation of the "hard" sort available to us, but fortunately the pages of this book will add important dimensions to what has been set down in retrospect about the early life of the man. From the recollections of Siao-yu (in earlier years known as Siao Shu-tung) we can perceive from one more vantage point how a small boy in revolt against his father has come to lead a nation in revolt against itself—and against much of the world as we in the West have known it.

The chief English language sources for Mao Tse-tung's life are Robert Payne, *Mao Tse-tung, Ruler of Red China* (New York: Henry Schuman, Inc., 1950); Emi Siao, *Mao Tse-tung, His Childhood and Youth* (Bombay: People's Publishing House Ltd., 1953); and the story which Mao dictated, partly with the aid of an interpreter, to Edgar Snow in 1936. This last material appeared in Mr. Snow's book *Red Star Over China* (New York: Random House, 1938), and also in *The Autobiography of Mao Tse-tung* (Canton: Truth Book Company, 1938, and revised in 1949). Translated back into Chinese, the *Autobiography* served for some time as the only source of any considerable length available in the Chinese language.

All three of these books emerge from recollections rather than from documents of the time or other contemporary evidence, and one is forced, therefore, to use them with even more caution than is usual for secondary sources, because of the possibility of partisan political propaganda. It is clear, also, that the *Autobiography* has served as a partially hidden source for the other two. In *Mao Tse-tung, Ruler of Red China*, for example, Mr. Payne draws from talks he had with Hsiao San (Emi Siao) in Kalgan, who, in turn, has very obviously refreshed his memory and supplemented it by reading the *Autobiography*.

Like these other sources, *Mao Tse-tung and I Were Beggars* rests wholly upon recollections—both Siao-yu's recollections of personal experiences, and his recollections of what third persons told him about Mao Tse-tung, particularly for that portion of his life before their friendship began. One recognizes many delightful similarities between this book and the story which Mao Tse-tung gave Edgar Snow, as in the parallel accounts of the way Mao and his friends packed themselves in bed and had to warn each other before turning over. There are discrepancies, too, but on the whole I think these tend to enhance the integrity of the book as an independent source.

The account also includes a further rare dimension in that Siao-yu and Emi Siao are bitter political antagonists—and also brothers.

Emi Siao, whom Mao knew in boyhood days as Siao Chih-fan, called himself Emil through deep admiration for Jean Jacques Rousseau. In later years he went to the Soviet Union, where he achieved recognition as a translator of Chinese poetry into Russian, and also as a poet in his own right. Here is what the author says about him: "You have asked about Emi Siao, which should be written Emil Siao. He was my brother, two years younger than me. He was with me at the First Normal School, and also a member of the Hsin Min Study Association. In 1919 he also went to

France [as part of the worker-student movement], where he made friends with the French Communists. When I returned to China, he had already inscribed in the French Communist Party. I completely broke relations with him forty years ago. My family is like China, divided into two, Nationalists and Communists. . . ."

So it is that the two unreconciled brothers emerge as the chief chroniclers —aside from Mao Tse-tung himself—of the Chinese Communist leader's early life. The story is a revealing one, and I commend it to all readers who search for some understanding of what has happened in China.

ROBERT C. NORTH
Stanford University, California
May 25, 1959

Page 5.

(1) Siao-yu gives Mao Tse-tung's birth date, November 19, according
to the lunar calendar, but "if one wishes to write it in the solar calendar, it
is 26 December, 1893." At the time of Mao Tse-tung's birth, Chinese
society had been grinding toward revolution for at least half a century.

In the course of the Ming Dynasty (A.D. 1368–1644) Chinese emperors
developed a highly institutionalized pattern of relationships with other
states, and with relatively minor adaptations it was this same pattern that
the Ch'ing, or Manchu, Dynasty (1644–1912) adopted. This diplomacy
depended upon the imperial tributary system which had emerged, in turn,
from ancient assumptions of Chinese superiority over foreign barbarians.

Until the Opium War of 1839 China had lived in virtual isolation, and
the Chinese people had come to view their empire as the only world order
that really counted. The society was one of the most ancient on the earth,
and its political, economic and social structures were almost wholly self-
contained. Generally speaking neither the emperors nor the state officials,
nor the people at large saw any reason for meeting foreigners except with
the condescension which great empires traditionally have displayed toward
barbarians on distant frontiers.

Western penetrations of East Asia gave rise to relations of a different
sort. By the middle of the nineteenth century the Chinese empire was face
to face with what amounted to the challenge of foreign conquest—though
it looked more like economic and technological invasion than the threat
of military power. For the Westerner won ground less by force of arms
than by building railroads and floating loans. The great campaigns were
construction jobs rather than military expeditions, and the old Empire
found itself nearly helpless against this kind of onslaught. Neither the
Chinese government nor any other part of the society had effective counter-
weapons, nor could they be obtained except from foreign sources.

In the course of the nineteenth century representatives of various European states succeeded in persuading the Manchu Empire to open a number
of Chinese ports to foreign trade, and then, from these footholds, they
worked their way inland—leasing, building railways, obtaining concessions,
and lending more and more money. For many Chinese there seemed to be
no way out of the dilemma. If China were to rebuild itself into a great
power along Western lines, the country needed both money and technology, but these could be acquired only from the West, and each new
agreement brought further indebtedness and deeper entrenchment of
foreign influence.

As time went on, the Manchu government increasingly revealed its inability to administer the affairs of the nation effectively. The leadership was
generally ineffectual, and there was virtually no concept of individual re-

sponsibility within the government. The civil service system became more and more corrupt, and even the examination system—upon which the whole administration of the Empire depended for its integrity—became increasingly debased. Toward the end of the nineteenth century it often appeared that China was on the verge of disintegration—and of partition among the western powers.

During the latter part of the nineteenth century various European states began competing with each other for political and economic advantage in China. Approaching the country by sea, Great Britain, France, Germany, and other states moved from the treaty ports into the interior, while Tsarist Russia, advancing overland, tried to halt British influence along vast Russian frontiers from Turkey and Iran and Afghanistan to Tibet and Sinkiang, and on to Mongolia, Manchuria, and Korea. It was also vital for Imperial Russia to obtain warm-water ports on the Pacific and to protect its Far Eastern flank against Japan.

China, under these circumstances, became more and more an economic and political jousting ground for the great powers of Europe—and also, as time went on, for Japan.

Individual Chinese leaders differed in their reactions to the Western challenge. Some hoped to withstand the shock through an inflexible preservation of the traditional structure; others wanted to keep the structure, but adapt it to cope with new conditions and foreign influences; still others came to the conclusion that the old society must be done away with and a new one built after Western models; a few—including Mao Tse-tung, as he grew into young manhood—began to reject the past of China and the West alike and to dream of something wholly new.

So it was that under foreign impact the old society began to fracture along lines of political, economic, social and intellectual cleavage—much as a huge rock is known to fracture under the point of a stone mason's chisel.

It was in a society of these many deepening cleavages that Mao Tse-tung was born and brought up.

Page 6.

(2) The village of Shao Shan, scattered along ten *li*, or nearly three and a half miles of countryside, commands a fine view of the hills and waters about. The houses, in times past, were few and widely spaced. There is a stream with a stone bridge across it, and nearby, in Mao's boyhood, stood a few small shops where meat, salt and other simple commodities were kept on sale. Most of the inhabitants of the village were honest, hard-working peasants.

Even today there stands near the stream a plain, tile-roofed house with high-walled courtyard and double wings where, at the turn of the century, the Mao and Tsou families lived. The house was sparsely furnished, but red peppers hanging from the roof beams gave the interior a touch of color, and the place was kept scrupulously clean. In those days the boundary line between the two families passed through the precise center of the living room.[1]

Page 6.

(3) Mao Tse-tung's father, who had once attended school for two years or so, knew a few characters and enough arithmetic to keep simple accounts. Mao's mother was wholly illiterate.[2]

Born a poor peasant, Mao Jen-sheng had been forced to join the army while still young because of debts. After several years as a soldier, he returned to Shao Shan to enter into small trading and other petty enterprises. Saving carefully, he managed eventually to buy back his land and, with 16 *mou* (1 *mou* = 1/6 acre), to achieve status as a middle peasant. On this acreage, Mao Tse-tung recalled years later, the father was able to raise sixty *picul* (1 *picul* = 133⅓ lbs.) of rice per year.

With five members—Mao Tse-tung, his parents, his grandfather and his brother—the family regularly consumed about thirty-five *picul* a year. Through sale of the surplus and by purchasing grain from his poorer neighbors, transporting it to the city, and selling it at a higher price, the elder Mao gradually accumulated further capital and bought seven more *mou*, which gave the family the status of rich peasants. The farm now yielded some eighty-four *picul* annually, and Mao Jen-sheng began to buy mortgages on other men's land. In this fashion he accumulated what, in Shao Shan, was a considerable fortune.[3]

Mao Tse-tung's grandfather died after a time, but then another boy was born, and later, a girl. All members of the family were expected to work on the farm. As he achieved rich peasant status, according to the *Autobiography*, Mao Jen-sheng kept a full-time laborer, and in winter, when the rice was being ground, he even took on a second hired hand. The family worked hard and ate frugally—though always enough.[4]

The elder Mao was a formidable man—tall, sturdily built, bearded in his later years,[5] and increasingly cantankerous. "He was a severe task master," Mao Tse-tung recalled years later. "He hated to see me idle. . . . He was a hot-tempered man and frequently beat both me and my brothers."[6]

---

[1] Emi Siao, *Mao Tse-tung, His Childhood and Youth* (Bombay: People's Publishing House Ltd., 1955), p. 1.

[2] *The Autobiography of Mao Tse-tung* (Canton: Truth Book Co., 1949), p. 3.

[3] *Ibid.*, p. 5.

[4] *Ibid.*, p. 3.

[5] Emi Siao, p. 2.

[6] *Autobiography*, p. 4.

The old man gave his children no money at all, according to Mao, and only the most meager food. "On the fifteenth of every month he made a concession to his laborers and gave them eggs with their rice," Mao records, "but never meat. To me he gave neither eggs nor meat."[7] As a small boy Mao was somewhat frail physically, and this may have been an element in his father's seeming dislike of him.

Mao Tse-tung's mother, on the other hand, had a placid, handsome round face and tender eyes. Surnamed Wen, she was a native of Tangchia-tuo, a district of Siangsiang.[8] Her duties were those of any other peasant woman—cooking, rearing children, collecting firewood, spinning, mending, starching and washing. Through the years she won for herself the reputation as a good woman and a thrifty housewife.[9] A Buddhist in her faith, she was deeply religious and opposed to violence and any sort of killing.[10] "My mother was a kind woman," Mao remembered in later life, "generous and sympathetic, and ever ready to share whatever she had. She pitied the poor and often gave them rice when they came to ask for it during famines. But she could not do so when my father was present."[11]

Old Mao Jen-sheng, who disapproved of charity, kept close account of the rice, and whenever he found that some had been given away, he burst into a temper.[12] "We had many quarrels in my home over this question," Mao Tse-tung told Edgar Snow in 1936.[13]

Inside the house Mao's mother kept a bronze Buddha; squatting on a blackwood table, it occupied a special place of honor.[14] For years during his childhood Mao Tse-tung went with his mother to Buddhist ceremonies and learned to sing Buddhist hymns. In those days he believed that it was a crime to kill any living thing. But as the boy grew older he became more and more skeptical, and his mother was finally left to hope that, if he was not destined for the priesthood, he might at least become a teacher.[15]

The father had other ideas. By the age of six Mao Tse-tung began working on the farm[16] where he helped to plant rice seeds or sat on a wicker platform in the fields to frighten birds away—a small boy with a shock of black hair and blue linen trousers.[17] Two years later he entered

[7] *Ibid.*, p. 4.
[8] Robert Payne, *Mao Tse-tung, Ruler of Red China* (New York: Henry Schuman, Inc., 1950), p. 25.
[9] Emi Siao, pp. 5–6.
[10] Payne, p. 25.
[11] *Autobiography*, p. 4.
[12] Payne, p. 25.
[13] *Autobiography*, p. 4.
[14] Payne, p. 25.
[15] *Ibid.*, p. 27.
[16] *Autobiography*, p. 3.
[17] Payne, p. 28.

a local primary school, which he attended until he was thirteen, but in the early morning and at night his father saw to it that he did chores about the farm. As soon as the youngster had learned a few characters, it occurred to Mao Jen-sheng that his son could be very useful at the abacus and at keeping the family books. "As my father insisted upon this," Mao recalled later, "I began to work at those accounts at night." [18]

Page 7.

(4) "There were two parties in the family," Mao told Edgar Snow. "One was my father, the Ruling Power. The Opposition was made up of myself, my mother, my brother, and sometimes even the laborer. In the 'united front' of the Opposition, however, there was a difference of opinion. My mother advocated a policy of indirect attack. She criticized any overt display of emotion and attempts at open rebellion against the Ruling Power. She said it was not the Chinese way." [19] Again and again Mao was distressed by his mother's helplessness, and the inequality he saw between man and wife, according to Emi Siao, "sowed the seeds for his later all-out rebellion against the oppressive character of the feudal patriarchal system." [20]

As the boy grew older, he found that his two brothers and sister were useful allies in his continual conflict with their father.[21] "The dialectical struggle in our family was constantly developing," Mao told Edgar Snow. "One incident I especially remember." [22]

When Mao Tse-tung was about thirteen years old, he and his father fell into violent argument in front of guests. "My father denounced me before the whole group," Mao remembered years later, "calling me lazy and useless. This infuriated me. I cursed him and left the house. My mother ran after me and tried to persuade me to return. My father also pursued me, cursing at the same time that he demanded me to come back. I reached the edge of a pond and threatened to jump in if he came any nearer. In this situation demands and counter demands were presented for cessation of the civil war. My father insisted that I apologize and k'ou-t'ou as a sign of submission. I agreed to give a one knee k'ou-t'ou if he would promise not to beat me. Thus the war ended, and from it I learned that when I defended my rights by open rebellion my father relented, but when I remained meek and submissive he only cursed and beat me more." [23]

At about this same time Mao discovered that he could neutralize much

[18] *Autobiography*, p. 4.
[19] *Ibid.*, p. 5.
[20] Emi Siao, p. 16.
[21] *Ibid.*, p. 27.
[22] *Autobiography*, p. 5.
[23] *Ibid.*, p. 5.

of his father's scolding with quotations from the Classics. When Mao Jen-sheng accused his son of laziness and unfilial conduct, the boy recited passages which urged older people to be kind and affectionate toward their children and exhorted them to set an example by working harder than their juniors. The father being three times older than the son, Mao argued, should do proportionately more work.[24]

Page 8.

(5) So the struggle between father and son continued. With passing years, however, Mao Tse-tung became more and more skillful, attacking and feinting and quietly sabotaging, while the old man pored over his accounts or sat grumbling by the stove in winter and hurling maxims of Confucius at his unwilling listeners.[25] "I hated Confucius from the age of eight," Mao confided to a friend in later years. "There was a Confucian temple in the village, and I wanted nothing more than to burn it to the ground." [26]

In his detestation of Confucius, as with his rebellion against patriarchial authority, the boy did not stand alone, but was simply one individual in a rising tide of protest. China, under influence of Western technology and Western thought, was rapidly breaking loose from tradition and authority —and this meant the traditional family and the traditional philosophies quite as much as the authority of the state.[27]

The elder Mao mellowed somewhat as he grew older, and a kind of weariness and resignation seemed to settle over him. In time he even developed a concern for religion, and more and more frequently he could be seen bowing before the bronze Buddha, a gaunt old man destined to live out his remaining years in a rebellious household. In time, too, the son became less and less concerned with the father, who began somehow to merge, perhaps, with the image of a larger adversary—the ancient and outmoded social and political order.[28]

Page 9.

(6) At school young Mao read the Confucian *Analects* and the Four Classics. In those days the students were expected to commit long passages to memory, whether or not they had any notion of the meaning, and long hours were devoted to parrot-like recitation. Mao's teacher in Shao Shan

[24] *Ibid.,* p. 5.
[25] Payne, p. 27.
[26] *Ibid.,* p. 30.
[27] See Wen-han Kiang, *The Chinese Student Movement* (New York: King's Crown Press, 1948).
[28] Payne, p. 27.

was harsh, frequently beating his pupils,[29] and because of this the boy, at the age of ten, ran away from home.

Afraid to come back lest his father give him an additional beating, young Mao set out in the direction of the city, which he believed to be located in a valley nearby. According to the *Autobiography*, he wandered for three days before he was found by his family. Then he discovered that he had been circling about and, in all his travels, had never proceeded more than about three miles from his home.[30]

In school Mao Tse-tung became rather proficient in the Classics, but as Siao Shu-tung points out, it was the romances of Old China—and especially the stories of rebellion—that particularly interested the boy, and also books about the "new" China that was just beginning to emerge. In the farmhouse at night he used to cover his window, so that his father would not see the candle burning, and read long after he was supposed to be asleep. His favorites among the authors were old "reformist" scholars —men who believed that China's weakness emerged from her lack of Western railways, telephones, telegraphs and steamships, which they wanted introduced as a first step in developing the country.[31]

The first attempts at reform were made during the period 1862–1894 by a number of high-ranking officials—including Tseng Kuo-fan, Tso Tsung-t'ang, and Li Hung-chang—who still had confidence in the old political system and thought that the introduction of Western technology would suffice to restore China to a position of power and eminence. The inadequacy of this approach became painfully evident with the Sino-Japanese War of 1894–1895 and the ignominious Chinese defeat.

In the wake of the Sino-Japanese War a number of scholars—particularly K'ang Yu-wei and his disciple Liang Ch'i-ch'ao—began to argue that China, if it were to survive as a sovereign nation, must undertake a wide sweep of reforms in administration, industry, agriculture, education and other fundamental spheres of life.

Born in 1858, K'ang Yu-wei was educated in the traditional manner, but at the age of fifteen he revolted against writing an eight-legged essay in the classic form, and somewhat later he began to read about the outside world and the history and geography of modern nations. In 1894 he organized a study group called the Society for Studying How to Strengthen the Nation.[32] Among the young men who came under his influence was Liang Ch'i-ch-ao. Born in 1873, Liang became active in various groups that

---

[29] Emi Siao, p. 8.

[30] *Autobiography*, p. 4.

[31] *Ibid.*, p. 6.

[32] See Arthur W. Hummel, "K'ang Yu-wei," *Pacific Historical Review*, Vol. IV, No. 4 (December, 1935), p. 345.

were interested in Western ways, and in 1895 he started a daily paper in order to discuss democratic ideas and argue for a constitution.[33]

K'ang and Liang advocated the gradual establishment of a constitutional monarchy which would provide a sufficiently modified structure for the carrying out of necessary reforms. Many younger officials in the Empire sympathized with the suggested changes—though some of them were less enthusiastic when they perceived that the reforms could not be achieved without cost to the privileges of the official and scholarly elites.

In 1898 the young Emperor, Kuang-hsü, was introduced to K'ang Yu-wei by his imperial tutor, and it was from this meeting that the so-called Hundred Days of Reform emerged. Deeply impressed by K'ang Yu-wei, the Emperor came under the scholar's dominance, and the two of them embarked upon an extensive program of reform. During that summer a whole series of edicts were issued to abolish time-honored sinecures, to reorganize the military forces, to alter the educational and examination systems, and to make other changes that were long overdue.[34]

Serious opposition to the reforms began to appear almost immediately, and in time the Empress Dowager, Tz'u-hsi, who had supposedly "retired" to the Summer Palace, began to intervene actively. The young Emperor was persuaded to move against Tz'u-hsi, and Yüan Shih-k'ai, former Chinese Resident in Seoul and later President of the Chinese Republic, was brought into conference with the reformers on the mistaken assumption that he was sympathetic. Instructed to put himself in command of troops at Tientsin, march on the Summer Palace and seize the Empress Dowager, he united his forces, instead, with those of a relative and devoted supporter of Tz'u-hsi and proceeded, under her orders, to seize the young Emperor, who was then kept in confinement until his death ten years later. This action put an end to the Hundred Days of Reform.

The reform movement had emerged as a reaction against the inability of a decaying order to deal effectively with rapidly changing conditions of domestic life and the active intrusion of foreign powers. When the conservatives came back into control, they had only one solution to offer—the restoration of isolationism and the traditionalism of the old order. Under these circumstances, it is not surprising, perhaps, that they tried to divert attention from their own shortcomings and impotency by encouraging antiforeignism.

During 1899 there were antiforeign outbreaks in nearly all parts of the country, and in most instances the incidents took an anti-Christian as well

[33] See Ralph Levenson, *Liang Chi-chao and the Mind of Modern China* (Cambridge: Harvard University Press, 1953).

[34] For a detailed English-language account of the Hundred Days, see M. E. Cameron, *The Reform Movement in China, 1898–1912* (Stanford: Stanford University Press, 1931).

as an anti-Western course. Indeed, many of the initial hostilities were directed against Chinese Christians rather than against foreigners. Of the various organized groups responsible for these hostilities, the most notorious was the "Society of Harmonious Fists," or Boxers, which had strong support from the Court in Peking and from many officials in the provinces.

As the Boxers achieved more and more control in Peking, the foreign legations found themselves in what amounted to a state of siege, and attempts were made by the respective powers to send more troops into the capital for the protection of their nationals. The siege lasted from June to August, when an allied expeditionary force finally came to the relief of the foreigners. Boxerism then collapsed, and China was forced to accept an indemnity charge secured on her Maritime Customs and certain domestic taxes; the punishment of some of her officials; the permanent quartering of foreign troops in Peking as legation guards; and various other obligations.

It was against this background that the Empire was forced into a program of educational reform. Beginning in 1901, the old system of examination was abolished, the provincial schools for older students were changed into colleges, the prefectural schools were transformed into middle schools, and the county schools became primary schools. With fond hopes and driving aspirations students poured into the schools from all parts of the country. In 1905 there were only about one hundred thousand students in modern schools; by 1911 the number had increased to more than two million; ten years later there were six million. In these schools, moreover, they came under the influence of teachers who had studied abroad—and had brought with them a whole spectrum of new ideas from the West.[35]

Page 9.

(7) In spite of certain moves made toward reorganizing some aspects of government administration, modifying the civil service examinations, and establishing a modern educational system, the despotic nature of the Empire was not altered, and many urgent reforms were further delayed until after the Russo-Japanese War of 1904–1905.[36]

Many Chinese were coming to believe that the chief explanation for Japan's success against Tsarist Russia lay in the new governmental efficiency which became evident under the newly adopted Japanese constitution. More and more Chinese students were attracted to Japan for study, and in June, 1905, the Imperial Government sent five high-ranking officials abroad to study constitutional government and see how it functioned

[35] Tsi C. Wang, The Youth Movement in China (New York: New Republic Inc., 1927), pp. 91–92.

[36] For an English text of the Imperial edict proclaiming reforms, see J. O. P. Bland and E. Backhouse, China under the Empress Dowager (Philadelphia: J. P. Lippincott Co., 1910), pp. 419–424.

in other nations. On their return the regime proclaimed its intention of establishing a constitutional government, and a number of preparatory measures were subsequently undertaken.[37]

In 1908 the Imperial Government promulgated the proposed "Principles of Constitution" and a "Nine Year Program (1908–17) of Preparation" which projected the year-by-year accomplishment of reforms in administration, taxation, auditing, budget formulation, the development of educational facilities, the introduction of local self-government and so forth.[38] On October 3, 1910, a National Assembly convened for the first time, and this body, together with various provincial assemblies, was able to prevail upon the Imperial Government to promise the convening of a Parliament as early as 1913. On May 8, 1911, the formation of a cabinet was announced, but the new body was dominated by the Manchu Court, and the National Assembly had no control over it. Under these circumstances, it was inevitable that those who looked for substantial reforms were further frustrated.

Page 10.

(8) In the days of Mao Tse-tung's boyhood very little news reached communities like Shao Shan except by word of mouth. Imperial rescripts were posted from time to time and read aloud by the schoolmaster, but these usually dealt with taxes, the conscription of soldiers from among the people, and the celebration of special events such as the Empress Dowager's birthday.[39]

On October 10, 1904—when Mao was eleven years old—the Empress Dowager's birthday was celebrated in the usual fashion. Incense was burned, local dignitaries made the usual speeches. But Mao, playing outside the little school in Shao Shan along with the other children, noticed a number of bean merchants returning early along the road from Changsha.[40] On the same days columns of soldiers began moving through the countryside on the way to the city,[41] and rumor had it that there had been an uprising. A delegation of starving people had approached the civil governor in Changsha, according to report, and had begged relief from famine that was sweeping the land. "Why haven't you any food?" the governor was said to have asked. "There is plenty in the city. I always have enough." [42]

Anger flared up, and there was a mass demonstration. Then word came to Shao Shan that Huang Hsing, a young Hunanese revolutionary, had

---

[37] *China Year Book*, 1912, p. 353.
[38] For English versions, see *Ibid.*, pp. 359–61.
[39] Payne, p. 28.
[40] *Autobiography*, p. 8.
[41] Payne, p. 28.
[42] *Autobiography*, p. 8.

attacked the yamen, or governor's residence, in Changsha with a band of peasant guerrillas.

A returned student from Japan, Huang Hsing had taken a teaching post in Hunan and then, in his off-duty hours, he had organized a secret society and a Japanese language school, which was used as a center for revolutionary propaganda. Revolution was in the air, and tens of thousands of Hunanese joined the group. A rebellion was then organized for October 10, 1904—the sixtieth birthday of the Empress Dowager. The plan was to capture Changsha and destroy the whole Provincialdom.[43]

According to word reaching Mao and his schoolmates in Shao Shan, the young revolutionary leader had succeeded in fighting his way into the yamen, only to be captured and thrown into a dungeon. Then, by some incredible subterfuge, he had managed to escape in disguise, and the city was thrown into an uproar. Martial law was proclaimed in Changsha, and soldiers began a systematic search of the villages nearby.[44]

The officials lost track of Huang Hsing, but in subsequent years he was to turn up again and again. Having escaped down the Siang River, he went to Hong Kong and thence to Japan, where he worked out a new set of plans. Some months later, in February, 1905, he proceeded up the river again by boat with forty-three rifles and some ammunition. Trouble started as soon as customs officials boarded his boat, and he fled once more to Japan. In ensuing years Huang Hsing, with help from Sun Yat-sen and the T'ung Meng Hui, or forerunner of the Kuomintang, undertook further rebellions in Hunan and later in southwest Kwangtung along the Indo-Chinese border.

According to Robert Payne's account, young Mao was not much impressed by Huang Hsing's first insurrection. At this time he still had much of the peasant's "contempt for disorder," and his loyalty to the monarch remained unshaken.[45] The *Autobiography* maintains, on the other hand, that it was the Changsha revolt which first stirred the boy's political consciousness. About that time, according to the *Autobiography*, he came upon a pamphlet which made a deep impression on him. Opening with the sentence, "Alas, China will be subjugated," this pamphlet described Japan's occupation of Korea and Formosa and of China's loss of sovereignty over Indo-China, Burma and elsewhere. Mao felt depressed by what he had read, and he began to feel that it was the duty of all Chinese people to help save their country.[46]

[43] Hsueh Chun-tu, "Huang Hsing and the Chinese Revolution," a Doctoral Dissertation Submitted to and Accepted by the Faculty of Political Science, Columbia University, 1958, pp. 24–37.

[44] *Autobiography*, p. 8.

[45] Payne, p. 28.

[46] *Autobiography*, p. 9.

Shortly after the Changsha uprising a conflict arose in Shao Shan between members of the Ke Lao Hui, a peasant secret society, and a local landlord who brought the dispute to court. Since he was a powerful man in the countryside, the landlord was able to secure a favorable decision, whereupon the Ke Lao Hui members, rather than submit, struck out against him and against the officials. Withdrawing to a nearby mountain called Liu Shan, they fortified themselves against attack. The landlord, according to Mao Tse-tung, spread the story that they had sacrificed a child when they raised their banner of revolt. The authorities dispatched troops against them, and the leader was subsequently beheaded. Mao remembers, however, that among the students this man became a hero.[47]

There were more troubles and more famine in the countryside. Both the poverty of the people and spirit of insurrection among many of them were unmistakable. A group of peasants again assaulted the yamen, and several of their leaders were executed. The whole province of Hunan was in ferment.

The effect on Mao this time was profound. How could innocent peasants be executed—officially and in broad daylight—by a monarchy which was supposed to have the interests of the people at heart? Discussing these things with other students in the small school, Mao found his belief in the monarch and his faith in Buddhism deeply shaken. He grew increasingly uneasy about his own family's comparative wealth, and even his delight in learning was somewhat subdued. What could he believe in now?[48]

Page 11.

(9) Mao's father, according to the *Autobiography*, had decided to apprentice his son to the proprietor of a rice shop, but the boy had heard about a "modern" school in Siangsiang where his mother's family lived. A cousin, who was studying there, had told about the "radical" methods which put less emphasis upon the classics and more on the "new knowledge" of the West.[49]

At first Mao Jen-sheng forbade his son to go, but the boy rebelled and reminded the old man that it was wholly proper for a young Chinese to emulate Confucius. A young scholar could find service in the Imperial Government and even reach high office, perhaps, and bring fame to his parents and to the village.[50]

---

[47] *Autobiography*, p. 12.
[48] Payne, p. 29.
[49] *Autobiography*, pp. 9–10.
[50] Payne, p. 33.

Page 12.

(10) So the boy set out on foot, a bundle of clothes and other odds and ends on his back, and made his way toward Siangsiang,[51] which lay some fifteen miles up river from Shao Shan.

Page 18.

(11) Leaving the city of Siangsiang, one passes through the Wangchun Gate and goes on down a stone terrace toward a river, the Lien Shui, where ferryboats are busy carrying people across. On the far bank one proceeds along a gravel path to a woody hill. Not far from the foot of the hill—and surrounded by a high, circular brick wall with thick, black-lacquered double doors—stands a neat and comfortable-looking house known formerly as the Tungshan Academy and later re-named the Tungshan High Primary School.[52]

Page 23.

(12) Mao Tse-tung was sixteen years old when he registered at the school. Having heard that the place was open only to local residents, he claimed at first—according to Emi Siao's account—to be a native of Siangsiang, but it turned out that admission was open to all, and so he was admitted as a Siangtan boy. He paid 1,400 coppers for five months' board, lodging and all the material needed for study, and in due course he was registered along with a maternal cousin named Wen, who had been admitted the previous year.[53]

Page 24.

(13) Both students and teachers began to notice Mao Tse-tung within a few days after his arrival. Many of his schoolmates, belonging to landlord families, were richly dressed in long gowns and dark jackets over colorful waistbands.[54] Many of them wore leather-soled brocade shoes to match. Mao, on the other hand, had only one suit of clothes—trousers and a jacket of blue cloth, homespun and exceedingly plain. He was a slender boy with friendly eyes and intelligent face. His accent betrayed the fact that he was not from Siangsiang.[55]

Until that time, Mao had never seen so many children together in one place. "Many of the richer students despised me because of my ragged suit and trousers," Mao told Edgar Snow many years later. "However, among

[51] Emi Siao, pp. 17–18.
[52] Emi Siao, p. 18.
[53] *Autobiography*, p. 10.
[54] Emi Siao, pp. 18–19. According to the *Autobiography*, p. 10, only the teachers wore gowns.
[55] Emi Siao, p. 19.

them I had friends, and two especially were my good comrades. One of these is now a writer living in the Soviet Union." [56]

The friend who later lived in the Soviet Union was Siao Chu-chang (often written Tzu-chang) sometimes called Siao San, the son of a well-to-do farmer in Siangsiang and the brother of Siao-yu whose school name was Siao Shu-tung. Two years younger than Mao, the boy was elegant and delicately boned with high forehead and slender, expressive hands. In subsequent years, as the translator of Chinese poetry into Russian, he became famous in the Soviet Union as Emi Siao. [57]

In the school, Mao recalled later, it was very important to be a native of Siangsiang. Indeed, it was important to come from a certain district in Siangsiang. "There were upper, lower and middle districts," according to Mao, "and the lower and upper were continually fighting on a regional basis. Neither could become reconciled to the existence of the other." [58] In retrospect, Mao considered that he "took a neutral position in this war," and consequently all factions despised him. "I felt spiritually very depressed," he told Edgar Snow in the *Autobiography*.

It appears that some of his experiences, at least, were not unpleasant. "In the evening," according to Emi Siao, "the cone-shaped Tungtaishan and a white, tapering, seven-storied pagoda were shimmeringly reflected in the round pond near the school. There, newcomer Mao Tse-tung would frequently loiter with his young friends. Leaning against the stone balustrade

---

[56] *Autobiography*, p. 10.

[57] Payne, p. 34. One of the problems which confronts historians is the multiplicity of names by which a Chinese, particularly a person of importance, may be known. He may acquire four or five names in a lifetime and two after death. A child is called by his "milk" name until he enters school, when he receives a school or "book" name which is analogous to what we in the West term "Christian" name. According to Han Yu-shan (see *Elements of Chinese Historiography*, Hollywood, California: W. M. Hawley, 1955, pp. 13–16) a courtesy name (tzu) is given at the time of a capping ceremony when a man reaches age twenty. "This name is often a literary, ethical, geographical, historical, or philosophical derivative of his book name. A second courtesy name, used as commonly as the first, is given by a friend or chosen by the person himself." Siao-yu, the author, had the school name of Shu-tung and his second name was Tzu-cheng. Siao-yu says of his brother: "Emil Siao, whom Mao knew in boyhood days was Siao Chih-fan, second name Tzu-chang. (My second name is Tzu-cheng.) Our father gave us these names which have a profound signification. Emil Siao used his name Chih-fan at the First Normal School and later in France. Then Siao Tzu-chang became more known than Siao Chih-fan, for he signed very often with his second name. That is to say that Siao Tzu-chang eventually became his official name. Siao San (Siao-the-Third) was originally his pseudonym, which he used when he wrote some articles in Chinese and did not wish to sign his true name. For articles in other lands he used the pseudonym Emil Siao." Emi is a corrupted form of Emil which the Communist writer chose out of admiration for Jean Jacques Rousseau's *Emil*.

[58] *Autobiography*, p. 10.

of the bridge, they would talk and look at the fish darting to and fro in the water. A little further off, on the playground, students were swinging, doing gymnastics, running, laughing. . . ." [59]

Page 26.

(14) Yet Mao seems to have done well at the Tungshan School. Most of the teachers liked him, and he was known for writing good essays in the classical manner.[60] But his mind was not on the classics. Day by day he continued his life-long habit of doing his own reading on the side, and although Chinese history—especially the history of rebellions—was his favorite field, he also dipped into the history and geography of foreign countries.[61] He was particularly impressed by two books presented to him by his cousin Wen[62]—one on Kang Yu-wei's Reform Movement of 1898, and the other was a bound volume of the New People's Miscellany edited by Liang Ch'i-ch'ao. These two books Mao read again and again,[63] and he was very grateful to his cousin, whom he then "thought very progressive, but who later became a counter-revolutionary, a member of the gentry, and joined the reactionaries in the period of the Great Revolution of 1925–27." [64]

By this time much of China was in political and social ferment. In recent years the war with Japan (1894–1895), then the Boxer Uprising (1900) and finally the Russo-Japanese War had stirred much of the nation. China, of course, had been deeply humiliated by her own military defeats, but this sense of humiliation had encouraged in the country a genuine admiration for Japan and a widespread determination on the part of young Chinese to follow the Japanese example in adopting ways of the West. What Japan could do, China could also do, and it was in this spirit that more and more young Chinese began going both to Japan, as well as to the West, for study.[65]

One of the teachers at the Tungshan School was a returned student from Japan who wore a false queue now that he was back once more in his own country.[66] Mao, according to Emi Siao, had already cut off his queue as a protest against the monarchy. Indeed, he had been among the first at Tungshan to do it. "He and another student who had done the same thing

[59] Emi Siao, p. 18.
[60] Autobiography, p. 11.
[61] Emi Siao, p. 19.
[62] Autobiography, p. 11.
[63] Emi Siao, p. 20.
[64] Autobiography, p. 11.
[65] See Tsi C. Wang, The Youth Movement in China (New York: New Republic, Inc., 1927), and Wen-han Kiang, The Chinese Student Movement (New York: King's Crown Press, 1948), especially p. 16.
[66] Autobiography, p. 10.

began to work on others," Emi Siao records, "and clipped off the queues of more than ten people who had previously entered into a 'queue-clipping pact' with them but lost courage at the last moment." [67]

It is no wonder then that Mao had only contempt for the teacher who wore a false queue. "It was quite easy to tell that the queue was false," Mao remembered later. "Everyone laughed at him and called him a False Foreign Devil." [68]

The Emperor Kuang Hsü and the Empress Dowager Tz'u-hsi both died in 1908. The Emperor's death was of no particular significance, but the Empress Dowager, who had ruled China since 1860, was a remarkable woman, and now there was no one to take her place. Prince Ch'un, who was named Regent, was a man of good intentions, but he possessed neither the knowledge nor the strength to save a rapidly disintegrating state. The only strong man left to the Manchus was Yüan Shik-k'ai, and he was in retirement. Because of his participation in the coup d'etat of 1898, Yüan had won the enmity of Kuang Hsü and the hostility of influential members of the Court. The Emperor, on his death bed, had demanded Yüan's life, and although Prince Ch'un had no intention of carrying out the order, he did not feel free, either, to make use of the man's undeniable talents.

It was at the Tungshan School that Mao heard for the first time that the Emperor and the Empress Dowager were both dead—although the new Emperor had already been ruling for some time. In the *Autobiography* Mao himself maintains that he was still not yet an "anti-monarchist"[69]— however much he may have been moved by poverty, famine and disorder in Hunan. "I considered the Emperor and most officials," he told Edgar Snow, "to be honest men, good and clever. They only needed the help of K'ang Yu-wei's reforms." Emi Siao recalls, however, that the schoolmaster used to give a little talk each morning when the students had gathered for roll-call. On these occasions he would speak of China's decline and of her "being bullied" by foreign powers, and many of the students were fired with indignation.[70]

In the course of his reading at Tungshan Mao began forming his early images of the West. Emi Siao tells one story this way:

"One evening when the children were through playing and were crowding into the study room at the sound of the bell, Mao Tse-tung found himself in the company of another boy as he made his way towards the second gate of the school. The boy was holding a book in his hand.

" 'What do you have there?' asked Mao Tse-tung gently.

" '*Heroes and Great Men of the World.*'

[67] Emi Siao, p. 25.
[68] *Autobiography*, p. 10.
[69] *Ibid.*, p. 11.
[70] Emi Siao, p. 19.

" 'May I have a look?'

"A few days later, Mao Tse-tung returned the book. His manners were apologetic. 'Forgive me for smearing your book.'

"The curious student opened the book and found many passages marked out with circles and dots. The most heavily marked were the biographies of Washington, Napoleon, Peter the Great, Catherine the Great, Wellington, Gladstone, Rousseau, Montesquieu and Lincoln." [71]

The owner of the book, apparently, was Emi Siao. Later Mao told him, "We need more great people like these. We ought to study them and find out how to make China rich and strong and so avoid becoming like Annam, Korea and India. . . ." [72]

Mao himself, in later years, had a similar recollection. "I had first heard of America," he told Edgar Snow, "in an article which told of the American revolution and contained a sentence like this, 'After eight years of difficult war, Washington won a victory and built up his nation.' In a book called *Great Heroes of the World* I read also of Napoleon, Catherine of Russia, Peter the Great, Wellington, Gladstone, Rousseau, Montesquieu and Lincoln." [73]

Page 26.

(15) Mao stayed at the Tungshan school about a year, according to Emi Siao, when a strong desire to travel seized him.[74] "I began to long to go to Changsha," Mao told Edgar Snow, "the great city, the capital of the province, which was 120 *li* (about 40 miles) from my home." [75] The city was known to contain many people, numerous schools and the yamen of the governor. From one of his teachers Mao obtained a letter of introduction.[76] Then he and Emi Siao headed for a senior primary school in Siangtan but, because of Mao's height, the principal there rejected him. So the two of them took a crowded little Siang River steamer third class to Changsha where there was a secondary school for children of Siangsiang. Mao was "speechless with excitement on seeing the city bustling with activity and immense crowds thronging the streets. For a while he was haunted by the fear that he might not be allowed to enter the Provincial Siangsiang Secondary School of which he had a high opinion. . . ." [77]

In the *Autobiography* Mao said nothing about his ill fortune in Siang-

[71] *Ibid.*, p. 205. In view of the similarities in text, it seems probable that Mr. Siao refreshed his recollections from the *Autobiography* here.

[72] Payne, p. 36.

[73] *Autobiography*, p. 12.

[74] Emi Siao, p. 22.

[75] *Autobiography*, p. 12.

[76] *Ibid.*, p. 12.

[77] Emi Siao, p. 22.

tan, but records merely that he "walked to Changsha, exceedingly excited, half fearing that I would be refused entrance, hardly daring to hope that I could actually become a student in this great school. To my astonishment, I was admitted without difficulty. But political events were moving rapidly, and I was to remain there only half a year." [78]

This was 1911, the year of the Great Revolution that overthrew the Manchu Empire.

In Changsha young Mao saw a newspaper for the first time. Called *People's Strength*, it was financed by Sun Yat-sen's revolutionary organization, the T'ung Meng Hui. Mao was deeply stirred by one article about seventy-two martyrs who had sacrificed themselves in an armed revolt in Canton against the Manchus. At the same time, he read the political platform put forward by Sun Yat-sen, and he was so impressed that he wrote an article himself and posted it on the school bulletin board. He proposed that Sun Yat-sen be called back from Japan to become President of a new government and that K'ang Yu-wei be made Prime Minister and Liang Ch'i-ch'ao be appointed Foreign Minister. "Needless to say," wrote Emi Siao in later years, "he had at that stage not grasped the difference between Sun Yat-sen's views and those of K'ang and Liang, but he did have a distinct feeling that all those who worked for the Reform and the Revolution should unite together in combatting the cowardly and despotic Manchu regime." [79]

In 1905 Sun Yat-sen had organized his followers into the T'ung Meng Hui, or Alliance Society, which became the forerunner of the Kuomintang. The organization promised to "oust the Manchus, regenerate China, establish a republic, and equalize land ownership." Members of the organization were recruits, for the most part, from Chinese living overseas, from students studying abroad, and from various secret societies which had existed for a long time—especially south of the Yangtze. Among the members drawn from secret societies there were few who had any clear notion of republicanism or democracy. Their interest in the revolution was largely anti-dynastic—or, more specifically, anti-Manchu—and in subsequent years Sun Yat-sen found it increasingly difficult to win their support for the sort of program he himself had in mind. [80]

By tradition, the province of Hunan had always been the scene of fierce struggles between the old and the new, and now, on the eve of the 1911 Revolution, Mao Tse-tung found himself in the center of political and social ferment. DRIVE OUT THE MANCHUS . . . SET CHINA

---

[78] *Autobiography*, p. 12.

[79] *Ibid.*, pp. 12–13; Emi Siao, p. 23.

[80] Franklin W. Houn, *Central Government in China, 1912–1928* (Madison: The University of Wisconsin Press, 1957), p. 8.

FREE . . . ESTABLISH A REPUBLIC . . . EQUALITY IN LAND
RIGHTS—these were only a few of the slogans that swept the countryside.

Much of the ferment arose in the army.

Until after her defeat in the Sino-Japanese War of 1894–95, China had
possessed no army in the modern sense. Reforms were attempted in 1895
and again in 1901, but it was not until Yüan Shih-k'ai began organizing
the New Model Army between 1903 and 1906 that real progress was made.
Four of Yüan Shih-k'ai's original six divisions were placed under a new
Ministry of War in 1906, and a plan was developed for the training of a
National Army of thirty-six divisions, which were to be ready by 1912.

By 1911 the various revolutionary movements had made considerable
headway in propagandizing and infiltrating the New Model Army stationed in southern China—especially in Wuchang, Hankow and Nanking.
Therefore, when groups of local gentry in Szechwan Province began op-
posing the Peking Government's railway nationalization program, revolutionary groups in Hankow and Wuchang felt strong enough to start a
revolt. On October 9, 1911, a bomb explosion in the Hankow headquarters
of a local revolutionary group led to an investigation and the execution of
several plotters. On the following day their fellow revolutionists among
New Model Army troops in Wuchang—just across the Yangtze—raised
the banner of revolt and forced their commander to assume leadership.
Within the next two days rebel forces had seized control of Wuchang,
Hankow and Hanyang.

The revolution spread to other parts of China, and when Nanking fell
into rebel hands, it was decided to proclaim that city as the seat of a new
Provisional Government. Sun Yat-sen, who had been in Denver, Colorado,
when the Wuchang Revolution broke out, returned to China at this junc-
ture, and on December 29, 1911, he was elected Provisional President.
Huang Hsing and eight other revolutionaries were then appointed heads
of departments by the new President, and the Provisional Government of
the Republic was duly proclaimed.

In Changsha on October 10, 1911, the atmosphere was tense. The governor of Hunan had proclaimed martial law, but the revolutionaries continued their secret activities inside the city walls—and without. Some gave
pro-Han, anti-Manchu lectures in the schools, and others worked on army
units stationed outside the city, inciting the men to mutiny.

Page 27.

(16) One day a revolutionary came to the school where Mao was a
student and, with the permission of the principal, made a speech which
fired the whole audience with excitement and fervor. A number of students
bitterly denounced the Manchus and called for the establishment of a

republic. Mao Tse-tung, deeply stirred by the speech, decided to join the revolution.[81]

After some days' reflection, Mao made up his mind to enlist in the Revolutionary Army under the command of Li Yüan-hung, who was governor of Hupeh. Borrowing money to travel from fellow-students, Mao and several friends set out for Hankow. Since they had heard that the streets were wet there, someone suggested that they should wear oilskin shoes. Mao Tse-tung remembered that he had a peasant friend who possessed a pair of such oilskin shoes. His friend, who came from the same village as he himself, was then a soldier in the New Model Army encamped outside the walls of Changsha. He called on him but was stopped by garrison sentries.[82]

There were new elements of excitement and suspense in the air. Members of the T'ung Meng Hui and other insurrectionists had already infiltrated units of the New Army stationed outside the city, and soon the 29th and 50th Brigades joined the revolution. As Mao arrived at the encampment, the two brigades had just received their ammunition and were preparing to march into Changsha.

"It was a Sunday morning," Emi Siao recorded many years later. "The New Army marched from their review ground outside the city towards one of the gates of Changsha. After firing a series of volleys, they sent one unit to take the arsenal at the 'Lotus Pond,' while the main body of troops entered the city through the gate and made its way directly towards the Governor's House. The guards did not put up any resistance, and the Governor was forced to surrender. A huge white flag was hoisted atop the Governor's House. Soon white flags of various sizes appeared over all the schools, offices and shops. By the time Mao Tse-tung returned to school, a white flag had already been hung over the gates, with a few soldiers on guard outside. Hunan declared itself independent of the Manchu government." [83]

News came in the afternoon that two members of the Ke Lao Hui of Hunan had been elected Governor and Vice Governor of the Province. "It was a cloudy day," Emi Siao recalled subsequently, "and people felt nervous and tense. But soon everybody brightened up—who had expected the revolution to 'come through' so easily?" [84]

The Governor and Vice Governor did not last long, according to Mao, who saw their corpses lying in the street a few days later.[85]

---

[81] *Autobiography*, p. 13; Emi Siao, p. 26.
[82] *Autobiography*, p. 14; Emi Siao, p. 26.
[83] Emi Siao, p. 27.
[84] *Loc. cit.*
[85] *Autobiography*, p. 15.

The Manchu regime had not been overthrown, and the war continued. Changsha buzzed with excitement and activity. Revolutionary leaders proposed to dispatch troops in support of Wuchang and to recruit new soldiers. A number of enthusiastic youngsters began to form a student army, but Mao was not much interested in it. According to Emi Siao, this was the way he reasoned it out: for a revolution to succeed, fighting was necessary and the best way to serve the revolution was to become a soldier —a soldier in the regular army.[86]

A student army had been organized to Changsha, and many of Mao's classmates were joining it. But Mao himself considered the student army "too confused" and decided to join the regular army instead—"to help complete the revolution." [87]

Page 27.

(17) Mao Tse-tung, now eighteen years old, had grown tall, and his height, which had been a liability when the principal of the Siangtan senior primary school turned him down, now proved to be an advantage. The army wanted tall men and he was accepted. Emi Siao records that "The company to which he belonged was quartered inside the Court of Justice which had not yet begun operating. Besides regular training, these new soldiers had to do all sorts of curious minor duties. They had to carry bed-boards, bedding, clothes-baskets, and other things for their officers when they moved to new quarters. On top of all this, some of them had to make daily journeys to the White Sand Well outside the city to fetch water for the mess as well as for the officers' tea." [88]

Mao's pay amounted to seven dollars a month—a small sum by Western standards, but "more than I get in the Red Army now," Mao told Edgar Snow in 1936.[89]

Most of the soldiers spent their money as soon as they had received it, eating, drinking and otherwise amusing themselves. Mao, on the other hand, was careful with what he earned. Each month he spent two dollars for food and a small amount for water—since he bought water from professional carriers rather than going to the White Sand Well himself. Newspaper subscriptions were his single luxury, and careful reading of the news became a lifetime habit. "He would read through all the four pages of an edition without skipping a word," Emi Siao recorded. "The variety of material contained in the newspapers especially delighted him—news items, commentaries on current affairs, miscellaneous articles and what not. He acquired quite a bit of useful knowledge through newspaper reading.

[86] Emi Siao, p. 28.
[87] *Autobiography*, p. 15.
[88] Emi Siao, p. 28.
[89] *Autobiography*, p. 15.

Most important of all, it led him to apply himself to the study of current affairs and social problems." [90]

During these days, Emi Siao recalls, Mao came upon an article about socialism, and somewhat later on he found some pamphlets on the same subject. These materials were sketchy and poorly written, according to Emi Siao, but still, "to Mao Tse-tung, with a sharp sense for what was new and his courage to stand by what he thought was the truth, they were a source of joy and inspiration. He immediately started discussing Socialism with other soldiers, holding it to be the best theory so far advanced for the salvation of the world and mankind." [91] He even wrote to some of his old friends at Tungshan and told them about the principles of Socialism.

Among the men in Mao's squad were a Hunan miner and an ironsmith, whom he liked, but the others he considered mediocre and, he recalled later, as rascals. "I persuaded two more students to join the army," Mao told Edgar Snow, "and became on friendly terms with the platoon commander and most of the soldiers. I could write, I knew something about books, and they respected my 'Great Learning.' I could help by writing letters for them or in other such ways." [92]

The momentary successes of the Revolution convinced students throughout much of China that their wildest expectations had come to pass. Excitement spread like fever through their ranks. They cut off their queues. They tore down the dragon flags of the old regime and ran up new banners in five colors representing "Benevolence, Righteousness, Harmony, Wisdom and Truth." They poised themselves—alert and ready for whatever might come next.

What came next was confusion . . . chaos.[93]

As the revolution proceeded, Yüan Shih-k'ai commanded Imperial forces —but attempted at the same time to maintain negotiations with the rebels, who were beginning to run short of funds. Toward the middle of January Sun Yat-sen, apparently on his own initiative, wired Yüan Shih-k'ai an offer of the Presidency if he would accept the Republic and persuade the Manchu Government to abdicate. Settlement terms were reached on February 12, 1912, the dynasty abdicated, power was transferred to Yüan Shih-k'ai, and Sun Yat-sen, resigning from the Presidency, himself advised the Nanking Assembly to elect the former Imperial general as provisional President of the Republic of China.

So it was that the first phase of the Chinese Revolution came to its somewhat anticlimactic finish.

[90] Emi Siao, p. 29.
[91] *Ibid.*, p. 30.
[92] *Autobiography*, p. 15.
[93] Wang, pp. 95–96.

On achieving the Presidency, Yüan Shih-k'ai tried to restore law and order, but he did not have at his disposal sufficient strength to disband the various nearly independent bodies of troops that had sprung up—nor the funds to buy them off. In order to bring these bands under some sort of control, therefore, Yüan legalized the positions of various commanders by giving them the official rank of Governor in the respective provinces. From this point on the warlords and Military Governors became powers to be reckoned with in the unstable circumstances of twentieth-century China.

In the meantime, Yüan Shih-k'ai used the Presidency to strengthen his personal position while plotting to restore the monarchy with himself as emperor. In late 1913, with the concurrence of his Cabinet, he ordered the dissolution of Sun Yat-sen's party on the grounds that it was a seditious organization, and this, for all practical purposes, brought an end to the new parliamentary government. Yüan's death on June 6, 1916 put a finish to his ambitions, but released a monotonous series of struggles for power on the part of various warlord factions.

Sun Yat-sen had been appealing to European countries and to the United States for support, but it soon became clear that aid was not likely to be made available in either quarter. He and his followers, reorganized as the Kuomintang, or Nationalist Party, made a number of abortive attempts against the ever-changing coalitions of warlords in Peking, but Sun Yat-sen had few funds and no troops that could be counted upon. As time went on, the procession of military men who gained and lost and regained power in Peking began to resemble a game of musical chairs.

It is small wonder that students and intellectuals in China became more and more disillusioned with events as they unfolded.

With the Chinese Revolution of 1911, indeed, a new kind of young scholar began to achieve prominence in the country. Inspired by "modern" schools and ideas from the West, these youngsters became the driving force of various new reform movements. They led attacks against almost every aspect of the old order—against Confucianism, the patriarchal family, ancestor worship, the old father-son relationship, the traditional role of women, and countless other aspects of the old society.[94]

"Our Chinese family is the source of all evils," one young man wrote. ". . . Political revolution is of no use; it is a failure! . . . The fundamental way to attack the evils in society is to begin with the 'family revolution.' "[95]

As leaders of the various movements suffered further disillusionment with the post-revolutionary government, they turned their attention more and more to the students with the hope of rebuilding the nation through

[94] *Ibid.*, pp. 91, 103–104.
[95] *Ibid.*, p. 104.

them. The National University of Peking became the center of this effort.

Organized after the Sino-Japanese War, the university had become a training school for officials, but during the next two or three decades it became even more famous as the birthplace of revolutionary movements. Members of its faculty were returned-students from the greatest universities of the world, and to their classrooms they brought ideas which they had absorbed in France and England and America.[96]

The whole of China seemed to be caught up in a renaissance which Hu Shih described as a new attitude—an attitude of criticism against the past. All the gnawing questions which had been raised since the turn of the century were asked again—bitter questions about the old customs, the inherited teachings, and all the most widely recognized beliefs and practices. In Nietzschean terms, it was a "transvaluation of values," and nothing was taken for granted. The ultimate purpose was to raze the old culture of China and rebuild it after the Western pattern.[97]

Page 31.

(18) After his brief experience in the army, Mao spent six months as a student in the First Middle School of Changsha, but the curriculum was limited, and he found the regulations objectionable. He decided that he could make better progress by reading and studying alone.[98]

While carrying on a program of independent study, Mao began to watch school advertisements in the newspapers. In those days the papers carried advertisements for all sorts of schools—law schools, business school, police academies, schools for soap-makers, and so forth. To be on the safe side, Mao paid application fees to five or six different institutions. The advertisement for the soap-making school was especially "attractive and inspiring." There was no tuition, board was free, and a small salary was provided. The advertisement described the great social benefits of soap-making and told how the country and its people could be enriched. Mao, who had been considering a police academy, now decided to become a soap-maker. In the end, however, he entered a business school—a provincial institution with good courses under respectable teachers.[99] As Mao sent in his application, he wrote also to his father, who was delighted, of course, to see his son embarking on a business career, and consented immediately.

It turned out, however, that the courses were conducted in English, and since Mao Tse-tung did not know the language well, he withdrew after a month's instruction.[100]

[96] *Ibid.*, p. 110.
[97] Kiang, p. 24–25.
[98] *Autobiography*, p. 17.
[99] *Ibid.*, p. 16.
[100] *Ibid.*, p. 17; Emi Siao, p. 35.

An old building on a small hill in Changsha had recently been converted into a provincial library—the first provincial library in Hunan. It had been opened to the public only a short time, and so far there were not many regular readers, but there was one whom the librarians had already come to count upon. Every day, as the library opened, a tall and plainly-dressed young man went in, found the book he wanted, sat down at a table in the reading room, and read almost without interruption until closing time.[101]

This faithful reader, of course, was Mao Tse-tung. "I was very regular and conscientious about it," he told Edgar Snow, "and the half year I spent in this way I consider to have been extremely valuable to me. I went to the library in the morning when it opened. At noon I paused only long enough to buy and consume two rice cakes, which were my daily lunch. I stayed in the library every day reading until it closed." [102]

During the course of this independent study Mao read Adam Smith's *Wealth of Nations,* Darwin's *Origin of Species,* and "a book on ethics by John Stuart Mill." He also read from the works of Rousseau, Montesquieu, Spencer, and Huxley. Beyond this, he "mixed poetry and romances and the tales of ancient Greece with a serious study of history and geography of Russia, America, England, France and other countries." [103]

Mao was fascinated by a huge map of the world which hung on the library wall, and he often stood studying it, oblivious to everything else.

He was living at this time in a guild house for natives of Siangsiang. Many of the other lodgers were disbanded soldiers who had neither work nor money. "Students and soldiers were always quarreling in the guild house," Mao recalls, "and one night this hostility between them broke out in physical violence. The soldiers attacked and tried to kill the students. I escaped by fleeing to the toilet, where I hid until the fight was over." [104]

Old Mao Jen-sheng was not pleased to find out that his son was neither studying regularly at school nor working at a job, and so he cut off the young man's allowance. Without any source of income, Mao saw his funds running low, and soon he found it impossible to meet his rent payments. He began searching the newspapers again, hoping to find a teaching job, perhaps, or some other means of support. Finally he came upon an encouraging advertisement:

First Normal School of Hunan
Tuition and Board Free
Educational Work after Graduation
Education Lays the Foundation of a Country, etc.

[101] Emi Siao, pp. 35–36.
[102] *Autobiography,* p. 18.
[103] *Loc. cit.*
[104] *Loc. cit.*

Mao Tse-tung was overjoyed: this seemed to be the answer. He took the school's entrance examination and was admitted forthwith.[105]

Page 32.

(19) While Mao Tse-tung was a student in the First Normal School (1912–1918), according to Emi Siao, he devoted much of his time to the natural sciences, but Mao himself insists that he did not like these courses, which were required, and that his marks in them were poor. "Most of all," he told Edgar Snow, "I hated a compulsory course in still-life drawing. I thought it extremely stupid. I used to think of the simplest subjects possible to draw, finish up quickly and leave the class." During one class he drew a simple oval and labeled it an egg. His final grade in the class was 40—an utter failure—but his marks in the social sciences were near the top, and in this fashion he was able to get by.[106]

Throughout his years at the Normal School Mao continued his practice of independent reading, and each day he paid particular attention to the newspapers. During the whole of this period, Mao recalls, he spent only $160—including his registration fees—and of this amount a third must have been spent on newspapers. Old Mao Jen-sheng cursed his son for this extravagance and complained about money wasted on paper.[107]

Emi Siao writes that Mao, after reading a newspaper through with great care, would snip off the blank margins and fasten them together. Then, on these long, slender strips he would note the geographical names he had found and, with help from a map, he would write them out in English. If a friend asked what he was up to, Mao would explain that he was practicing the writing of English. " 'Also, I want to memorize all the important cities, ports, oceans, rivers and mountains in the world. . . . I want to accumulate my general knowledge, as newspapers are a source of living history.' "[108]

Frequently Mao engrossed himself in a newspaper for hours. With a Chinese atlas on one side and a world atlas on the other, he made a point of looking up every place he found a reference to. "He has a retentive memory," Emi Siao records, "and if one brings up the name of a place now he can immediately tell in what province and in what *hsien* of China it is, or its precise location in a foreign country. . . . In making a special study of geography, he used the same methods with which he studied history—grasping the crux of the matter, collecting extensive data but never flying off on a tangent. . . . This tireless pursuit of knowledge characterized Mao Tse-tung from the very early days, and his painstaking meth-

---

[105] Emi Siao, p. 37.
[106] *Autobiography*, p. 19.
[107] *Ibid.*, p. 23.
[108] Emi Siao, p. 46.

ods of study and research eventually made him a man of immense erudition." [109]

Page 35.

(20) It was during his years at the First Normal School from 1912 to 1918 when he took his degree that Mao's political views began to take shape, and it was at this time, too, that he had his first experience with "social action."

There was a special study hall for the students, and often in the evening, when it was ablaze with lights, one could find Mao browsing there among the newspapers. World War I had broken out, and China was already beginning to feel the impact. In 1914 Japan took possession of German holdings in Kiaochow and Tsingtao, and in 1915 she sent the Twenty-one Demands, which China was forced to accept.[110]

"At this time," Mao recalls, "my mind was a curious mixture of ideas of liberalism, democratic reformism and Utopian Socialism. I had somewhat vague passions about 'nineteenth-century democracy,' Utopianism and old-fashioned liberalism, and I was definitely anti-militarist and anti-imperialist." [111]

Emi Siao remembers, however, that Mao could explain "in a clear and analytical manner" the situation facing both China and the world in general, which he knew "like the back of his hand." His fellow students listened to him as though to a formal weekly report on current military and political affairs. "He went into everything: how the Crown Prince of the Austrian-Hungarian Empire was assassinated at Sarajevo; how Kaiser Wilhelm II mobilized his army; how war was declared between Germany and Russia, between Germany and France, and between Germany and England; how a pitched battle was fought at Verdun; how Japan seized the opportunity to impose the Twenty-one Demands, designed to subjugate China, and so on and so forth." [112]

It was also during his years at the First Normal School that Mao's genius at organizing first began to be apparent. When others talked he listened, Emi Siao remembers, "with his head slightly inclined, often confining himself to monosyllabic answers like 'um' or 'yes.' Afterwards he would make an orderly analysis, pick out the important points and sum up the problem on hand, all with a minimum of words. His remarks were all to the point and always inspiring. People often came to him with problems. After a brief talk with him, things seemed to clear up and straighten themselves out marvellously." [113]

[109] *Ibid.*, pp. 46–47.
[110] Wang, p. 160.
[111] *Autobiography*, p. 22.
[112] Emi Siao, p. 45.
[113] *Ibid.*, p. 49.

Even in those days he had an ability to spot, encourage and develop other people's possibilities. "There are two kinds of people in the world," Mao told one of his school mates, "those who are good at individual things and those who are good at organization. There are more of the former than the latter. However, everyone has his strong points. He should be encouraged to develop and put to good use these strong points however limited they may be. . . ." He explained, "Even the lame, the dumb, the deaf and the blind could all come in useful for the revolutionary cause." [114]

In addition to his friends at the First Normal School, Mao began making contacts elsewhere. "Feeling expansive and the need for a few intimate companions," he told Edgar Snow, "I one day inserted an advertisement in a Changsha newspaper, inviting young men interested in patriotic work to make contact with me. I specified youths who were hardened and determined and ready to make sacrifices for their country. To the advertisement I received three and one-half replies. One was from Liu Chiang-lung, who later was to join the Communist Party and afterward to betray it. Two others were from young men who later were to become ultra-reactionaries. The 'half' reply came from a non-committal youth named Li Li-san. Li listened to all I had to say, and then went away without making any definite proposals himself, and our friendship never developed." [115]

Gradually, in this way Mao Tse-tung built a group of students which became the nucleus of a larger society. "It was a serious-minded little group of men," Mao recalls, "and they had no time to discuss trivialities. Everything they did or said must have a purpose. They had no time for love or 'romance' and considered the times too critical and the need for knowledge too urgent to discuss women or personal matters." [116] In later years Mao told Edgar Snow how, when he was visiting in the house of another young man, his host began to talk about the problem of buying some meat. "I was annoyed and did not see this fellow again. My friends and I preferred to talk only of large matters—the nature of men, of human society, of China, the world and the universe!" [117]

In those intense days, Mao told Edgar Snow, he was not even interested in women. "My parents had married me when I was fourteen to a girl of twenty, but I never lived with her—and subsequently never did. I did not consider her my wife and at this time gave little thought to her." [118] The problems of mankind loomed much larger.

---

[114] *Loc. cit.*
[115] *Autobiography*, p. 20.
[116] *Ibid.*, p. 21.
[117] *Loc. cit.*
[118] *Loc. cit.*

Page 38.

(21) A native of Changsha, Yang was deeply rooted in the Chinese Classics and had made the philosophers of the Sung Dynasty his specialty. Among Western philosophers Kant, Spencer and Rousseau were his favorites. In the First Normal School he taught ethics, logic, psychology, and education. "He was not a brilliant speaker," Emi Siao recalls, "but neither did he have tiresome mannerisms, and his audience was always most respectfully attentive. His enthusiasm for learning drew around him a circle of thoughtful, studious young men among whom were Mao Tse-tung, Ts'ai Ho-shen and Ch'en Chang." [119]

Yang had a powerful influence upon the way his students lived, as well as upon their academic interests. In rejecting traditional customs, he advocated living in a new, "democratic" and "scientific" manner. He thought that breakfast should be omitted and urged his students to go in for deep breathing, meditation and year-around cold baths. Mao Tse-tung, Ts'ai Ho-shen, and a number of other students accepted Yang as their model. "In the winter holidays," Mao told Edgar Snow, "we tramped through the fields, up and down mountains, along city walls, and across the streams and rivers. If it rained, we took off our shirts and called it a rain-bath. When the sun was hot we also doffed our shirts and called it a sun-bath. In the spring winds we shouted that this was a new sport called 'wind-bathing.' We slept in the open when frost was still falling and even in November swam in cold rivers. All this went under the title of 'body-training.' Perhaps it helped much to build the physique which I was to need so badly later on in my marches back and forth across South China, and on the Long March from Kiangsi to the Northwest." [120]

One year, Emi Siao records, Mao, Ts'ai Ho-shen and a student named Chang Kung-ti shared a pavilion on the top of Yao-lu Mountain, on the river bank opposite Changsha. They dispensed with both breakfast and supper, and their diet consisted largely of fresh broad beans. Each morning early they climbed to the hilltop in order to meditate, and then they

[119] Emi Siao, p. 39, 57–58. Ch'en Chang was an outstanding debater, and in later years he made a name for himself as a political agitator. "He was arrested after the defeat of the Revolution," Emi Siao records, "but before he met his death he made a fiery speech in which he lashed the Kuomintang executioners and called on the people dauntlessly to carry on the struggle." Ts'ai Ho-shen, who was one of Mao's closest friends at the First Normal School, was a native of Siangsiang. Born of a poor family, he was unusually studious, and later on he went to France and organized Communist groups there among Chinese laborers and students. Upon his return to China, he became a propagandist for the Central Committee of the Chinese Communist Party. Arrested in Hong Kong in 1931, he was extradited to Canton and executed for his revolutionary activities.

[120] *Autobiography*, p. 21.

came down for a cold swim in a pond or in the river nearby. Another hobby was "voice training," Emi Siao recalls. "They would go to the hills and shout, or recite the poets of the T'ang Dynasty, or climb up the city walls and there inflate their lungs and yell to the roaring winds." [121]

During their stay in the pavilion each of the students possessed little more than a towel, an umbrella, and a minimum of clothes. Mao, at that time, usually wore a long, gray gown which set him apart from the rest.

Even when they later returned to school, Mao and his friends slept out on the playground until winter set in.[122]

Page 43.

(22) Emi Siao remembers Yang K'ai-hui as a "very quiet, serious-minded girl" who had been given an excellent education by her parents. Mao and K'ai-hui were married in Changsha.[123] Some years later, when Mao was organizing his guerrillas in the mountains, his wife stayed behind in Hunan, was arrested by Nationalist authorities and executed.

Page 61.

(23) As he built up his correspondence with students and friends in other towns and cities, Mao began to realize the importance of a more closely knit organization. "In 1917 with some other friends," he told Edgar Snow, "I helped to found the Hsin Min Hsüeh Hui (New People's Study Society). It had from seventy to eighty members, and of these many were later to become famous names in Chinese Communism, and in the history of the Chinese Revolution. Among the better-known Communists who were in the Hsin Min Hsüeh Hui were: Lo Man, now secretary of the Party Organization Committee; Hsia Hsi, now in the Second Front Red Army; Ho Hsien-hon, who became high judge of the Supreme Court in the Central Soviet regions and was later killed by Chiang Kai-shek; Kuo Liang, a famous labor organizer, killed by General Ho Chien in 1930; Hsiao Chu-chang [Emi Siao], a writer now in Soviet Russia; Ts'ai Ho-shen, a member of the Central Committee of the Communist Party, killed by Chiang Kai-shek in 1927; Yeh Li-yün, who became a member of the Central Committee and later 'betrayed' to the Kuomintang, and became a capitalist trade-union organizer; and Hsiao Ch'en [Hsiao Chung-chen?], a prominent Party leader, one of the six signers of the original agreement of the formation of the Party, but who died not long ago from illness. The

[121] Emi Siao, p. 41.
[122] *Ibid.,* p. 42.
[123] Emi Siao, p. 65.

majority of the members of the Hsin Min Hsüeh Hui were killed in the counter-revolution of 1927." [124]

Page 64.

(24) The Hsin Min Hsüeh Hui was only one of numerous such organizations that were coming to life among the Chinese at this time, and sooner or later nearly all of them were profoundly influenced by a magazine known as *La Jeunesse* published by Ch'en Tu-hsiu, a newly returned student who had recently been appointed Dean of the National University in Peking.

The appearance of Ch'en Tu-hsiu's first article, "My Solemn Appeal to Youth," marked the beginning of a new movement which spread far and wide over the face of China.

"Oh, young men of China!" wrote Ch'en Tu-hsiu. "Will you be able to understand me? Five out of every ten I see are young in age, but old in spirit; nine out of every ten are young in health, but they are also old in spirit. . . . When this happens to a body, the body is dying. When it happens to a society, the society is perishing. Such a sickness cannot be cured by sighing in words; it can only be cured by those who are young, and in addition to being young are courageous. . . . We must have youth if we are to survive, we must have youth if we are to get rid of corruption. Here lies the only hope of our society." [125]

The appearance of this single article had the effect of a bombshell. Copies were snatched up wherever they appeared, and students rushed to the publishers or sent orders off posthaste to Peking. It is now difficult to establish how many times the first issue was reprinted, but the number of copies circulated probably ran into the hundreds of thousands. "I began to read this magazine when I was a student in the normal college," Mao Tse-tung recalls, "and admired the articles of Hu Shih and Ch'en Tu-hsiu very much. They became for a while my models, replacing Liang Ch'i-ch'ao and K'ang Yu-wei, whom I had already discarded." [126]

The influence of Hu Shih and Ch'en Tu-hsiu was enormous. The former, of course, became a leading literary figure of post-World War I China, while the latter founded the Chinese Communist Party and became its first General Secretary.

In its attacks on the old social structure and its customs and institutions

---

[124] *Autobiography*, pp. 21–22. Mao also refers here to the Social Welfare Society of Hupeh, which contributed substantially to Communist leadership. Among these men were Wen Teh-ying, the Society's leader, who was killed by Chiang Kai-shek's forces in 1927; and Lin Piao, who later served as president of the Chinese Red Army Academy and as an outstanding general.

[125] *New Youth*, Vol. I, No. 1, September, 1915, as quoted in Wang, p. 99.

[126] *Autobiography*, p. 22.

the youth movement was bitter and relentless. "In order to support Mr. Democracy," wrote Ch'en Tu-hsiu before he had become a Communist, "we are obliged to oppose Confucianism, the code of rituals, chastity, traditional ethics, old politics; and in order to support Mr. Science, we are compelled to oppose traditional arts, traditional religion; and in order to support Mr. Democracy and Mr. Science, we just have to oppose the so-called national heritage and old literature. . . ." [127]

Page 81.

(25) On one occasion Mao read a story about two Chinese students who had made their way across China to the borders of Tibet. Traveling caught his fancy, and he wanted very much to make a similar trip himself, but having little money to spend, he decided it would be better to see Hunan first.

The following summer he and Siao-yu set out across the province on foot. "We walked through . . . five counties without using a single copper," Mao told Edgar Snow. "The peasants fed us and gave us a place to sleep; wherever we went we were kindly treated and welcomed." [128]

In the course of another summer Mao and Ts'ai Ho-shen made a similar journey over the countryside—"each armed only with an umbrella, a towel wrapped around it, and a pair of sandals." Before they left, Ts'ai told his mother and his sister Ts'ai Ch'ang (later Chairman of the All China Democratic Women's Federation), " 'We'll be back in two or three days.' " But they did not reappear until almost two months later.[129] During their wanderings they investigated the manners and customs of the various villages, observed the life of the peasants, and inquired into rent conditions, relations between landlords and tenants, and the poverty and destitution of the landless peasants. Often, according to Emi Siao, the peasants would offer them food and lodging, but more often they slept out in the open and subsisted on hill haws and berries.[130]

Page 165.

(26) As early as 1912 several returned-students from France had organized an association to promote "frugal study" in that country. Normally the costs of studying abroad were almost prohibitive for a Chinese student of moderate circumstances, but the founders of this organization proposed a program of strict frugality which would make it possible for larger numbers of Chinese to attend universities and other institutions in France.

[127] Quoted in Kiang, p. 25.
[128] *Autobiography*, p. 20.
[129] Emi Siao, p. 44.
[130] *Ibid.*, p. 44.

Within a year more than eighty students went and undertook such a program under the association's auspices. In 1915 a second organization was established in order to combine work and study in France. Under this plan, Chinese students were encouraged to secure work in French factories and use their earnings in order to complete their studies. Special arrangements were made in order to enable these students to make the journey to France and return at very low cost.[131]

Page 166.
(27) As Mao Tse-tung was preparing to graduate from the Normal School, according to Emi Siao, "some printed matter about a self-help program for studying in France came to Hunan." To Mao Tse-tung and his friends, and also to many other young Chinese like them in neighboring provinces—all of them anxious to continue their studies, but lacking the funds to do so—this seemed to afford a magnificent opportunity. Therefore, "Mao Tse-tung, Ts'ai Ho-shen and others started a campaign in Hunan and organized a lot of young people. The plan provided that they first go up to Paoting or Peking to acquire a smattering of French. Then they would travel to France on a French liner in the so-called 'fourth class cabin' (i.e., the steerage)." [132]

Mao traveled to Peking with some of the Hunanese students who were bound for France, but he himself had decided not to study abroad. "I felt that I did not know enough about my own country," Mao told Edgar Snow, "and that my time could be more profitably spent in China." [133] He made the trip to Peking by borrowing money from friends, and on his arrival he had to look for work at once. The capital seemed to be an extremely expensive place indeed.

By that time Yang Huai-chung had moved from the First Normal School to the faculty of Peking National University in Peking.[134] Mao went to him for help in finding a job and was introduced by the professor to Li Ta-chao, the university librarian,[135] who later became one of the founders of the Chinese Communist Party and was strangled to death, after the Peking raids of 1927 by Chang Tso-lin.[136]

Page 166.
(28) Mao remembers the experience this way: "My own living conditions in Peking were quite miserable, and in contrast the beauty of the

[131] Kiang, p. 19.
[132] Emi Siao, p. 62.
[133] *Autobiography*, p. 23.
[134] Emi Siao, p. 65.
[135] *Autogiography*, p. 24.
[136] Emi Siao, p. 65.

old capital was a vivid and living compensation. I stayed in a place called San Yen-ching ("Three Eyes Well"), in a little room which held seven other people. When we were all packed fast on the k'ang there was scarcely room enough for any of us to breathe. I used to have to warn the people on each side of me when I wanted to turn over." [137]

Actually, Mao spent much of his spare time in the parks and in the grounds of the old imperial palace where "I saw the early northern spring, I saw the white plum blossoms flower while the ice was still solid over the North Sea." [138] He watched the willows with ice crystals hanging from them and remembered a description of the same scene by a T'ang Dynasty poet, Ch'en Tzu-ang, who wrote about winter-jeweled trees looking like ten thousand peach trees blossoming. [139]

Page 172.

(29) The job provided a salary of eight dollars a month. "My office was so low," Mao told Edgar Snow, "that people avoided me. One of my tasks was to register the names of people who came to read newspapers, but to most of them I did not exist as a human being." [140] Some of those who came to read had names that were famous in the renaissance movement. "I tried to begin conversations with them on political and cultural subjects," Mao remembers, "but they were very busy men. They had no time to listen to an assistant librarian speaking southern dialect." [141]

Mao was not discouraged, however. He continued his independent studies—reading, studying maps and asking questions, and Professor Yang introduced him and several of his student friends from Hunan to some of the foremost intellectuals in Peking. [142] He joined the Philosophical Society and the Journalism Society in order to be able to attend classes in the university, and through these organizations he met fellow students like Ch'en Kung-po, who became a high Kuomintang official; T'an P'ing-shan, who later emerged as a leading Communist and still later as a prominent member of the Third Party; and Shao P'iao-p'ing, a lecturer in the Journalism Society who was killed by Chang Tso-lin in 1926. "While I was working in the library," Mao told Edgar Snow, "I also met Chang Kuo-t'ao, now vice-chairman of the Soviet Government, [143] K'ang P'ei-ch'en, who later joined the Ku Klux Klan in California (!!!—E.S.); and Tuan Hsi-

---

[137] *Autobiography*, p. 25.
[138] *Autobiography*, p. 25.
[139] *Ibid.*, p. 25.
[140] *Autobiography*, p. 24.
[141] *Ibid.*, p. 24.
[142] Emi Siao, p. 66.
[143] Chang Kuo-t'ao later broke with Communism and, at this writing, is preparing his memoirs in Hong Kong.

p'en, now Vice Minister of Education in Nanking. And here also I met and fell in love with Yang K'ai-hui. She was the daughter of my former ethics teacher, Yang Chen-ch'i [Yang Huai-chung] who had made a great impression on me in my youth. . . ." [144]

The intellectual life of Peking began to have its effect upon Mao. "My interest in politics continued to increase," he records, "and my mind turned more and more radical. I have told you some of the background for this. But just now I was still confused, looking for a road, as we say. I read some pamphlets on anarchy and was much influenced by them. With a student named Chu Hsun-pei, who used to visit me, I often discussed anarchism and its possibilities in China. At that time I favored many of its proposals." [145]

Page 174.

(30) Mao began devoting a large part of his time to student politics. He was active in organizing the Hunan Students' Association and soon became editor of its news organ, the *Hsiang Chiang Review*. The foreword of the *Review*, written by Mao, took up more than half the space of the periodical, and according to Emi Siao, its fiery eloquence held the readers spellbound. "As a publication which opposed imperialism and warlordism and advocated democracy, science and the new culture, the *Hsiang Chiang Review* greatly stimulated the student and youth movements in Hunan and elsewhere and influenced all intellectual, academic and educational circles in Hunan in their great march of progress and revolution." [146]

Page 174.

(31) The Hunanese warlord, Chang Ching-yao, opposed the various movements, whereupon, according to Mao, "we led a general student strike against Chang, demanding his removal, and sent delegations to Peking and the Southwest, where Sun Yat-sen was then active, to agitate against him. In retaliation to the students' opposition, Chang Ching-yao suppressed the *Hsiang Chiang Review*." [147] Mao then returned to Peking as representative of the Hsin Min Hsüeh Hui, which began organizing an anti-militarist movement, and there he became head of the society's news agency. Chang was overthrown by another militarist, T'an Yen-k'ai who, in turn, was driven out of Hunan somewhat later by a warlord named Chao Heng-t'i. The whole countryside was in political tumult.

[144] *Autobiography*, p. 24.
[145] *Autobiography*, p. 24.
[146] Emi Siao, p. 70.
[147] *Autobiography*, p. 26.

Page 176.

(32) At the close of World War I the Chinese Renaissance with its uncritical enthusiasm for the West began to suffer a series of rude and embittering shocks.

For many young Chinese, Woodrow Wilson had seemed to be speaking with the voice of a prophet when he condemned secret covenants and forced agreements and when he called for self-determination among all peoples and peace for the world. In the new postwar era that was coming, they told themselves, it would be possible at last for less powerful nations like China to develop their cultures, their industries and their national welfare and take their places in the sun.[148]

Chinese hopes remained high during Armistice negotiations, but the Peace Conference brushed aside a Chinese request for the cancellation of Japan's Twenty-one Demands. The issue, according to Western nations, lay outside the area of consideration which the Conference had set for itself. Yet Japan—which, from the Chinese viewpoint, had taken advantage of the war to rob China of its territory—was nevertheless allowed to retain special rights which Germany had previously enjoyed in Shantung.

". . . when the news of the Paris Peace Conference finally reached us," a Peking University student wrote in *The Renaissance,* "we were greatly shocked. We at once awoke to the fact that foreign nations were still selfish and militaristic and that they were all great liars. I remember that in the evening of May 2 [1919] very few of us slept. I and a group of my friends talked almost the whole night. We came to the conclusion that a greater world war would be coming sooner or later, and that this great war would be fought in the East. We had nothing to do with our Government, that we knew very well, and at the same time we could no longer depend upon the principle of any so-called great leader like Woodrow Wilson, for example. Looking at our people and at the pitiful ignorant masses, we couldn't help but feel that we must struggle." [149]

On May 4, 1919 five thousand students and citizens demonstrated in Peking. Shouting slogans, they advanced into the legation quarter to demand the intercession of American and European diplomats against the aggressive policies of Japan. "Cancel the Twenty-one Demands," they shouted, "Down with power politics" and "Down with Japan." Denied admission to the legation quarter, they marched toward the homes of Chinese Cabinet members who were supposed to be the tools of Japan. "Down with all traitors," they shouted, "We will not sign the Peace Treaty." The house of Ts'ao Ju-lin, the Minister of Finance and the most notorious of the pro-Japanese Cabinet members, was partially wrecked

[148] Kiang, p. 36.
[149] As quoted in Kiang, p. 37.

while the Minister himself made good his escape and took refuge with the Japanese.

Police began rounding up the students, but disorders continued—even after the jails were filled. For every student who was imprisoned, a dozen or more were ready to continue the demonstrations. "The movement electrified the whole country," according to Emi Siao. "Students of Tientsin, Shanghai, Nanking and Wuhan, in the provinces of Kwangtung, Kwangsi, Fukien, Shansi, Chekiang, Kiangsi and Hunan and in the Northeast rose in indignation. Strikes, protest meetings and the boycott of Japanese goods spread like wildfire. Students and intellectuals from every corner of the country threw themselves into this anti-Japanese movement. The demand for organization and action was universal." [150]

It was often difficult for the observer to determine how much of this anger was directed against Japan and how much was deflected against countries of the West.

The implications of the Russian Revolution began to dawn on many Chinese intellectuals just at the moment when disillusionment with the West was thus reaching a climax. Men like Ch'en Tu-hsiu and Li Ta-chao hailed this event as the beginning of another "New Tide" in thought. The real victory, according to Li Ta-chao, had been won by Lenin, Trotsky and Marx rather than by Woodrow Wilson, and supporters of the new Bolshevism hailed it as a gospel of salvation.[151]

"It was at the summons of this world revolutionary upheaval, of the Russian revolution, and at the call of Lenin," Mao wrote years later in the *New Democracy*, "that the 'May 4th' movement actually took place." [152]

Page 177.

(33) Sometime early in 1919 Mao went to Shanghai with a student who was on his way to France. "I had a ticket only to Tientsin, and I did not know how I was to get any farther. But, as the Chinese proverb says, 'heaven will not delay a traveler. . . .'" [153] A fellow student loaned him ten dollars which was sufficient to take him as far as P'u-k'ou [Pukow]. On the way he stopped at Ch'ü-fou [Küfow] and visited the grave of Confucius. "I saw the small stream where Confucius' disciples bathed their feet and the little town where the sage lived as a child. He is supposed to have planted a famous tree near the historic temple dedicated to him, and I saw that. I also stopped by the river where Yen Hui, one of Confucius' famous disciples, had once lived, and I saw the birth-

---

[150] Emi Siao, p. 69.

[151] Kiang, p. 76.

[152] Mao Tse-tung, "The New Democracy," in *The Strategy and Tactics of World Communism,* Supplement III, "Communism in China" (Washington, 1949), p. 86.

[153] *Autobiography,* p. 25.

place of Mencius. On this trip I climbed T'ai Shan, the sacred mountain of Shantung. . . ." [154]

On reaching P'u-k'ou, Mao found himself penniless again. "Nobody had any money to lend me; I did not know how I was to get out of town. But the worst of the tragedy happened when a thief stole my only pair of shoes! Ai-ya! What was I to do? But again, Heaven will not delay a traveler, and I had a very good piece of luck. Outside the railway station I met an old friend from Hunan, and he proved to be my 'good angel.' He lent me money for a pair of shoes, and enough to buy a ticket to Shanghai. Thus I safely completed my journey—keeping an eye on my new shoes." [155]

In Shanghai Mao learned that a considerable sum of money had been raised for sending students to France and an allowance set aside to cover his own return to Hunan. So he saw his friends off on their ship bound for France, and then set out for Changsha. Upon his arrival there he found lodgings across the Siang River from the city and returned to his old austere life of one meal of broad beans and rice a day—and took up political activities again. [156]

Somewhat later in 1919 Mao made a second visit to Shanghai, where he discussed with Ch'en Tu-hsiu the possibility of organizing a League for Reconstruction of Hunan. "Then I returned to Changsha and began to organize it. I took a place as a teacher there, meanwhile continuing my activity in the Hsin Min Hsüeh Hui. The society had a program then for the 'independence' of Hunan, meaning, really, autonomy. Disgusted with the Northern [Peking] Government, and believing that Hunan could modernize more rapidly if freed from connections with Peking, our group organized for separation. I was then a strong supporter of America's Monroe Doctrine and the Open Door." [157]

Group by group, Chinese students were still leaving Shanghai for study in France. As one of Hunan's groups happened to be leaving at the time of Mao's second visit to Shanghai, he went down to the dock to see them off. "The sun," according to Emi Siao, "was shining on the rippling waves in the Whangpoo River. Both those who were leaving behind their Motherland and those who had come to say goodbye felt sad. They found it hard to raise their heads, but they kept looking at each other for a long time. . . . Mao Tse-tung, in a pale blue gown, waved briefly to those on deck. Then, without waiting for the boat to weigh anchor, he turned around and went up the sloping jetty. Soon he was lost in noisy, jostly crowds of people." [158]

[154] *Ibid.,* p. 25.
[155] *Ibid.,* pp. 25–26.
[156] Emi Siao, p. 67.
[157] *Autobiography,* p. 27.
[158] Emi Siao, p. 70.

Page 188.

(34) Sympathy for the Russian Revolution was growing in many parts of China. "I remember an episode in 1920," Mao recalls in the *Autobiography*, "when the Hsin Min Hsüeh Hui organized a demonstration to celebrate the third anniversary of the Russian October Revolution. It was suppressed by the police. Some of the demonstrators had attempted to raise the Red flag at the meeting, but were prohibited from doing so by the police. They then pointed out that according to Article 12 of the (then) Constitution, the people had the right to assemble, organize, and speak, but the police were not impressed. They replied that they were not there to be taught the Constitution, but to carry out the orders of the governor, Chao Heng-t'i. From this time on I became more and more convinced that only mass political power, secured through mass action, could guarantee the realization of dynamic reforms." [159]

It was during the winter of 1920 that Mao, beginning to organize the workers, was guided for the first time by Marxist theory and by the example of the Russian Revolution. During the course of his second visit to Peking he read about developments in Russia and made every effort to lay hands on what little Communist literature was then available in Chinese. "Three books especially deeply carved my mind," Mao told Edgar Snow in 1936, "and built up in me a faith in Marxism from which, once I had accepted it as the correct interpretation of history, I did not afterward waver. These books were *The Communist Manifesto*, translated by Ch'en Wang-tao, the first Marxist book ever published in Chinese; *Class Struggle*, by Kautsky; and a *History of Socialism*, by Kirkupp. By the summer of 1920 I had become, in theory and to some extent in action, a Marxist, and from this time on I considered myself a Marxist. In the same year I married Yang K'ai-hui." [160]

Page 198.

(35) Many years later another participant, Ch'en T'an-ch'iu, wrote an account of the meetings for *The Communist International*:[161]

"In the second half of July, 1921, nine guests unexpectedly arrived at a private Ladies' School in Pubalu Street on the territory of the French Concession in Shanghai. They all settled in the top story of this school. On the ground floor, there was nobody with the exception of the cook who was at the same time the watchman, since the students and teachers had left for their summer holidays. On instruction from an acquaintance, the watchman prepared dinners for the newly arrived guests every day. In

---

[159] *Autobiography*, p. 28.

[160] *Ibid.*, p. 28.

[161] Chen Pan-tsu, "Reminiscences of the First Congress of the Communist Party in China," *The Communist International*, October 1936, pp. 1361–1364.

addition to this it was his task to see that no outsiders entered the school. If his acquaintance had not explained who the guests were, he would not have known, since he did not understand their dialect. Some spoke Hunan dialect, others Hupeh dialect, while others spoke Peking dialect.

"The arrivals were the representatives of the Communist circles of various districts in China. They came to Shanghai with a view to officially organizing the Communist Party of China. . . . The Congress lasted four days. The following questions were discussed there: (1) the current political situation; (2) the basic tasks of the Party; (3) the Party statutes; and (4) organizational questions.

"During the discussion of these questions, serious disagreements arose, particularly on the question of the basic tasks of the Party and organizational principles. On the one hand a tendency of legal Marxists headed by Li Han-tsin [Li Han-chün] came to the fore, which considered that the Chinese proletariat was too young and did not understand the ideas of Marxism, and required a lengthy period of propagandist and educational work. On this basis Li Han-tsin did not consider it necessary to establish a real proletarian party, and declared himself against the dictatorship of the proletariat, and for bourgeois democracy.

"He asserted that it was possible within the bounds of bourgeois democracy legally to organize and educate the proletariat, that therefore there was no reason for immediately proceeding to build up workers' trade union organizations, and that it would be better to direct all our strength to the development of the student movement and cultural educational work. Li Han-tsin declared that what was first of all necessary was really to organize the intellectuals, and arm them with Marxist theory, and then when Marxism had won the minds of the intellectuals, it would be possible with their assistance to set about organizing and educating the workers. Therefore, he did not consider it necessary to have a disciplined and fighting party of the proletariat, and as against that proposed the unification of the advanced intellectuals, and a legal organization of a wide peaceful party to occupy itself with the study of the theory of Marxism.

"Making this his starting point, he came to the conclusion that anybody who recognizes and spreads the principles of Marxism may be a member of the Party. He considered that it was not obligatory for a member to belong to a definite party organization and to take part in its practical work. The line of Li Han-tsin was also supported by Li Ta and Chen Chun-bo [Ch'en Kung-po].

"Another line was an extremely "Left" one. It was headed by Lu Chen-tsin [Liu Jen-ch'ing] who considered the dictatorship of the proletariat to be the immediate aim of the struggle, and opposed all legal forms of work. He relegated the whole of the intelligentsia to the role of ideological representatives of the bourgeoisie, and considered it necessary as a rule to refuse to accept them into the Party. Bao Hwei-shen [Pao Hui-seng] also declared himself in agreement with this point of view.

"The majority of the delegates of the Congress opposed both incorrect points of view. At last the general line was accepted, in which the main task of the Party was recognized to be the struggle for the dictatorship of the proletariat. In defining the tactics of the struggle in the transition period, it was pointed out that the Party not only cannot reject but, on the contrary, must actively call on the proletariat to take part in and to lead the bourgeois democratic movement as well. The line was adopted demanding the organization of a militant and disciplined Party of the proletariat. The development of the trade union movement was put forward as a central task of the work of the Communist Party. In relation to legal forms of work, it was stated that the Party should make use of them under definite circumstances beneficial to the proletariat. As regards the organizational principles and conditions of the acceptance of membership to the Party, it was decided to make use of the experience of the Russian Bolshevik Party.

"The adoption of these lines laid the basis for the establishment of a Bolshevik Party in China. The final endorsement of the Party statutes was transferred to the fourth day of the Congress. On this day, however, after supper, when the delegates gathered together at eight o'clock in the evening in Li Han-tsin's apartment, and the chairman announced the continuation of the work of the Congress, a suspicious person in a long coat appeared in a neighboring room. Li Han-tsin was sent along to find out who was the unknown. This person replied that he was seeking for the chairman of the Association of Social Organizations, Wan by name, and then said he was mistaken and speedily left. It is true that the Association of Social Organizations was three houses away from Li Han-tsin's apartment, but everybody knew that it had no chairman, and least of all one named Wan. The appearance of this person appeared suspicious to us, and so we quickly gathered together our documents and disappeared. Only Li Han-tsin and Chen Chun-bo stayed behind, and it was a fact that before ten minutes had passed after our departure, nine spies and policemen turned up at Li Han-tsin's apartment to institute a search. Apart from legal Marxist literature, they found nothing there, and were therefore unable to arrest anybody.

"Each of us, however, had to search for a night's lodging. We could not return to the Ladies' School, since we presumed that spies had discovered our Congress by traces leading from the school."

Page 199.

(36) Years later Ch'en T'an-ch'iu described the event for *The Communist International:*

"At the beginning we counted on finishing the work of the Congress in seven days, but in connection with this incident it was decided to cut the time down to five days. However, we could not find a suitable place in which to continue the work of the Congress in Shanghai. It was decided to move to Sihu (the Western Lake) in Hanchow, but before our departure we came to the conclusion that Sihu was not a suitable place, since many holiday-makers come there. We therefore decided on Naihu [Nan Hu], which is close to Tsiasin [Chiahsing], 300 li away from Shanghai. Lovers of nature also come to this place, but in smaller numbers. When we arrived at this place we hired a big boat, bought food and wine, and carried through the work of the Congress in a boat, under the guise of having an outing on the lake.

"This was the last day of the Congress. Li Han-tsin [Li Han-chün] and Chen Chun-bo [Chen Kung-po] did not attend on this day, since a watch was kept on them after the search had taken place. The weather that day was dull. However, many holiday-makers appeared after eight o'clock. And this, of course, made our work more difficult. At half past nine a light rain began. The holiday-makers departed and this made it easier for us to continue our work in peace. We discussed the questions facing us during the whole day, until eleven o'clock at night. Apart from the final endorsement of the Party statutes, we discussed the question of our attitude towards Sun Yat-sen, the question of the establishment of a temporary Central Bureau of the Party, and then carried through the elections to the Bureau. The question of Sun Yat-sen gave rise to a small discussion. Bao Hwei-shen [Pao Hai-seng] considered that the Communist Party and Sun Yat-sen represented two diametrically opposed classes, between which there could be no compromises, and therefore the attitude towards Sun Yat-sen must be the same as towards the Beiyan militarists, and even still more negative, since he confused the masses by his demagogy. This conception was rejected by the delegates of the Congress. The following line was adopted towards this question: In general a critical attitude must be adopted towards the teachings of Sun Yat-sen, but his various practical and progressive actions should be supported, by adopting forms of non-Party collaboration. The adoption of this principle laid the basis for further collaboration between the Communist Party and the Kuomintang and for the development of the anti-militarist and anti-imperialist movement. . . ." [162]

---

[162] *Ibid.*, p. 1364. The list of those present is believed to comprise Chang Kuo-t'ao, Ch'en Kung-po, Ch'en T'an-ch'iu, Chou Fu-hai, Ho Shu-heng, Li Han-chün, Li Ta, Liu Jen-ch'ing, Mao Tse-tung, Pao Hui-seng, T'eng En-ming, Tung Pi-wu and Wang Ch'iu-meng. Also present was Hendricus Sneevliet (Maring), who represented the Comintern.

A Brief Biographical Chronology
of Siao-yu and His Relationship with Mao Tse-tung

1894
Siao-yu was born on July 20 (lunar calendar) in Siangsiang District of Hunan Province. Mao Tse-tung was born eight months earlier in Siangtan District forty miles away.

1911
(Last year of the Ch'ing Dynasty.) Siao-yu entered the new Provincial Normal School of the Central Zone in Changsha. Schools were temporarily closed in the latter part of the year due to revolution.

1912
(First year of the Republic of China.) Schools reopened in February. Siao and Mao began their friendship as fellow students in the same school.

1914
During the course of an all-night discussion, Siao-yu and Mao Tse-tung planned the organization of the *Hsin Min Hsueh Hui* (The New People's Study Association).

1915–1918
Siao-yu completed his studies and became a teacher, first in the Hsiu Yeh School and later in the Ch'u Yi School.

1917
During the summer, Siao-yu and Mao Tse-tung journeyed together as beggars through Hunan Province.

255

1918

Fall, Peking: Siao sought a way for Hsin Min members to study abroad. He accepted the post of Secretary of the French-Chinese Society of Education which was offered to him by Ts'ai Yuan-p'ei, President of the National University of Peking and also President of the Society. Mao Tse-tung joined Siao-yu and lived with him while in Peking, but decided to remain in China when Siao sailed for France early in the following year.

1919

From headquarters at Paris, Siao-yu dealt with the problems of nearly 3,000 Chinese student-workers then in France.

1920

Siao-yu worked toward establishing a French-Chinese Institute and a Belgic-Chinese Institute. Late in the year he presided over a meeting of Hsin Min in Montargis Forest before returning to Peking to report on conditions in Europe. Throughout 1919 and 1920, Siao-yu carried on an extensive correspondence with Mao Tse-tung.

1921

Siao-yu remained at Peking to confer about petitioning France and Belgium to apply the Boxer indemnity to the education of Chinese students in Europe. In the spring he traveled to Changsha and lived there with Mao and other Hsin Min members. Siao-yu traveled with Mao to Shanghai, where the first secret conference of regional delegates to organize the Communist Party was held, and to Chiahsing, where the conference reconvened in a boat on South Lake. Throughout this period, Siao-yu disputed Mao's adherence to Russian Communism, and refrained from attending the meetings.

1922

Mao Tse-tung became the secret leader of the Changsha Communists. Siao-yu remained in Peking.

1923

Siao-yu returned to Paris to carry on his work as Secretary of the French-Chinese Society of Education and as European correspondent of the National University of Peking.

1924

Siao-yu returned to Peking in the winter to accept the post of First Secretary of the Minister of National Education.

1925

When a change of government prevented his becoming First Secretary at that time, Siao-yu accepted a position as Professor in the French-Chinese University of Peking. He also became editor of *Ming Pao* (News of the People), the organ of the Kuomintang in Peking. Two months later, because of an article against the Military Government, the paper was forcibly closed, his colleague imprisoned and Siao forced to hide for some months in the Foreign Concession of Tientsin. When the government changed in the autumn, Siao-yu became First Secretary of the Ministry of National Education. The correspondence between Siao and Mao continued throughout this period.

1926

Siao-yu was appointed General Censor of all school books in the Ministry of National Education. As the secret work of the revolution progressed, secret police surveillance over him increased. Siao's mail was censored and correspondence with Mao came to an end.

1927

From within the diplomatic concessions at Peking, Siao worked actively in the revolutionary movement against militarism. When the Kuomintang army under Chiang Kai-shek ousted the Military Government in July, Siao and four other members of the National Party were for several weeks the highest authority in Peking. After the establishment of the new government of the Republic at Nanking under Chiang Kai-shek, Siao became Consul of the Ministry of Agriculture and Mines and High Commissioner of Agriculture and Mines in Hopeh Province.

1928–1930

Siao-yu was alternately at Peking and Nanking in the following positions: Vice Minister of Agriculture and Mines of the Republic, Dean of the College of Agriculture, Director of the National Museum of Natural History, President of the University of Hwa Pei, Professor in the French-Chinese University, and General Secretary of the Mixed Commission on French-Chinese education.

1931–1932

With the change of government, Siao-yu withdrew from the political sphere, but continued in his educational posts. He accepted a commission from the Central Government to study agriculture and forests in Europe.

1933

In June at Shanghai Siao married Phyllis Ling-cho. In August they sailed for Europe.

1937

Sino-Japanese war was declared. In winter Siao returned to China alone to aid the national defense from headquarters in Hongkong.

1938

In September Siao left Hongkong for his fourth journey to France.

1941

Siao was elected Vice President of the Institute of Higher Chinese Studies at the Sorbonne.

1943

When France and China broke diplomatic relations, Siao, in his post as University Professor, became China's sole representative in France. He served four years as President of the Committee of Aid for Chinese Students. In Lyons, Siao, as Vice President, directed the French-Chinese Institute.

1945–1948

After returning to Paris, Siao traveled to London to attend UNESCO conferences. Four times he was the chief delegate from China to assist at general assemblies of the World Federation of United Nations Associations, and was elected vice president of this federation when Jan Masaryk was president.

1947

Elected Vice President of the French-Chinese Society of Education in Paris.

1948

Elected Director of the Sino-International Library at Geneva.

1951

Preparations started to transfer Library to Montevideo on the invitation of the government of Uruguay.

1953

In June the Siao-yus arrived at Montevideo.

1957

Mrs. Siao passed away on May 21.